Inference and Understanding

The process of inference is essential for everyday communication and understanding. It is also central to scientific reasoning, and is the focus of research in many different areas, most recently in cognitive science. This wide-ranging and up-to-date review of empirical and theoretical work on reasoning and linguistic inference will be an invaluable introduction for students of language and thought.

Focusing on the relationship between what people *do* and what, according to logic, people are *supposed* to do when making inferences, the authors bring together two disciplines which have much to tell us about the subject – psychology and philosophical logic. They explore the subtle link between the two perspectives to shed light on how inference is expected to work and how it works in reality. They extend their coverage to make links with the wider theoretical context, and show how their work has implications in areas such as the debates about human rationality, child development, evolutionary influences, and artificial versus human intelligence.

Essential reading for students of cognitive psychology and philosophical logic, *Inference and Understanding* will also be of great interest to those working in social and developmental psychology, psycholinguistics, general philosophy, and cognitive science.

The Authors

Both authors teach at Sunderland Polytechnic, where K.I. Manktelow is Senior Lecturer in Psychology and D.E. Over is Principal Lecturer in Philosophy. Their previous collaborations include articles and essays on the psychology of thinking and mental logic.

International Library of Psychology

Inference and Understanding

A Philosophical and Psychological Perspective

K.I. Manktelow and D.E. Over

London and New York

First published 1990
by Routledge
11 New Fetter Lane, London EC4P 4EE

Simultaneously published in the USA and Canada
by Routledge
a division of Routledge, Chapman and Hall, Inc.
29 West 35th Street, New York, NY 10001

Typeset by LaserScript, Mitcham, Surrey

Printed and bound in Great Britain by
Biddles Ltd, Guildford and King's Lynn

British Library Cataloguing in Publication Data

Manktelow, K. I., *1952–*
  Inference and understanding : a philosophical and
  psychological perspective. – (International library of psychology)
  1. Inference   I. Title   II. Over, D. E., *1946–*   III. Series
  160

Library of Congress Cataloging in Publication Data

Manktelow, K. I., 1952–
  Inference and understanding : a philosophical and
  psychological perspective / by K.I. Manktelow and D.E. Over.
  p. cm. — (International library of psychology)
  Includes bibliographical references.
  1. Thought and thinking. 2. Inference. I. Over, D. E., 1946–
  II. Title. III. Series.
  BF441.M14 1990   89-70206
  153.4′32—dc20   CIP

ISBN 0–415–00784–4
      0–415–00785–2

Contents

Preface

This book is an introduction to the philosophical and psychological study of inference. Not everything that we learn about ourselves and the world lies on the surface; often we must draw conclusions from that to gain deeper understanding. This process of inference is essential for our communication with each other and the development of our everyday, as well as advanced scientific, knowledge. To have a good theory of it must be one of the central goals of *cognitive science*, the interdisciplinary study of the mind. Philosophy and psychology are two of the disciplines which have an important contribution to make to this new science, and in particular to its account of inference, as we hope to demonstrate.

There is an especially subtle link between descriptive examinations of inference, primarily the concern of cognitive psychology, and normative theories of it, where philosophical logic mainly comes in. Philosophers and logicians have tried to tell us how we ought to reason by specifying rules of inference, and this had two effects on psychologists. First, it has suggested to some that we actually perform inferences by following these inference rules explicitly, after having internalised them in some way. But second, it has also led some to test experimentally whether we do tend to conform to those rules, and the results have had an effect in turn on views of how we really perform inferences. We shall look at these effects in the book, and at another issue of great interest. Our rationality depends on the extent to which we conform to justified inference rules, at least implicitly. Thus, experiments on reasoning can tell us how far, and in what respects, if any, we are rational, and this is of significance not just for philosophy. It has much wider educational, social, and political implications; one object we have in this book is to introduce the basic research which will ultimately reveal what these implications are.

Part 1

Inference in language

1 Inference and linguistic understanding

In this chapter we shall illustrate how inference is necessary for understanding language, even at the most apparently elementary level. To make the point, our first case study will be the use of single words. Not just any word: while it is true in a trivial sense that no one word on its own means anything much, there are some words which owe their very existence to their inferential properties. We shall take as examples the negative, *not*, and the conditional, *if*. Here the use of inference is by no means trivial: in a very real sense, to understand these words is to be able to perform certain inferences.

Just as a single word does not mean much in isolation from a context, so the use of a single sentence generally acquires its full significance from its linguistic or other context. Grasping this significance in context is also an inferential process, and once again we shall select some examples from the range available to illustrate how this happens. We shall look at the use of definite and indefinite articles, at the way pronouns are used, and at bridging inferences. These inferences concern relations within and between sentences. The topic of inference and general knowledge of the world will be dealt with in Chapter 2, while inference dependent on tacit agreements between people when they communicate will be described in Chapter 3.

Negation

Negation is one of the earliest notions a young child encounters. Yet it is a fundamental logical concept which has puzzled logicians and philosophers for 2,500 years; and in this century it provided an early and valuable lesson for psycholinguists in the necessity of taking inference into account when trying to explain linguistic understanding. In this section, we shall focus on the work of Wason and his colleagues (e.g. 1959, 1961, 1965, 1972;

Wason and Johnson-Laird 1972; Wason and Jones 1963), and the phenomenon of implicit negation.

There are many ways of expressing negation in language and many functions it can perform. One way is simply to use the word *not* in what is known as *explicit negation*, e.g. '6 is not an odd number' is the explicit negation of '6 is an odd number'. Even in this apparently simple case inferences are crucial for understanding what is said; and sometimes these inferences are not very easy to perform. Wason's work on negation was not entirely a theoretical matter: he was also interested in the sources of difficulty in understanding official regulations, which to most of us quickly reduce to pure gibberish. This example appears in Wason and Johnson-Laird (1972):

> A Class 1 contribution is not payable for employment by any one
> employer for not more than eight hours in any week – but if you
> normally work for more than eight hours in any week for any
> employer, a Class 1 contribution is payable except for any week when
> you do not do more than four hours work for that employer.

Most people find that comprehension of this passage effectively ceases at the arrival of the second *not*. In Wason's research, the question of why people have difficulty in such cases was addressed by exploring their grasp of the relation between negation and truth. Obviously, there is such a relation : '6 is not odd' is true if and only if '6 is odd' is false. To understand negation is, in part, to have the ability to perform inferences in line with this relation; and in a series of experiments, a *verification task* was used to examine this ability in a variety of contexts.

The task, which has become a widely used experimental technique, requires subjects to infer whether a sentence is true or false with respect to a state of affairs. This state can be artificial, as in the 'sentence-picture' version of the task.

Sentence	*Picture*	
* is before B	* B	(true)
* is not before B	* B	(false)

Alternatively, a sentence alone is given, and knowledge of the state of affairs is evoked from memory. In the following example, the interest lies in how long it takes subjects to infer that the first sentence is true, and then how long it takes them to infer that the second is false, just from what they remember.

7 is an odd number
7 is not an odd number

We can see from these examples that the first sentence in each case is a *true affirmative* and the second is a *false negative*; the two remaining possibilities are *false affirmative* ('6 is an odd number'; 'B is before *') and *true negative* ('6 is not an odd number'; 'B is not before *'). In simple verification tasks like this, subjects are under instruction not to make mistakes, and the time taken to make a correct response to a sentence measures the difficulty in understanding it.

The results of such studies, by Wason and many others, are clear and consistent. In terms of speed of response, from fastest to slowest, the order of increasing difficulty of the four sentence types is:

True affirmative < False affirmative < False negative < True negative

There are two things which need explaining in this result. One is why negative sentences in general are the more difficult to process, and the other is why true negatives are more difficult than false negatives.

Several explanations have been advanced to account for both these results, ranging from the idea that *not* contains emotional echoes from its prohibitive use in childhood (Eifermann 1961) to the linguistic scope argument of Clark (1974). Very precise information-processing models have been developed to account for performance in these verification tasks, and readers interested in them may refer to Carpenter and Just (1975) or Clark and Chase (1972) for seminal examples. These models, though, bear little relation to the use of negation in natural language, and since this is our main concern here, we shall proceed straight to the most convincing explanation based on an aspect of this use, called by Wason *plausible denial.*

There are two strands to this explanation, linguistic and contextual. The first, the linguistic element, derives from Greene (1970). She held that the function of negation in natural language, as opposed to verification experiments, is not merely to state a truth, but also to deny a statement which has already been made or implied, thereby 'reversing its meaning'. For example, the point of saying 'not guilty' at a trial is to deny a charge which has already been made against one, with some plausibility, in public.

Greene used judgment tasks to test this proposal: subjects had to judge whether two sentences presented on cards had the same or different meanings. Response time was the dependent measure. The results showed that it was significantly easier for subjects to deal with negated sentences when they were performing their predicted natural function of denial and reversing meaning than when they were not. This held for both abstract sentences and sentences containing realistic materials.

The second component of the explanation, in terms of plausible denial, is really a subtle instance of the first. Under what conditions do we consider it appropriate to utter the negation of a sentence? As Wason pointed out, we do not necessarily find it appropriate to do so merely because we believe the sentence to be false. But if, in addition, it has itself been plausibly uttered as true, or some reason is given or exists in context for thinking it might be true, then we conclude that a denial of it is in order. In his experiments, Wason (1965) used artificial response-time tasks and showed that subjects found negated statements easier to process when they referred to exceptional perceptual features. It is easier to process 'Circle 6 is not red' when circles 1–5 *are* red and 6 is blue, than to say that, for instance, circle 1 is not blue. The fact that most of the circles are red might be a reason for concluding that circle 6 is red, but since it is not, a denial is natural and easy to understand. On the other hand, no reason exists in context for thinking that circle 1 is blue, and no one says it is; thus the inappropriateness of saying it is not blue is bound to make us pause.

Wason also gave some examples from ordinary discourse to reinforce the point. For instance, one would only remark, on arriving punctually to work, 'The train was not late this morning,' if there was a prior expectation that the train would be late. Another real-life example was used by Clark and Clark (1977), who attributed the speed of President Nixon's downfall partly to his appearing on television and announcing, 'I am not a crook.' By saying this, he encouraged people to infer that he had been plausibly called a crook, and that may have helped them to the belief that he really was one.

It must not be concluded that an appropriate plausible denial is as easy to understand as a simple affirmative statement. There is, in fact, an extra computational step to make whenever *not* is encountered: this is explicit in the artificial experiments, and reflected in the lengthened response times observed in these studies. A connection has to be made between two sentences when one is the negation of the other. Moreover, people who hear such denials in the sort of situation exemplified by Nixon's remark have to perform further inferences. This tends to be an automatic part of one's linguistic abilities, and usually proceeds without awareness or difficulty in ordinary affairs. But the experiments we have discussed in this section demonstrate that true negatives can be especially difficult to understand outside a context in which they are appropriate. This could be so because a vain attempt is made to perform inferences which would reveal these utterances as appropriate. It is almost as if we pause to ask ourselves, 'What is the point of saying that 6 is not odd when no one has claimed that it is?' (We say more in Chapter 3 about plausible denial and the appropriateness of utterances in context.)

In some ways artificial experiments involving sentence-picture judgments and the like can be quite misleading, in that they omit an element – namely, realistic context – which is vital in accounting for the way people use one of the most basic units of language. However, one might counter this charge by pointing out that artificial experiments did, after a while, arrive at the right conclusion, and in fact the work we have just reported can be seen as ahead of its time.

Implicit negation

The explicit negation which we have just been considering is an example of what Klima (1964) called 'sentential negation': that is, *not* influences the comprehension of the whole sentence. In this section we shall look at examples from Klima's second category, 'constituent negation'. This is where the sense of the negative is restricted, as the term implies, only to constituent parts of a sentence. Constituent negation is often an instance of *implicit negation*, which we will take to be a broad category of negation in a wide sense.

Implicit negatives come in many shapes and sizes. Some examples are the sentential connective *unless*; adjectives or verbs beginning with prefixes such as *dis-*, or *un-*; adjectives such as *absent* and *different*; and verbs such as *prohibit, ignore*, and *fail*. This last category is closely related to the family of 'marked' words (see Sherman 1976, for experimental evidence) which we shall also consider below.

It is not only linguistic intuition which qualifies these words as negatives. Some experiments have also examined their cognitive properties. In general, they tend to be treated in very similar ways to *not*. For instance, in sentence-verification and judgment tasks like the ones referred to in the previous section, but using implicit instead of explicit negatives, the same overall effect of negation was observed, including the interaction with truth and falsity. This was also true of other positive–negative pairs such as 'same–different' (Clark 1974; Just and Clark 1973).

However, there is more to the role of implicit negatives than simply to characterise them as constituent equivalents of *not*, i.e. as words which reverse the meanings of other words. In some cases, the reversal is only partial, as the following example (adapted from Clark and Clark 1977) makes clear. Consider the verb *persuade* and its implicit negative partner, *dissuade*. The latter is not a simple reversal of the former: if you say, 'I dissuaded her from going,' you are saying rather more than, 'I did not persuade her to go.'

Lexical marking, as we hinted above, is a further example of the subtlety of implicit negation. Once again, research on this topic is largely the province of Clark (see Clark and Clark 1977, for a review and detailed references). Marking is usually applied to distinctions such as 'good–bad', 'high–low', and so on. In these pairs, the second term is an implicit negative, and it is these terms which are referred to as the marked items, the others being unmarked. They are known as marked and unmarked for a specific reason: a marked term negates, or indicates the absence of, the property expressed by the neutral, unmarked term. If a father asks his daughter how good a rock concert was, he is not expressing a judgment himself, but if he asks how bad it was, he indicates his own negative attitude. Again, verification studies have shown that unmarked terms are easier to process than marked ones with their implicit negations.

Learning to be negative

While such inferential processes seem automatic in adults, they have to be learned at some stage. Negation does seem a natural, and indeed pervasive, part of adults' talk to children, so how do children themselves acquire the ability to produce and understand explicit and implicit negatives? There has been quite a lot of research on this question, using both naturalistic observation of the utterances of young children and experimental techniques, though hardly any of it concerns implicit negation. This may imply that mastery of implicit negation is a late-developing ability and therefore beyond the range of ages which are usually studied in developmental psycholinguistic research (children under 5 are the most often studied group).

Some of the best-known observational data come from the studies of Klima and Bellugi (1966) and Bloom (1970). At the earliest stages of beginning to speak, single-word negative utterances – including ones such as 'allgone' and 'byebye' as well as 'no' – are combined with gestures and restricted largely to conveying refusal, as every parent knows. True sentential negation begins when *no* or *not* are attached to words expressing the proposition being negated: the earliest this can be observed is, naturally, at the two-word stage. Klima and Bellugi observed that, at this stage (around the second birthday), negated utterances had a consistent structure: the proposition, or 'nucleus', with the explicit negative either before or after it (e.g. 'No mitten'; 'No sit there'; 'Wear mitten no'). If the nucleus consisted of more than one word, the negative never split them. At the second stage, children began to use auxiliaries such as *can't* and *don't*, and also started to include the negative inside phrases, such as 'He no bite you.' Stage 3 (around the third birthday) is characterised by the understanding of most of the negative utterances children hear, even those which they cannot reproduce accurately themselves, and by the extensive use of auxiliaries. There are still errors, though – for instance, the use of *not* in sentences already containing negative expressions. Standard English is, in fact, unusual in prohibiting double negation of this kind.

Bloom (1970) analysed the function of different types of negated utterances as they emerged in children's language. Three such functions were found, and Bloom suggests that they develop at different stages. In order of emergence, they are:

1. Non-existence   e.g. allgone milk, no more light
2. Rejection   e.g. no meat, no go outside
3. Denial   e.g. no truck, no Daddy hungry

Bloom explains the differential development of these three negative functions as being due to the differing cognitive demands which they place on a young child. Non-existence utterances simply comment on a change in current perceptual experience; rejection involves a recording and assessment of someone else's action or speech; and denial requires a judgment of the truth value of another person's utterance. Bloom (1970) studied three children; Bloom, Lightbrown and Hood (1975) studied another four and reported a similar pattern; Pea (1979) proposes a similar distinction in his study of six children. Some consistency seems to be emerging here, and it appears that the idea of different forms of negation becoming available at different developmental stages for reasons of cognitive complexity may be a sound one.

An example of experimental work in this area comes from Kim (1985). She argues that the production of a particular piece of language is not sufficient evidence that children really understand its meaning. She therefore used the verification task to assess this. The subjects, aged between 3 and 5, were shown pictures of common objects along with affirmative or negative, true or false sentences which a puppet was said to have used to describe them. The children had to tell the puppet whether he was right or wrong. Thirty-six English-speaking and ten Korean-speaking subjects were used, so this was a large sample compared to those in the observational studies. Korean places the negative at the end of the sentence instead of between the subject and main verb, so a cognitive comparison across linguistic conventions was possible.

Both groups of subjects produced similar response profiles: subjects at all ages were quick to judge the truth value of affirmative sentences and significantly slower with negative sentences, and these latencies were correlated with errors: more with negatives than with affirmatives. There was also the familiar interaction of negation with truth value: true affirmatives were more easily processed than false affirmatives, but true negatives were harder than false negatives. Thus, the number of subjects who gave correct judgments to all four sentence forms increased with age. Even among the 3-year-olds, though, a quarter made no errors.

We can conclude that the ability to handle the relation between negation and truth develops early: in some children it is there at 3, though for the majority it is acquired around the age of 5. It appears that, when one looks at these findings alongside those of the observational studies above, there is an apparent lag between the appearance of negative expressions in children's speech and competence in using negation to make judgments. One cannot be too definite about this because the individual differences between children in all these studies are so wide. Whether there are differences between languages is not clear: Kim's research suggests not, but Akiyama (1984) found that Japanese children (the syntax of negation in Japanese and Korean is similar) performed better with true negative than with false negative sentences, the reverse of the usual pattern. In this study, though, the sentences were verified against knowledge rather than pictures, and therefore differed in content. As we shall see when we come to examine reasoning in Part 2, problem content can be a crucial variable.

Conditionality

As we have seen, to understand negation – on the surface, a simple aspect of language – it is necessary to perform a variety of inferences. The same is true of *conditionality*, the concept we usually express using the word *if* (on its own or in the the pair *if–then*). This is an even more fundamental concept in logic than negation, and its importance in natural language can hardly be exaggerated. We shall see that understanding it requires even more inference than understanding negation, and that the inferences necessary are subtle indeed.

The study of the conditional in natural language has led to a great deal of philosophical debate and psychological experiment. We shall defer our review of this work until Part 2, where it will have a prominent place. But at this stage we can introduce the topic, and make some basic points, by asking how we learn to use *if* in the first place.

Let us then consider the developmental literature, which has been reviewed recently by Bowerman (1986) and Braine and Rumain (1983). One fact is immediately apparent when looking at the large amount of research which has been done in this area. Young children seem to understand conditional relations a long time before they use *if* in their speech, which is a comparatively late arrival in their spontaneous utterances. Uses of *if* typically appear in children's speech in the months just before their third birthday, which is significantly later than the use of closely related words, such as *when* and *because* (Bowerman 1986).

Researchers commonly characterise a child's utterance as conditional if it can be reasonably paraphrased using *if* (Braine and Rumain 1983). Thus, Hood, Lahey, Lifter and Bloom (1978) classify

I gonna step in the puddle with sandals and get it all wet

as conditional, since it can be read 'If I step in the puddle with sandals I'll get it all wet.' And Bowerman (1986) holds that a 2-year-old, eight months before his first recorded use of *if*, expresses a conditional by saying of his toy dog which barks if its handle is pulled:

Puppy dog go wuff-wuff. Hold [the] handle, puppy dog go wuff-wuff.

It is by no means clear what causes the apparent delay in the spontaneous use of *if*. Children seem to use the major elements of conditionality prior to their use of *if* in speech. Bowerman groups these under four headings, and in each case she gives evidence of their use by 'pre-conditional' children. Here are her categories, with some examples:

> *Contingency*: This includes causality and temporality, e.g. 'Daddy like some when he come home' (by a child aged 2 years 2 months).
> *Hypotheticality*: This is the use of the conditional to make statements about the possible rather than the actual, e.g. 'I thought me do that' by a child aged 1 year 10 months when her mother did something she normally does; 'I think Daddy could do it' by the same child aged 2 years 2 months.
> *Inference*: e.g. a child aged 1 year 10 months said 'Mommy shirt wet' when she noticed that her mother had changed her shirt.
> *Generic events*: This is the use of the conditional to state general facts, such as the one about the toy dog. We should also include here general deontic rules, such as ones about what a child has permission to do under certain conditions.

There is plenty of evidence that very young children are in some sense cognitively 'prepared' for the use of *if*, although they do not use it until quite late in their linguistic development. Bowerman is rightly puzzled by this. But part of the explanation must lie in the range of different interpretations of *if*, which we shall begin to explore in depth in Chapter 4.

When *if* does appear in children's speech, two uses are said to predominate: the *predictive* and the *threat/promise*. The first recorded conditionals of two children in Bowerman's sample are of the predictive type:

> If we go out there we haf' wear hats [child aged 2 years 4 months].
> The sheep might run away if I don't pat them [child aged 2 years 7 months].

We should note that the first example above is not really a prediction. It is a deontic rule, requiring the children to wear hats if they go out. Children have to learn many such rules as soon as possible, and it is not surprising that some of their earliest uses of *if* are of this type. More developmental research needs to be done on deontic conditionals; as we shall also begin to bring out in Chapter 4, these conditionals remain crucial in adult reasoning.

Examples of threat/promise uses – 'inducements', as Fillenbaum (1978, 1986) calls them – are 'If you don't tidy your room I'll take your toys away' and 'If you do I'll take you to the park'. These are obviously used, if not over-used, in parents' speech to children. They become frequent in the speech of children themselves, once conditionals appear; but Bowerman comments that they do not often appear as first conditionals. We would add that these uses also bring with them the deontic concepts of obligation and permission. To understand them, one must be able to infer what one is obliged to do, or has permission to do, as a result of a threat or promise.

Another kind of research in this area has been on children's ability to infer whether conditionals presented to them were true or false. These studies in semantic evaluation or verification seem to reveal that this ability develops much later than the spontaneous use of *if* in speech. Bowerman's survey reports some use of conditional-type expressions before the second birthday, and even the late-arriving *if* present at 3. But evaluation experiments imply that full understanding of presented conditionals does not emerge until 7 or 8 at least. Braine and Rumain (1983) report some work by Emerson and her colleagues which provides a good example of experiments which have been done.

Emerson presented children with 'sensible' conditionals (naturally thought of as true) and 'silly' ones (naturally thought of as false), such as:

If it starts to rain, I put up my umbrella (sensible).
If I put up my umbrella, it starts to rain (silly).

Children had to judge which sentences were sensible and which were silly, and paraphrase them into the opposite kind, i.e. make sensible ones silly, and vice versa. This is quite a strict test. To pass it, children must understand that 'If A then B' is not the same as 'If B then A' – a point which sometimes eludes adults, as we shall see in Chapter 6. There are also two sorts of performance required here: judgment and paraphrasing. Taking both together gives an estimate of total competence in the test as emerging at age 7 or 8. But Braine and Rumain point out that if judgments alone are taken into account, the 5-year-olds are correct 75 per cent of the time, indicating an earlier competence.

Tasks like this point up the difficulty of collecting psycholinguistic data, especially from children. On the one hand, naturalistic observation leaves the researcher open to the overestimation of a child's ability, because of the problem of 'rich interpretation' (see Foss and Hakes 1978). What this means is that, because researchers are people too, and therefore liable to interpret the context as well as the utterance, more cognitive competence may be attributed to children than is their due. The opposite problem occurs in experimental studies: it is evident that some of the tasks are highly artificial – indeed, quite alien to the subjects' prior experience. In the experiment we have just used as an example, children were presented with conditionals outside a realistic context in which their use would be appropriate, such as when it was actually raining, and the children wanted to go outdoors. This is not a minor methodological quibble, but is of the first importance in interpreting the observed performance.

In the case of children, one has to be especially sensitive to the nature of the task as a communicative act. Understanding an utterance, as we shall see in Chapter 3, is generally founded on what is agreed to be appropriate by a speaker and a hearer in a particular context. If appropriateness is violated, or even just ignored, we shall not get useful data.

Referential continuity: anaphora and bridging

The material we shall consider under this heading marks a change of focus in this chapter. Up to this point, we have been concerned with the inferences we must perform in order to understand the use of words like *not* and *if* in sentences and utterances. Now the focus will not be so much on individual words, as on how unity and continuity are achieved in sentences, utterances, and longer pieces of discourse. Because of space limitations, we shall look at just two of the major topics in this area, *anaphora* and *bridging*. There is no rigid dividing line between these categories, nor between them and some of the subject-matter of the next two chapters: we shall in some cases be crossing the border into the influence of general rather than linguistic knowledge on language understanding.

One of the most important tasks a person has to do in constructing a coherent mental representation from a segment of language is to relate what is now being read or heard to what has gone before or, less frequently, to what is about to appear. This is the process of anaphora. There are many ways in which this is accomplished, and detailed treatments of anaphora may be found elsewhere – for instance, in Halliday and Hasan (1976) or Sag (1979) from the standpoint of linguistics, in Johnson-Laird (1983) or Stevenson (1988) from that of psychology. The most common anaphoric device is the pronoun (Clancy 1980), so we shall look at this, and also at the use of definite and indefinite noun phrases. The latter will lead us naturally to bridging.

Pronouns

Anaphora is one of the two major functions of pronouns, the other being *deixis*, which we shall not go into in any detail. A simple example of an *anaphoric pronoun* is:

I met Rosemary this morning. *She* gave me a black eye.

The following is a *deictic pronoun*:

She hit David.

It is uttered when pointing out the culprit as its referent. The use of the deictic pronoun does not depend on some expression in the preceding discourse, while the use of the anaphoric pronoun depends on its grammatical *antecedent* – in the example, the proper name *Rosemary*.

Explaining how we infer what a deictic or anaphoric pronoun refers to or has as its antecedent is far from straightforward. We shall simplify matters and begin with what have been called *pragmatic* or *social factors* (see Stevenson 1988).

These factors are present in the roles people occupy in a conversation, where there are potentially three types of participant: the speaker, the listener, and the bystander. If I am speaking to you, I am the speaker, you are the listener, and your friend is the bystander. When you speak to me, our roles reverse. When your friend speaks to me, you become the bystander, and so on. Obviously, the pronouns people use depend on these roles: the speaker uses *I/me*, refers to the listener using *you*, and refers to the bystander using *he/him* or *she/her*; this usage moves around the group with the turns in the conversation. One can easily imagine the difficulties a young child would encounter in learning the appropriate use of these pronouns, and in fact parents seem to allow for this in their speech to children. One of the prime characteristics of 'baby talk' is the anomalous use of pronouns, usually in the shape of omitting them (see Snow and Ferguson 1977). Daddy might say to his insomniac toddler:

Daddy wants to go to sleep now.

If he were speaking to an older child or an adult, he would use *I*. Clearly, this factor will mainly operate in the deictic use of pronouns, and we shall not pursue it any further.

There are also *linguistic factors* which can affect pronoun use. These can be subdivided into *lexical* and *syntactic* factors. The former have to do with properties of the pronouns themselves, such as gender (*she* is feminine) and number (*they* is plural). Syntactic factors are to do with the structure of language. Stevenson (1988) gives this example:

John said that Bill liked him.

A syntactic rule specifies that *John*, and not *Bill*, must be the antecedent of *him*. One way to try to account for this is by means of the constituent-command, or *c-command*, rule introduced by Reinhart (1983). The application of this rule depends on a grammatical structure for a sentence as given by what is called its *phrase structure*. Figure 1.1 shows a simple example of a phrase structure from Stevenson (1988). Each point in this tree structure is called a node. S is the sentence, NP is a noun phrase, and VP is a verb phrase. At the bottom of the tree are the words which go to make up the sentence.

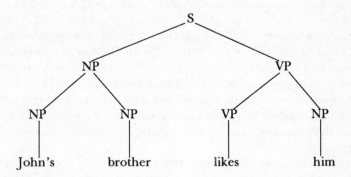

FIGURE 1.1

The c-command rule is that a personal pronoun, such as *him*, cannot have as its antecedent a noun which is higher up in the phrase structure tree and in the same 'local domain' (Chomsky 1981), which roughly means the same clause. Higher nodes are said to dominate lower ones, and one node c-commands a second if the next higher branching node which dominates the first also dominates the second. In Figure 1.1, the higher node for the NP *John's brother* is S, and this also dominates the VP which includes *him*. The higher branching node for *John*, though, is the NP *John's brother*, which does not dominate the VP *likes him*. The NP *John's brother* c-commands *him* but the NP *John* does not: thus, *him* has *John* and not *John's brother* as its antecedent. In the original example, *Bill* c-commands *him* and *John* does not, so *him* must have *John* as its antecedent again.

Of course, intuition tells us that if we wanted to refer to Bill or the brother in our two examples, we would use *himself*. This is a *reflexive pronoun*, which must in general be used to refer to the subject of the clause in which it occurs. In other words, the antecedent of a reflexive pronoun must c-command it.

We do not necessarily wish to endorse these rules as the correct explanation of pronoun anaphora in the examples we give. But they serve to illustrate linguistic rules we must, in some sense, follow if we are to infer what are the antecedents of anaphoric pronouns. (In Parts 2 and 3, we discuss different senses in which it might be said that we follow apparently complex rules in our reasoning.)

Finally, there are *heuristic factors* to consider before we can have a full account of anaphora. These become significant when one considers larger units of discourse, or when linguistic factors fail to decide the reference of a pronoun, as in the following example from Sanford and Garrod (1981):

Steven blamed Frank because he spilled the coffee.

There are no linguistic grounds for deciding whether the antecedent of *he* is *Steven* or *Frank* – 'he' is in an entirely separate clause and neither *Steven* nor *Frank* c-commands it. Psychological research shows that people usually infer that *Frank* should be the antecedent. To do this they need to employ their general knowledge of the type of state of affairs described – it would be unusual to blame Frank for one of Steven's actions. Of course, Steven might, rationally or irrationally, blame Frank if he had startled Steven, who had consequently spilled the coffee. In that case, knowing more about the context of the utterance would help us to infer that *Steven* was the antecedent.

Pronouns which occur a long time after their intended antecedents are a particular problem; it is difficult, if not impossible, to state rules for their assignment with the same precision as one can at the sentence level. Sanford and Garrod (1981) give a set of three heuristics for inferring what are the antecedents of pronouns under these circumstances:

1. An expression for the current topic is more likely to be an antecedent than other expressions;
2. A proximal expression is more likely to be an antecedent than a distant expression;
3. An expression repeatedly used earlier in the discourse as an antecedent is more likely to be the current antecedent than an expression not so used.

These are clearly rules which are generally and not universally true, and we would expect more errors of assignment when they are in operation as a result. Such heuristic procedures are a feature of some well-known computer programs for understanding language (see Winograd 1972). Sometimes, the best program or mind will be defeated, as with this example from a car manual:

If the pad is worn and has damaged the disc, replace it.

Replace what? Your cognitions about brake mechanisms will be of little help here; the best advice might be to replace both.

Heuristic procedures do not always help, but young children must learn to follow them in general, just as they learn to follow stricter linguistic rules, like the c-command rule. Which of these different kinds of rules do they learn to follow first? The unfortunate state of affairs at present is that not enough research has been done for a consensus to emerge. Some studies find that linguistic knowledge precedes heuristic knowledge of pronoun use, others find the opposite. Different ages and stages for pronoun acquisition are proposed as a result. As Stevenson (1988) indicates, methodological differences preclude a real comparison between studies in any case, and there have been few attempts to compare linguistic and heuristic factors directly in a single study. Stevenson herself has made a beginning in this direction (Stevenson and Pickering 1987): she concludes that linguistic knowledge is used earlier than heuristic knowledge, and that the ability to combine the two is a late-developing ability. It would be of great educational value to know more about this question.

Definite and indefinite noun phrases

One of the most common anaphoric devices is the use of the definite article *the* at the head of a noun phrase, following a previous noun phrase headed by the indefinite article *a* or *an*:

> In a local match in Lancashire in 1898 a batsman hit a ball over a cliff. The umpire refused to signal 'Lost ball' and while the fielders climbed down and retrieved the ball the batsman scored 264 runs.

> (Mell 1982)

We automatically infer that *the ball* and *the batsman* in the second sentence have *a ball* and *a batsman* in the first sentence as their respective antecedents. However, this brief passage – which is given in its entirety – also illustrates some of the complexities of noun phrase anaphora. There are two other definite noun phrases, *the umpire* and *the fielders*, which have no explicit antecedents in the text. Using our knowledge of cricket or ball games generally, we infer by *default* (see Chapter 2) what these phrases refer to. If we were not familiar with games like cricket, definite noun phrases like these would cause difficulty.

One general rule about indefinite and definite noun phrases is simply that indefinite noun phrases introduce new items into the reader's representation of a text, and that definite noun phrases can have those items as their antecedents. As we have seen, the representation can include information stated in the text or evoked as background knowledge; we address this relation in detail in Chapter 2.

Naturally, there is more to this kind of anaphora. A definite noun phrase may contain a different kind of term from its antecedent. Here is another example from Mell's cricket book:

> Bernard W. Bentinck ... was bowled by a ball ... which hit a swallow on
> the wing and was deflected on to his wicket. The bird was killed.

Sanford and Garrod (1981) found that reading time is faster for
sentence pairs such as this, where a specific noun (*swallow*) is followed by a
more general one (*bird*) than for pairs where the general noun comes first.
People seem to introduce information at an appropriate level of specificity,
and do not become more specific unless there is a particular reason.
Sanford and Garrod also suggest that very general terms are harder to refer
back to and so noun phrase anaphora will tend to proceed in the direction
specific-to-general.

There are many other aspects of noun phrase anaphora which the limits
of space prevent us from going into. We hope that this brief discussion
conveys the essence of the explanatory problem. However, we shall not
leave the topic entirely, but conclude this chapter with a topic which in
many ways subsumes this one, that of *bridging inferences.*

Bridging

Our discussion of *bridging* is based largely on the work of Clark (e.g. 1977a).
Let us use the following passage from a recent adaptation of Anna Sewell's
Black Beauty (McKinley 1986) as an example.

> One day, when I was still quite young, I heard the cry of dogs.
> 'They have found a hare,' said my mother, 'and if it comes this way,
> we shall see the hunt.' A hare wild with fright rushed by, then came
> the dogs, who leaped over the brook below our meadow. After them
> came men and women on horseback. The hare tried to get through
> the fence around the meadow; but it was too late, and the dogs were
> upon her. Two horses were down by the brook. One of the riders was
> getting out of the water covered with mud; the other lay still. It was
> Squire Gordon's only son, and his neck was broken. The farrier came
> to look at the horses; he shook his head over the one, for he had a
> broken leg. Someone came with a gun; there was a loud bang and the
> black horse moved no more.
>   Not many days after, we heard the church bell tolling for a long
> time; they were carrying young Gordon to the churchyard to bury him.

This passage, which comes from the third and fourth paragraphs of the
book, requires a number of bridging inferences.

We infer easily that *the hare* has *a hare* as its antecedent, but other
bridging inferences connect expressions with antecedents in a less obvious
way, as when *the riders* is connected both with *two horses* and, before that,

with *men and women on horseback*. Further down we meet *the farrier*. This has no antecedent, and so to infer why it is introduced here, we must rely totally on our knowledge of what a farrier is. Why does the shaking of the farrier's head lead to someone coming with a gun? Who had the broken leg? Why did the black horse move no more? Finally, *they*, a pronoun without an antecedent, has to be taken to refer to a group of people who go to bury young Gordon, whose death we must also infer.

As adults, we can make the required inferences without too much effort, but bear in mind that *Black Beauty* is supposed to be a children's story, and note that this is an abridged version. Very little work has been done on children's bridging inferences, although it is known that the ability to make them is correlated with reading ability. Good readers in a sample of children aged 7 – 8 confused inferred material with what they had explicitly heard in stories to a greater extent than did average readers (Oakhill 1982). It seems that, to read well, a reader is required to make many inferences, though not necessarily to distinguish between what is stated explicitly in the text and what is inferred. It would be interesting to analyse the sort of abridged versions of books children are given to read. These obviously contain words that are easier to understand, but do they also call for *more* bridging inferences of some type?

Bridging inferences have been studied in great detail, as we said at the outset, by Clark and his colleagues. He has presented what is in effect a classified catalogue of them in terms of their forms and functions, and the reader who wants a detailed account can refer to Clark (1977a). We shall present two examples here.

One interesting category which occurs in the *Black Beauty* passage is that of *set membership*: we infer that *the black horse* refers to one of the two horses mentioned before the term is used. Even more interesting are those inferences in our example that are to do with *reasons, causes, and consequences*, though they are more indirect than the examples given by Clark. Thus, the fact that the black horse moved no more is a consequence of what causes the loud bang, which is, in turn, a consequence of the arrival of someone with a gun. Young Gordon's death is the reason for the burial; and this is the reason for the bell's tolling.

There are numerous other types and cases, but for the moment all we want to do is describe in essence what bridging is. A description is not an explanation, but what we can say from these examples is that there is something quite general going on both here and in the other examples of anaphora outlined above. Part of the explanation for these inferential processes lies in the ways large units of text are understood, and we shall be looking at these in the next chapter.

Justification

We want to end this chapter, however, with a word about the *justification* of inferences. We have introduced a variety of inferences, and these cannot all be justified in the same way. That '6 is odd' is false *logically implies* that '6 is not odd' is true, and this means that one can never be mistaken in inferring the latter from the former. Such a *valid* inference is absolutely justified: it *always* preserves truth. (We deal with logical implication and validity in Chapter 4.) On the other hand, one *could* be mistaken in inferring that Nixon had been plausibly called a crook from the fact that he said he was not one. At best, this type of inference leads, in general though not always, to true conclusions. (We hereby state that we are not crooks, and if you infer from this that someone has plausibly called us crooks, you are mistaken.) But one can argue that its conclusion is *probably* true to some extent, and that at least it can be justified to that extent. (We return to this type of inference in Chapter 3, and discuss probability and inference in Chapter 7.)

Bridging in itself covers very different types of inference. Consider those inferences which assign antecedents to anaphoric pronouns: to justify these one must show how this process can preserve truth. (We discuss how this is to be done, using Kamp (1981), at the end of Chapter 4.) But those inferences based on our knowledge of causes and effects must be justified in a different way: one which connects the concept of causation with that of probability (this is touched on in Chapter 7).

The essential point is that our inferences must have true – or at least probably true – conclusions, given our premises. If this is not so, we make a lot of mistakes, and understanding and communication cannot be built on mistakes.

2   Inference and general knowledge

In this chapter, we shall ask how our general knowledge of the world enables us to understand extended pieces of discourse or texts by performing inferences.

Few topics mark the beginnings of modern-day cognitive research quite so clearly as the shift in focus in cognitive psychology from word-list or single-sentence memory studies and neo-Chomskian psycholinguistics to the study of text comprehension. This work really took off in the early 1970s with some pioneering demonstrations of the power of the reader's knowledge in determining what or how much of a passage of text could be understood. The most famous of these studies is probably that of Bransford and Johnson (1973), using the 'washing clothes' passage. Here a set of ideas (18 in all) expressed in deliberately vague terms was recalled with much greater ease by subjects when they were given a title for the passage than when they were not. This and similar research is well reviewed in most cognitive psychology or psycholinguistics books of the recent past.

This early work was rapidly followed by several significant theoretical advances, which in turn generated large amounts of empirical research, so that a veritable industry devoted to this area was created. Obviously we cannot be exhaustive in our treatment of this now vast topic so we have been highly selective. We shall therefore begin with one of the theoretical approaches which greatly stimulated the area, that of *story grammars*, and then continue with some of the explanations which compete with it.

Story grammars

As we have noted, the theory of story grammars gave an impetus to the field of text comprehension and excited enormous interest, resulting inevitably in the establishment of pro and anti factions. We cannot refer to all such statements: for accessible reviews, readers are referred to Mandler (1984),

Thorndyke (1977), or, more critically, Johnson-Laird (1983); Wilensky (1983) is useful as it is followed by several replies and ripostes.

Why stories, and why grammars? To take the latter point first, the usage of the word *grammar* in this context has, it must be admitted, been rather inexact. This has led to some rather technical arguments, which it will not serve our purpose to bother with, concerning the equivalence of the term in linguistics and the psychological study of story comprehension. Although in some writers' hands the analogy with linguistic grammar was deliberate, in others' the term has come to overlap with *schema* (see Mandler 1984) to mean a certain kind of mental representation of the structure of stories. (We cover schemas below in this chapter, and refer to them throughout the book.) Seen in this way, the debate about story grammars becomes nicely focused around the central issue of whether we need to presume this type of representation in order to explain story comprehension.

So why stories? The answer lies partly in the fact that initial progress in this area was made outside cognitive science and 'bought in' (see Lakoff (1972) and Propp (1968), for initial moves of this kind); secondly, stories are highly amenable to arguments and experiments about structure because they are a particularly strongly structured and familiar sort of text. They also have a long history, and are found in most cultures, literate or not. The stories which story grammarians refer to are, in fact, usually short folk-tale-type stories rather than, say, the novels of Henry James. The main developments in story grammars were provided by Mandler and Johnson (1977), Rumelhart (1975, 1977), and Thorndyke (1977). While each of these contributions is distinctive in its own way, they have enough in common for us to be able to treat them as a set. The most influential work on story grammars is probably that of Rumelhart, so we shall base our review on this.

Rumelhart's story grammar

Consider a grammar in linguistics containing *rewrite rules*, in which the constituents of a piece of language are given in terms of syntactic categories. We might state the following in a simple grammar:

Sentence → Noun phrase + Verb phrase

The arrow here means 'can be rewritten as', and this tells us that a sentence has a noun phrase and a verb phrase as its grammatical constituents. From there, the rewrite rules would become more specific, as in the following:

Noun phrase → Article + Adjective + Noun

These rules are hierarchical, as we can see from even these simple examples, and *recursive*, in that their constituent structures are capable of self-embedding, as when a verb phrase is broken down into verb + noun phrase. Supporters of story grammars, such as Rumelhart (1980a), hold that structures like these are present in stories.

The following are the rules in Rumelhart's story grammar:

1. Story → Setting + Episode
2. Setting → State * (the asterisk indicates that more than one is possible)
3. Episode → Event + Reaction
4. Event → Episode or Change-of-state or Action or Event + Event
5. Reaction → Internal response + Overt response
6. Internal response → Emotion or Desire

These grammar-like rules are paralleled by what are supposed to be semantic-like rules. The numbering below equates with the numbering above.

1. Setting *allows* Episode
2. State + State ... (i.e. conjunction of states is possible)
3. Event *initiates* Reaction
4. Event *causes* Event or Event *allows* Event
5. Internal response *motivates* Overt response

Here is the standard example, taken from Rumelhart (1975), showing how the story grammar is used to analyse a simple story. First, the story is given in numbered sections for a reason which will become apparent.

Margie was holding tightly to the string of her beautiful new balloon (1). Suddenly a gust of wind caught it (2) and carried it into a tree (3). It hit a branch (4) and burst (5). Margie cried and cried (6).

Figure 2.1 shows in graphic form how the story elements, or *propositions*, are compiled into a story-grammatical structure. The theory is that people possess mental story grammars and understand stories by processing them in this way. These mental representations and processes are supposed to constitute general knowledge of the structure of stories and of what they purport to describe in the world; and the rules of the story grammar are supposed to be the basis of inferences people perform about stories. In the next section, we shall trace some of the consequences of this way of trying to explain the comprehension of stories, before proceeding to some of the problems resulting from it and some alternative views.

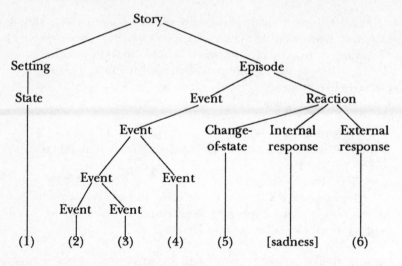

FIGURE 2.1 *Syntactic structure of the 'Margie' story* (after Rumelhart 1975)

Implications of a story grammar analysis

The depiction of Rumelhart's 'Margie' story in its syntactic form in Figure 2.1 brings out certain characteristics of the analysis straightaway. First, one can see how an interesting inference is possible: an internal response (sadness) is not mentioned in the story but, as a part of the grammar, is entered with those propositions which are explicitly stated. This leads to some fairly straightforward predictions concerning, for instance, reconstructive errors when the story is memorised: we might find that subjects claimed that Margie was said to be sad, though they actually inferred this from what was explicit in the story. Similarly, the hierarchical structure of the grammar is apparent. This, as we shall see, leads to some further testable predictions concerning memory for stories. Let us look at the empirical consequences of a story grammar analysis more closely.

The most elementary such prediction is that disruption of the grammatical structure should upset comprehension and memory (recall is the most often used dependent measure in these investigations); it has been known for a long time that a word string inflected to give it an apparent grammatical structure is better remembered than an uninflected or jumbled string (see Slobin 1974, for a review). Jumbled stories are indeed harder to understand and recall: this has been demonstrated many times and reported in almost all the publications on story grammar experiments; no sentient human would be surprised by this. But there are many possible routes to this prediction besides story grammars: to give one example, Johnson-Laird and his colleagues (Johnson-Laird 1980, 1983; Garnham, Oakhill and Johnson-Laird 1982) point out that jumbling stories disrupts more than a putative grammatical structure.

They look specifically at *referential continuity*, the way in which, for instance, pronouns are linked to nouns already used (see Chapter 1), and *plausibility*, which is the degree to which the stated sequence of events relates to familiar experience of the world. Restoring referential continuity removes some, though not all, of the difficulty of remembering jumbled stories (and other texts: Garnham, Oakhill and Johnson-Laird 1982). Plausibility is a slightly more complex matter as it involves issues concerning the application of memory of everyday events; this does not ease the problem for story grammars, though, since other approaches aim to capture precisely this relation. We shall consider those approaches later.

Some of the problems which dog the empirical testing of the theory of story grammars are apparent even at this stage. How do we know that the observed behaviour derives from mental story grammars rather than from some other type of mental structure? However, we should remember that story grammars are about *stories*. Before we pass on to these other approaches, let us consider the empirical question of whether story grammars pick out something particular about stories which distinguishes them successfully from other forms of text and discourse in a way which other explanations cannot. The general issue is whether knowledge of abstract story structure, as opposed to knowledge of the content of texts, is necessary for understanding. A few representative arguments from the large number which have been advanced will suffice to convey the essence of the problem.

'Storyness'

One of the claims which a theory of story grammars ought to be able to make is that they capture some essential property of stories – their 'storyness' (Mandler 1984) or 'storihood' (Wilensky 1983), if you like – which other forms of textual analysis omit. To be specific, the kinds of *structure* proposed to constitute story grammars ought to differentiate stories from non-stories and, to be useful and interesting, ought to capture storyness in general. Such claims exist and have been tested.

In the first case, Mandler (1984) reports and extends the findings of Pollard-Gott, McCloskey and Todres (1979), who asked naive subjects to sort stories into what they considered to be coherent units. Pollard-Gott *et al.* had found good, though not perfect, agreement between the structures the subjects had produced in this way and those derived from the story grammar of Mandler and Johnson (1977); Mandler (1984) used a later version of the grammar and a refined version of the experimental technique of Pollard-Gott *et al.* and again obtained a strong correlation between subjects' structures and those of the grammar. This is not proof positive of course. Subjective judgments are, as we shall see later in the book, problematical as evidence for cognitive structures, but these findings are quite consistent with the story grammar analysis. On this evidence, when asked to make evaluations people do have some sort of structural understanding of stories that is quite distinct from their understanding of content.

Levels effects

The hierarchical organisation of story grammars also implies something more detailed about people's responses to stories: it implies that there should be detectable differences in the ways people process the information represented at various *levels* in the hierarchy. If we look again at the graphical breakdown of the 'Margie' story in Figure 2.1, we see how various propositions occupy different positions in the vertical structure of the grammar: proposition 1 is higher than propositions 5 and 6, which in turn are higher than proposition 4, and so on. The theory of story grammars makes the specific prediction that, in memory experiments, higher-level propositions will be better recalled than lower-level propositions. This is because the higher levels subsume the information in the lower levels or, to put it another way, lower-level information puts detailed flesh on the global bones of the higher levels. For instance, propositions 2 – 6 in the 'Margie' story could be summed up as the *episode* 'She lost it'; lower-level propositions convey how this happened and what was the result. In other words, high-level propositions express the *gist* of the story.

There have been numerous tests of predicted levels effects, both within the story grammar domain (e.g. Rumelhart 1977; Thorndyke 1977) and without (e.g. Kintsch and van Dijk 1978). In general, the data are in line with the predictions of a levels effect. However, in reviewing these experiments, Mandler (1984) sounds a warning: the levels effect is not as straightforward as it seems, because the vertical structure in a story grammar hierarchy can express more than one textual relation. For instance, in Thorndyke's work the levels correspond to the relative importance of propositions (higher = more), but he states that importance includes consideration of scope and generality (Yekovich and Thorndyke 1981). In other studies, some propositions contain elaborations of others at the same level, some represent causal chains, and so on. Mandler concludes that it is safest simply to equate the levels in story grammars with importance and gist, or 'essential points', and to try to link the various kinds of levels analysis in a more complete explanation of story processing.

Thus, as with the investigations of storyness, we have evidence which is in the right general direction as far as story grammars are concerned, but where there is more to the issue than is immediately apparent. The question is further complicated by another possibility to which we have already alluded: that the evidence for the mental existence of story grammars might be just as good evidence for other explanations. There seem to be at least two options here. One is that other sorts of language-specific knowledge, either peculiar to stories or not, are involved in story comprehension and can deal with the empirical evidence. Another is that storyness is not confined to language, and therefore that theories not specific to language processing may be applicable. In examining these possibilities we shall confront some of the constructs which will recur in other areas reviewed in later chapters. For the moment, we remain in story-land.

Content-based approaches to story understanding

One central question about story comprehension is whether it makes use of information specifically about the structure of stories, or whether it is basically a matter of the interpretation of the *content* of stories. Several theorists have argued for the latter, often in answer to the proposals of the story grammarians. We shall look at the following: plot units, story points, and the general question of the affective (emotional) response to stories.

Content approaches, based on plot units (Lehnert 1981) or story points (Wilensky 1983; see also Schank, Collins, Davis, Johnson, Lytinen and Reiser 1982), emanate from research in artificial intelligence on the application of high-level knowledge to the interpretation of new material. Stories are only one such possible area of application – visual perception, for instance, could be another. As with the various story grammars, proposals about plot units or story points have similarities as well as differences (the reader can refer to Lehnert (1983) and Wilensky (1983: 579–91 and 617–18) for an explicit comparison). Both have the property of assigning a pre-eminent role to the content of the story: what the story actually concerns. The common proposal is that readers respond to this and do not analyse the supposed grammatical structure of the story.

Like grammars, Lehnert's plot units also form themselves into a structure, though we should note that this structure is not to do with the way a story is compiled, but rather it is to do with the ordering of types of occurrence in the story. Plot units are closely tied to the affective states of the story characters (one of the universal properties of stories which all theories recognise is the inclusion of human or quasi-human characters); these states in turn excite affective responses in readers. There are three governing states: events that cause positive affect (pleasure); events that cause negative affect (displeasure); and events of neutral affective consequence. Thus, problems (negative) motivate actions (neutral) which lead to resolutions (positive), and so on. It is possible to specify general, prototypical plot units which come under these headings, such as 'Fleeting Success', 'Fortuitous Problem Resolution' and 'Double-Cross'. The next level is actual bits of stories which perform these plot functions. Lehnert (1981, 1982) provides empirical support in memory experiments for the importance of these notions in story comprehension, and has applied them successfully in computer summarisation programs.

Wilensky's story points enter similar territory. Points are those aspects of a story which give it what Wilensky (1983) calls 'intrinsic interest', its 'important content'. It is also a hierarchical theory: a story has a point or set of points (a reason or reasons for it to have been told in the first place); the constituent events of these points are the next level, then a level of related, non-pointful events (elaborations and connections), then the actual words of the discourse.

This theory makes similar empirical claims to Lehnert's. It is not so well specified, though, and neither has it been subjected to such extensive experimental testing or computer implementation (Wilensky himself only quotes one or two rather sketchy and not wholly successful examples of such tests). Plainly, where they diverge at all, the divergence is around the question of storyness. Both appeal to the reader's affective response as the touchstone by which to judge whether or not a text is to be considered as a story. Story points are by definition those centrally interesting (to the reader) aspects of a story; plot units are defined more with respect to the mental states of the characters, with which the reader is assumed to identify. This relation may be more complex than Lehnert makes out (Wilensky 1983: 585) and plot units may just as well apply to non-stories as to stories, but then the distinction between texts which are stories and texts which are not is far from black-and-white (Lehnert 1983: 603).

The relation between affect and understanding has also been explored in an interesting set of studies by Brewer and Lichtenstein (1981; Lichtenstein and Brewer 1980). They make the case that both knowledge of story structure and of story content are important in understanding stories. We shall conclude our discussion of this particular area of research with their work and with a few summary points about story comprehension as approached from this angle.

Brewer and Lichtenstein contend that story grammars describe the sequences of plans of the main characters in a story, whatever else they are intended to describe. Two points arise from this. First, non-story narratives as well as stories will, as long as they adhere to this type of sequence, fit a story grammar analysis, and so will not be distinguished by story grammars (this argument is also a part of Wilensky's critique). Second, plan sequences of characters are an attribute of other media of communication besides verbal or written stories: mimes, films and cartoon strips, for instance, can equally well qualify as 'stories' in this sense. Lichtenstein and Brewer (1980) used both verbally and non-verbally expressed (videotaped) action sequences in a memory experiment and found that, as predicted by this second line of argument, both forms exhibited the recall patterns typical of memory experiments inspired by the theory of story grammars.

This brings us back to the concept of storyness. What is it that distinguishes stories from similarly structured non-story discourses? Brewer and Lichtenstein (1981), like Lehnert and Wilensky above, refer to how interesting or important the content is to the reader. Some topics are intrinsically more interesting or important: a passage about a butler murdering a lord is more interesting, and more of a story, than one about a butler losing his pencil (Brewer 1983). In the terminology of Brewer and Lichtenstein, the content of a story consists of described *events* – such as those in an isolated house on a foggy night, leading up to the murder of a lord or the loss of a pencil – and hearing about certain of these events creates affect. However, they also propose that *discourse structure* – that is, *how* the event information is conveyed in the words of the story – can itself create affect independent of that produced by the content.

They suggest three such categories of affect: suspense, surprise and curiosity. In an experimental test of the first two of these, Brewer and Lichtenstein found that subjects rated different kinds of stories significantly more highly on these dimensions when the stories had been structured to produce these responses than when they had not. They also found that stories arranged for surprise and suspense were more highly rated as stories, and better liked, compared to 'stories' about the same events missing these affective components.

Intriguingly, it seems that people's responses to story structure and content may develop independently. Bereiter (1983) reports that while younger children are sensitive to how well formed a story is, older children are also sensitive to 'story points', in Wilensky's term. One can get this impression when reading bedtime stories to young children: they sometimes seem less concerned with details of the plot than with whether the story makes the right moves.

Concluding comments

The general theory of story grammars has been remarkably successful in one of the most vital scientific functions of a theory: that of stimulating intense productivity in a new area. However, its explanatory status is less clear. There are so many problems in principle with the analogy between linguistic grammar and story grammar (see particularly Garnham 1983, 1984; Johnson-Laird 1983; Mandler 1984) that it seems fruitless to pursue the effort to cast them in the same light. Rather, it seems more profitable to think of this general theory, as Rumelhart did, as one which implies the existence of a certain type of mental representation.

That said, we are left with assessing the explanatory value of the general theory. It seems to explain little which other schools of thought cannot explain as well, and there seem to be some aspects of story comprehension which it fails to reach. Equally, though, there is the evidence for the application of some sort of knowledge of story structure in the understanding of stories – Bereiter's developmental evidence is perhaps the most suggestive here. And there are parallels with other areas of cognition, where knowledge of structure is demonstrably significant (Mandler 1984). Story grammarians gave themselves every advantage by investigating a type of discourse with inherent structure; but they have not advanced the case for the unique nature of stories, let alone described it, which their efforts once promised. It seems that story understanding may better be considered as a particular instance of more general kinds of understanding, linguistic and non-linguistic, and it is to some of these more general systems to which we turn in the second half of this chapter.

The propositional theory of Kintsch and van Dijk

We have seen how the theory of story grammars initiated a debate about the relative importance of story structure and of story content in the understanding of stories. The balance between these two factors is a problem emphasised both by supporters of story grammars (e.g. Mandler 1984) and by critics (e.g. Garnham 1983). The *propositional theory* of Kintsch and van Dijk (see e.g. van Dijk 1977; van Dijk and Kintsch 1983; Kintsch 1977; Kintsch and van Dijk 1978) is an attempt to take a unified approach to structure and content, representing both in terms of propositions. Indeed, van Dijk (1977) begins and ends by stating that the propositional approach is valid for other cognitive domains such as vision and problem solving, but – as we noted above – he and Kintsch have developed their theory exclusively with respect to language. (The generality of propositional representations in cognitive psychology has been argued by Anderson (1983) and Pylyshyn (1984) and is reviewed by Johnson-Laird (1983).)

In this approach, *propositions* are thought of as descriptions of what is expressed in a text. (This is a different usage of *proposition* from the one we shall encounter in Chapter 4 and use later in the book.) They are written in a notation which is common in propositional analyses, as in the following example, taken from Kintsch (1977), of a passage from Boccaccio. J is the Judge ('he' in the passage), S is Simona ('she'), P is Pasquino; thus '(Create, J, disturbance)' means that J creates a disturbance. The numbers in the proposition brackets are those of other propositions in the list; other details are not important.

1	(Create, J, disturbance)	Without creating any disturbance,
2	(Not, 1)	he therefore had her conveyed to
3	(Order, J, 4)	the spot where Pasquino's body
4	(Bring, $, S, to spot)	lay, swollen up like a barrel,
5	(Therefore, , 3)	and shortly afterwards he went
6	(Loc: where, spot, 7)	there himself.
7	(Lie, body)	
8	(Part of, body, P)	
9	(Still, 10)	
10	(Swollen, body)	
11	(Like, body, barrel)	
12	(After, 3, 13)	
13	(Go, J, to spot)	
14	(Shortly, 12)	

The fine details of this system need not concern us, but this example illustrates what we need: what a propositional analysis looks like, and how its propositions (in this usage) consist of *predicates*, e.g. 'Create' in proposition 1, which take *arguments*, e.g. 'J' and 'Disturbance', in proposition 1. (In Chapter 4, we shall call such expressions *declarative sentences*, and point out how they can be strictly formulated, using predicates and arguments, in the language of first-order predicate logic.)

Of course, people do not understand a text just by turning it into a list of propositions. In the theory of Kintsch and van Dijk, there are two basic forms of structural relation into which the propositions enter, *microstructure* and *macrostructure*, and which people must grasp before they can understand a text. Once the propositions have been constructed, the next stage in text comprehension is to abstract the microstructure: this is done largely, though not exclusively (van Dijk and Kintsch 1983), through the detection of *argument overlap*, or repetition, and is governed by the limits on working memory. A reader can hold only up to four propositions in working memory at one time; if the argument in one of these is the same as the argument in one now being read, the two propositions become linked. Failing to find such an overlap initiates a search through the text itself, or through one's long-term memory of it.

Obviously, there must be more to understanding text structure than noting overlapping (co-referential) links: if people speak only with this constraint in passing from one proposition to the next, we generally accuse them of rambling and failing to keep to the point. This is where macrostructure comes in: it is the component of the theory which deals with the overall point, or gist, of a text. The macrostructure of a text is

generated from the microstructure by the application of certain operations, called *macrorules*, such as Generalization, Deletion, and Integration
(van Dijk 1977; Kintsch and van Dijk 1978). Van Dijk (1977) illustrates the
operation of the Generalization rule thus: from the sequence of sentences
John was moving the chairs, John was moving the table, John was moving the chest,
we may infer the macroproposition that John was moving the furniture.
Other macrorules are derived by readers from a schema containing
information about their goals and assumptions, and then they use these
rules to infer the point or gist of a text.

This propositional theory has been applied and tested in a number of
ways, and has also been criticised. We shall consider the credits before the
debits. For an example of the former, Kintsch (1979) used the theory as an
approach to the topic of *readability*. Readability indices have been around
for a while. They aim to quantify that common subjective experience that
some texts are harder to understand than others. Prior to Kintsch's work,
these measures consisted of word and sentence length and word frequency
(i.e. use of rare or common words). Kintsch used his theory to make and
test predictions about the effects of structure on text readability.

Following the Kintsch and van Dijk theory, Kintsch (1979) argues that
readability depends both on the text and a reader's macrorules. How well
the text is understood depends on how well the macrostructure is
represented in memory, given the process of linkage between propositions
in the macrostructure and the limits of working memory. As we saw, where
there is no argument overlap, the reader must search either the text itself
or long-term memory (Kintsch calls this a *reinstatement search*) until a link
for the new proposition can be found. It follows fairly plainly that texts with
lots of argument overlap should be easier to understand than texts which
require a lot of reinstatement searches. Similarly, a text which is highly
relevant to a reader's macrorules will be easier to read than one which is
not. There is good empirical support for these basic predictions: see, for
instance, Lesgold, Roth and Curtis (1979) as well as Kintsch (1979) on the
first prediction, and the pioneering memory-for-gist studies of Bransford
and others, referred to at the beginning of this chapter and in the next
section, on the second.

Another prediction concerns the number of inferences necessary to
understand a text: texts which require more inferences will be harder to
read than texts which call for fewer. Here is an example of the opening of
a story (from Kintsch 1979) to illustrate this point: 'The Swazi tribe was at
war with a neighbouring tribe because of a dispute over cattle. Among the
warriors were two unmarried men ...' An inference is required to relate the
warriors mentioned in the second sentence to the war mentioned in the
first (see Chapter 1 for other examples of this type of inference). Using
measures of reading time and recall, Kintsch found that these inferences
also affected readability.

Structural approaches to the role of inference in readability are not the exclusive province of Kintsch (see, for instance, Wason and Johnson-Laird 1972: ch. 17), but the Kintsch and van Dijk theory is probably as good an attempt as any at an interactive view and an integration of both reader and text factors in explaining and predicting text readability. However, it will not come as any great surprise to hear that the theory has been subject to a number of criticisms. In particular, there is the point made by Garnham (1984) and Johnson-Laird (1983) concerning the means of extracting propositions, the starting-point for the theory, and the co-referential links which determine argument overlap. There is no algorithm in the theory to specify how propositions are to be extracted and compiled. Johnson-Laird (1983: 379) is particularly scathing on this point, calling the analysis of Kintsch and van Dijk 'an exercise of the theorists' intuitions'. Johnson-Laird goes on to point out that argument overlap and co-reference are simply not the same thing (van Dijk and Kintsch (1983) have gone some way in accommodating this point). There can be argument overlap without co-reference, e.g. *the man* may refer to different men in different parts of the text, and co-reference without argument overlap, e.g. *the man* and *the murderer* may refer to the same man in the narrative. This point reinforces the need to consider representations both for the sense of a text and its *reference*. (We say more about the distinction between sense and reference in Chapter 3. It is related to the distinction between intension and extension, which we cover in Chapter 4.) Discourse may initially be represented propositionally, but sense and reference together are best captured, in Johnson-Laird's view, by what he calls mental models, which we introduce below.

Indeed, a distinction of this sort has been adopted in a more recent version of the Kintsch and van Dijk theory (see van Dijk and Kintsch 1983; also Perrig and Kintsch 1985). Here the distinction is made between three levels of memory representation for text: a *surface trace*, corresponding to a verbatim record; the *textbase*, which is a propositional record; and the *situation model*, which corresponds to the mental model in the sense of Johnson-Laird. In the next section we consider mental models in more detail.

Mental models

Mental models (as in Garnham (1981) and Johnson-Laird (1983)) go by other names: situation models (van Dijk and Kintsch 1983), or scenarios (Sanford and Garrod 1981) are examples. We prefer to use *mental model*, because we shall be returning to this notion in the context of logical reasoning (beginning in Chapter 4), where it has a particular application. Whatever you call them, the idea behind mental models, in the present context, is that understanding a piece of discourse requires a particular kind of representation of its content. What is supposed to be required is a mental representation of the actual or possible states of affairs described in the discourse, and such a mental model must have some kind of structural similarity to the state of affairs it is a model of. Part of the theoretical interest of mental models lies in the source of the information used to compile them: it can come from the discourse, from the reader's long-term memory, or from current perceptual experience. Part also comes from the dynamic nature of mental models, which can be revised and reconstructed during the course of understanding.

The necessity for a representation of the state of affairs described by sentences has been brought out in a number of experiments. Once again, some of the clearest evidence comes from the pioneering work of Bransford and his colleagues, in this case Bransford, Barclay and Franks (1972). They compared recognition memory for single sentences taken from two sorts of sentence pairs, confusable and non-confusable. Here is an example of a confusable pair:

1a Three turtles rested on a floating log, and a fish swam beneath them.
1b Three turtles rested on a floating log, and a fish swam beneath it.

Here is a non-confusable pair:

2a Three turtles rested beside a floating log, and a fish swam beneath them.
2b Three turtles rested beside a floating log, and a fish swam beneath it.

In both cases, the propositional content of each member of a pair is identical, except in one respect: the final proposition giving the location of the swimming fish has it as being beneath the turtles in 1a and 2a, and beneath the log in 1b and 2b (see Glenberg, Meyer and Lindem (1987) for a complete propositional analysis). However, subjects were significantly more likely to have difficulty in judging whether 1a or 1b was the one they had seen, in a memory task, than they were with 2a and 2b. The reason may be that the mental model derivable from sentences 1a and 1b is likely to be the same. Representations of turtles, log and fish may occupy a 'vertical stack' in mental space, in such a way that it hardly matters whether the fish is said to be beneath turtles or log. In the case of 2a and 2b, though, different mental models may be equally likely. Representations of turtles and log may be 'displaced horizontally' and the fish could be beneath one and not the other. Mental models may be based on spatial imagery in cases like this; but Garnham (1981) provides a similar demonstration with non-spatial materials, which seems to show that the notion of a mental model must be wider than that of spatial imagery.

A mental model of what a text is about is supposed to be distinct from a propositional analysis of the text, as given by a propositional theory of text understanding. The mental model does not have to be a mental image, but is supposed to have a structural similarity, not possessed by the propositional analysis, to the possible state of affairs described by the text. It follows from this that there may be two possible 'readings' of a text: one may come from its propositional analysis, and the other from the construction of an appropriate mental model (Johnson-Laird 1980, 1983). It further follows that texts should differ with respect to the ease with which they allow the building of a mental model, and that this difference can be detected experimentally.

According to Johnson-Laird, difficulty in compiling a mental model can be brought about in more than one way. He reports in one case the effect of continuity in a spatial description (Johnson-Laird 1980). Here is a spatial description in which it is possible to build a model continuously, as each new component follows from the next:

The knife is in front of the spoon.
The spoon is on the left of the glass.
The glass is behind the dish.

Subjects were much better at producing an accurate drawing of the table layout so described than when the third sentence was presented first, disrupting the continuity of the description. In the same vein, using similar materials, Johnson-Laird (1983: ch. 7) reports a confirmation of the apparent utility of mental models. In this study, the comparison was between determinate and indeterminate descriptions. A determinate description is consistent with only a single model, while an indeterminate description can lead to more than one model. Here is an example of the former:

The spoon is to the left of the knife.
The plate is to the right of the knife.
The fork is in front of the spoon.
The cup is in front of the knife.

This is consistent with the single model:

Spoon	Knife	Plate
Fork	Cup	

An indeterminate description is as follows:

> The spoon is to the left of the knife.
> The plate is to the right of the spoon.
> The fork is in front of the spoon.
> The cup is in front of the knife.

It is consistent with two models:

(a)	Spoon	Knife	Plate	(b)	Spoon	Plate	Knife
	Fork	Cup			Fork		Cup

Subjects were given pictures of table layouts and judged their consistency with the verbal descriptions, followed by an unexpected memory test for the descriptions themselves. The hypothesis was that subjects would construct a mental model for the determinate but not the indeterminate descriptions, and that (i) memory for gist should therefore be better for the determinate than the indeterminate descriptions, but (ii) memory for wording should be better for the *indeterminate* than the determinate descriptions. This is because subjects should retain only a propositional analysis of the former, but would lose this in favour of a mental model of the latter. In other words, an *interaction* between materials and memory was predicted, a stringent test of the hypothesis. It was duly observed: subjects' memories did indeed differ significantly in the predicted ways.

The idea that there is a difference between being able to remember the words of a piece of text and being able to reconstruct its meaning will be familiar to students and tutors alike: the difference between an exam answer which regurgitates a body of information 'parrot fashion' and one which actually addresses the question is precisely of this kind. But the extent to which the theory of mental models can account for this difference is still a matter of debate. (Perrig and Kintsch (1985) describe some interesting experiments which may have some bearing on this question.)

A different type of evidence for the existence of mental models can be found in Glenberg, Meyer and Lindem (1987), who investigated the possible formation of mental models during reading. They examined the phenomenon of *foregrounding*, which is where some items seem to be kept active in working memory – in the foreground – while others slip away into the background. Garnham (1981) gives this example:

> The little puppy trod on a wasp. The puppy was very upset.

The puppy, not the wasp, is foregrounded, so were the next sentence to be:

> It started to buzz furiously

it would seem anomalous. In their experiments, Glenberg *et al.*, echoing the earlier studies of Bransford, Barclay and Franks (1972) and Garnham (1981), kept sentences constant while varying associated (spatial) models. Subjects performed an item recognition task and answered questions about pronoun reference, where time taken to answer the question was the dependent measure. In both cases, differences in the models successfully predicted differences in performance, confirming the hypothesis that something like mental model construction can occur during reading.

We must remember that empirical evidence in favour of Johnson-Laird's theory might be equally evidence in favour of some other theory, which merely has different terminology. Part of the trouble is that Johnson-Laird's idea of a mental model is not completely clear – its clearest application is to logical inference (which, as we have said, will come up in Chapter 4). The phrase *mental model* itself can and has been used in a very wide sense to cover a whole range of mental representations, including what have been called schemas, frames and scripts. The latter are to be the topic of the next section, but it cannot be said that there is a precise distinction between these concepts as they are found in the literature.

Schemas, frames and scripts

The original use of *frame* and *script* was in research on artificial intelligence, where these terms expressed precise concepts. (On frames, see Minsky 1975a; on scripts, Abelson 1981; Schank 1982; Schank and Abelson 1977.) It would be hard to overestimate the impact of these concepts on cognitive psychology, but one result of this is that these terms have come to be used by some in a more general or generic sense, covering a range of related concepts. It might be best if *schema* were used as the generic term, as it seems to be by some, but as we have said, there is no general agreement on the exact use of this family of terms.

The frame concept is generally credited these days to the important work of Minsky (1975a), though a glance through a collection of papers of the period, such as Bobrow and Collins (1975), shows that other theorists were pursuing similar ideas. A *frame* is 'a data-structure for representing a stereotyped situation like being in a certain kind of living room or going to a child's birthday party' (Minsky 1975b). For a psychologist taking up this concept, a frame would be a mental representation of a stereotyped state of affairs, and would be evoked from long-term memory when appropriate.

A number of frames can be organised into a hierarchy. Each frame would have a top level of fixed information about a type of situation. At a lower level would be slots, or *terminals*, which would have to be filled with specific pieces of information from any particular instance of the situation type. Such slots could be filled from memory *by default* – that is, they would have automatic values taken to be correct unless information were presented to the contrary. For example, in a standard, stereotyped living room there is at least one chair; and with the right frame in mind, we would consequently expect to find a chair in any living room we entered. In this frame, the value *chair* would fill a terminal in default of information that we were entering an unusual bohemian house. At a higher level, frames can be linked in *frame-systems*, which would represent stereotyped states of affairs which were taken to be objectively related to each other – an example would be the arrangement of a standard house, with its standard rooms related in the standard way.

Another example that Minsky uses is that of a child's birthday party. A number of questions immediately come to mind when we hear that our children have been invited to one of these. Whose party is it? Where is it to be? On which day? We ask these questions, according to psychologists inspired by Minsky, because we have a frame for representing standard birthday parties. They hold that such a frame embodies the core of our general knowledge about birthday parties. We are ready to ask the questions we do because we are attempting to fill the terminals in this frame. We infer that the party will take place comfortably before bedtime, since that condition is a default value in the frame. In a computer, computational processes have the function of filling the terminals of a frame with values. Psychologists who use frames in their theories must assume that we also have computational processes with this function. Without these processes, the mental frame would be dead within us, and could not be said to embody knowledge in any sense. (These psychologists, even more obviously than the others we have discussed in this chapter, must have a computational theory of the mind; we discuss such theories in Chapter 9.)

A *script* is the same sort of structure as a frame. Scripts were originally used to try to explain how it is possible to understand stories or other discourse about stereotyped states of affairs, and as such are of particular interest to us in this chapter. Schank and Abelson (1977) used a restaurant script as an example. This script has four so-called *scenes*: entering, ordering, eating and exiting. Each of these scenes is itself a subscript for the specific actions and dramatis personae associated with them. For example, the 'ordering' subscript contains a sequence of picking up a menu (or being handed one by a waiter), looking at a list of things to eat, choosing, signalling or responding to the waiter, giving the waiter the order, and so on. These are the default values of this part of the restaurant script: those stereotypical elements which we expect to happen when we go out for a meal, or which we assume when reading or listening to an account of a visit to a restaurant.

The intuitive appeal of this theory is obvious, but its power is all the more apparent when one considers the relation between scripts and inference: scripts do not just enable us to understand complete, coherent accounts readily, they also allow us to infer a great deal from fragmentary texts. An elementary example is given in Sanford and Garrod (1981):

Feeling hungry, John went into a restaurant.
The waiter brought him the menu.

None of the items in the first sentence is mentioned in the second, but there is no problem in seeing them as a coherent pair, nor in the use of definite noun phrases in the second sentence: this is not anomalous, as it would be with two genuinely unconnected sentences. The reason, given by an account based on scripts, is that the second sentence brings out items in the activated restaurant script: we infer that there was a waiter because we are able to access this script in our memories.

Inferences based on scripts can be quite subtle. Consider the following fragment (adapted from Abelson 1981):

John entered the restaurant and sat down.
Suddenly, however, he realised he'd forgotten his reading glasses.

A possessor of a standard restaurant script will have little difficulty here: poor John would be unable to read the menu and hence order his meal. This process is not unlimited of course. If the second sentence were:

Suddenly, however, he realised he'd forgotten to take off his shoes

we might be foxed, not being in possession of the appropriate Japanese-restaurant script.

Intuitively plausible arguments do not, of course, constitute scientific evidence in themselves, so now we pass on to the empirical testing of the script theory. There is a lot of positive evidence, though there are some problems, as we shall see.

Various testable predictions can be derived from the script theory. Perhaps the most basic sort of evidence is the finding that people really do seem to have stereotypical representations of common event and action sequences in memory. This was established by Bower, Black and Turner (1979), who asked subjects to list the actions comprising events such as going to the doctor or attending a lecture. There was a high degree of agreement between the subjects as to the composition of these suggested scripts, showing that it was likely that there were existing memory representations for them. In fact, only just over 3 per cent of mentioned actions were specific to single individuals.

After establishing the existence of scripts as psychologically plausible, the next most fundamental prediction concerns their use in understanding. Here we can invoke again the phenomenon of 'gap-filling' in recall, which we have met on previous pages and which has been noted in research on text memory down the ages, from Bartlett (1932) via Bransford and Johnson (1973) to Bower, Black and Turner (1979), to give three seminal examples. This occurs when people claim that certain information was explicitly given in some discourse, but which they really *inferred* from what was explicitly stated there. The existence of a mental script would explain how this gap-filling takes place.

There is another, subtler side to this particular coin: that of the 'weird list' discussed by Schank and Abelson (1977). Such a list refers to a 'weird event' which does not fit the stereotype represented in a script evoked by the list as a whole. John's realisation that he had forgotten to take off his shoes would seem 'weird' in a list about what happened in an ordinary restaurant. There are several possible kinds of such anomalies, but the question arises as to how they are handled by people. Bower, Black and Turner (1979) found what on the surface may appear to be a surprising fact: 'weird events' are recalled better than ones which fit stereotypes. Schank (1982) deftly explains this effect by pointing out how important it is to notice failures. Scripts are only useful if they help us to infer accurately what is the case. When they fail to do this, we need to notice the fact and remember it, so that we have the chance to make them more accurate.

Schank's point is an extremely important one. Script-like structures must yield *justified* inferences, and this means that these inferences must, at least in general, have true conclusions. Evolution has apparently given us at least some ability to *evaluate* the output of any script-like structures we possess, and to modify them when they do not yield justified inferences. The importance of evaluation and justification will come up again and again later in the book.

Finally, let us briefly consider some possible criticisms of the use of frames and scripts in the study of inference and understanding. Must we propose a script for every intelligible report we read or hear? Schank and Abelson (1977) never in fact allowed this, and confront the problem head-on, by proposing that understanding can also come about through a knowledge of goals and plans, with scripts as an instance of this larger category. Sanford and Garrod (1981) neatly point out one possible diagnostic test for whether or not a script or some lower-level inference procedure is being used in comprehension, with the following example from Wilks (1976):

At the puberty rite, little Kamathi's mother dropped her shoga.
The crowd drew back in horror.

Obviously we cannot have a script for an esoteric ceremony made up by Wilks, yet we can understand this passage to some extent, using a simple inference rule about public horror and *faux pas*. This understanding is limited, and there is little we can infer: what on earth is a shoga? However, we can display more than what Sanford and Garrod call minimal comprehension if we read (our example):

At the christening, little Kamathi's mother dropped her baby.
The crowd drew back in horror.

We do need some explanation of where this richer understanding comes from, and perhaps the theory of mental scripts can supply this.

But another problem for scripts, and one which has led to a major revision of the theory, emerged from the research of Bower, Black and Turner (1979). They found that people confused, in recall, common items from scripts about similar stereotyped states of affairs, such as visiting the doctor or the dentist. They might, for instance, forget whether an incident in a waiting room was part of a dentist or doctor episode. This cannot be accommodated in the original formulation of Schank and Abelson (1977). Schank (1982) accordingly proposed that scripts do not exist as fixed entities, but rather are constructed as necessary by higher-level memory processes called MOPs (memory organisation packets). The fine detail of this version of the theory is interesting, but not the concern of this book; whether scripts or frames are fixed or fluid is, for our purposes, not crucial. What is important is the influence which this idea, like the others reviewed in this chapter, has had on research about inference and understanding.

In this chapter we have introduced some important concepts which we shall return to later in the book, but we now need to bring speakers and hearers into our study of language use.

3 Co-operation and inference

In this chapter we shall explain how some linguistic inference is based on co-operation between listeners (or readers) and speakers (or writers). This will help us to see better how linguistic concepts we have already introduced, such as anaphora and negation, operate, and how general knowledge is used in linguistic understanding. Our subject will be the practical use and interpretation of language and is known as *pragmatics*. It is the study of what speakers intend to convey when they utter sentences, and it depends on, but is distinct from, studies of the grammar and the semantics of those sentences.

Consider the following example (from Hodges 1977):

Launching the ship with impressive ceremony, the Admiral's lovely daughter smashed a bottle of champagne over her stern as she slid gracefully down the slipways.

A speaker who produced this utterance would not intend us to interpret it in the way we find amusing. The oddity here is fairly easy to explain in the light of the inferential processes we have already discussed. The use of 'she' in the utterance has two possible antecedents, but there is a linguistic bias in favour of the one which is in explicit focus (Sanford and Garrod 1981), in this case the most recent feminine noun phrase, which refers to a woman. At the same time, we would have no difficulty inferring what the speaker really intended to say. Our ability to perform this different kind of inference would be based on our understanding of general pragmatic principles, as applied to this particular speaker, and not solely on our understanding of the grammar and semantics of the above sentence. Later in this chapter we shall introduce general principles which enable us to infer what speakers intend to convey.

However, we often fail to be troubled by unintended interpretations of sentences used by speakers. More than that, we are often untroubled by outright grammatical or semantic mistakes in those sentences. We seem, at such times, to grasp easily what the speaker intends to say and to correct or 'normalise' the sentence in line with that.

Pragmatic normalisation and verbal illusions

The earliest example of *normalisation* seems to occur in the work of Fillenbaum (1971, 1974), and it is he who coined the term. Fillenbaum was investigating the usage of simple logical connectives as they are represented in natural language, such as *and* and *or*. Part of his methodology involved asking subjects to paraphrase sentences containing such connectives. Some of these sentences were 'pragmatically extraordinary', in that the actual semantic content of the sentences differed from what speakers who used them would normally intend to convey. Here is the example Fillenbaum (1974) gives of one such 'disordered' utterence, which he calls a 'perverse threat':

Clean up the mess or I won't report you.

This is perverse because it strictly implies that you will *not* be reported if you do not clean up, whereas you would normally expect to be reported in that case. Fillenbaum classified subjects' paraphrases of such sentences in terms of whether they preserved the 'disordered' content or converted it into an 'ordered' or *normalised* content. In the above example, subjects would normalise the content by paraphrasing it as the statement that you will be reported if you do not clean up. He also asked subjects whether their paraphrases did or did not preserve the meaning of the original utterance. He found that normally ordered utterances hardly ever had their meaning changed in the paraphrases, but that two-thirds of the disordered utterances were normalised. Furthermore, up to 43 per cent of the normalised *and* and 34 per cent of the normalised *or* utterances were not recognised as such: people did not realise that any change in meaning had been made.

Fillenbaum explains these findings as being due to people regarding the sentences as bad descriptions of normal events: they corrected, sometimes without being aware they were doing it, a perceived inadequacy in the form of words they received. 'It is', says Fillenbaum (1974), 'as though people focus not on linguistic messages per se, but on the information they embody or appear to convey'; they assume that the speaker was trying to be sensible but suffered a temporary fault. This explanation is consistent with the theories we shall review later in this chapter, particularly with that of Grice.

A similar sort of effect was observed by Wason and Reich (1979; see also

Natsopoulos 1985). Subjects were presented with complex injunctions such as

No message is too urgent to be ignored

and, as in Fillenbaum's research, were asked to paraphrase them. In some cases – for instance, the above example – the utterances were pragmatically anomalous: that one appears to instruct the reader to ignore all messages, however urgent, which is not what we would expect to hear. In others, though, the utterances were pragmatically congruent, as in:

No missile is too small to be banned

which enjoins us to ban all missiles, even the tiniest. Wason and Reich predicted, and observed, that the anomalous utterances would be normalised (they do not use the term, nor cite Fillenbaum) more often than the congruent utterances. Again, then, we have the case of a conflict between the semantics of sentences and the pragmatics of utterances – that is, between the content of sentences and what the speakers who used them would normally intend to convey. And we have the same outcome: pragmatics wins.

Similar effects have been independently observed over a longer period in studies of child language, though their findings have not always been interpreted in this way. For example, children have been found to have difficulty responding correctly to experimental instructions containing the comparatives *more* and *less*: they usually respond as if both words mean *more* (e.g. Donaldson and Balfour 1968). Similarly, children experience difficulty with the prepositions *in*, *on* and *under* (e.g. Clark 1973).

In the case of *more* and *less*, Carey (1978) used a condition in which a nonsense syllable replaced these words to test the then commonly held conclusion that young children treat *less* as if it meant *more*. Children were given glasses of water and a jug with more water in it and asked to 'make it so that there is more/less/tiv'. She found that the children in each condition indeed responded as if each word meant *more*: they poured some water from the jug into the glass. The significance of the nonsense syllable condition is that we cannot presume that the subjects really thought *less* meant *more*, or even, as Foss and Hakes (1978) note, that they knew what *more* meant: they behaved in what they construed to be a pragmatically appropriate manner, given the demand characteristics of the experiment. Confronted by glasses of water and a jug containing more, they seem to have presumed that the situation concerned the adding of water to glasses, so the instruction sentences reduced to the command: 'go'. Testing whether children truly understood the meaning of *less* would require a different sort of context.

Clark (1973) observed a similar phenomenon with *in*, *on* and *under*. For instance, given the instruction 'Put the mouse under the table,' children tended to put it *on* the table. Clark surmised that the children were using two pragmatic rules: (i) if the object governed by a preposition is a container, put the small object *in* it; (ii) if the governed object is a surface, put the small object *on* it.

As we can see, there is nothing specifically childlike about this behaviour, although it takes distinct forms in children's and adults' language: both adults and children normalise the messages that they receive to fit their understanding of the context. In the face of this, one can conclude that an understanding of the pragmatics of the experimental situation is absolutely essential in interpreting language comprehension, especially where children are concerned: their pragmatics may differ from those of the adult experimenter. A context-free language experiment probably does not exist. There is a similarity here with the 'pragmatic' explanations of reasoning which we shall be reviewing in Part 2.

Clearly, the effect of pragmatic inferences to do with the sharing and transmission of knowledge between participants is a powerful factor in language understanding, and one which is present from early childhood through adulthood. We shall now consider some theories which aim to explain understanding in these terms, beginning with an extension of Clark's bridging construct, which we met in Chapter 1.

Bridging and the given–new contract

Strictly speaking, the first approach we shall deal with is not so much an extension of the idea of bridging, as a more general framework of which bridging is a part. It is the *given–new contract* proposed by Clark and his colleagues (Clark 1977a, 1977b; Clark and Clark 1977; Haviland and Clark 1974).

The general concern of the given–new contract is with reference, both deictic and anaphoric (see Chapter 1). How do we relate the content of utterances to their referents as represented in perception, memory, or other utterances? What we do, according to Clark, is invoke a linguistic convention by which we partition our utterance into two sections: given information and new information. Hearers, in turn, assume that speakers are doing this. Given information is what we assume our hearer already to know; new information is what we assume our hearer does not know. Bridging inferences serve to connect these two forms of information, and to connect the given information with its intended antecedent, or referent. As we saw in Chapter 1, these bridges can take many forms.

The partitioning of an utterance into given and new information is by syntax and intonation. Identifying which is given and which is new is the first step in applying the contract; the next is to search memory (or perception) for a term (or object) matching the given information and to call it the antecedent; the last is to add the new information to memory by replacing the given information by its antecedent (Clark 1977b). Sometimes the antecedent and the given information match directly, as in (examples from Clark 1977a, 1977b):

I met a man yesterday. The man I met yesterday told me a story.

The given information in this example easily allows us to connect 'the man I met yesterday' in the second utterance with its antecedent in the first. We can then add the new information we receive about that man in the second utterance to our memory. Sometimes the match is indirect, and we are required to perform a bridging inference based on our general knowledge:

I went shopping yesterday. The walk did me good.
John died yesterday. The murderer got away.

In some cases, the match is so indirect that we can become conscious of the inference being made in a way which we might not be with the examples above:

Max lives in New York. Moritz is crazy too.

Inferential indirectness seems to lead to amusement in instances like this: perhaps when someone says of such an intended joke, 'I don't get it,' what they are signalling is that they cannot make the necessary bridge. We shall return to this point below when we consider how these processes can be used wilfully by people in, for instance, *concealing* meaning from hearers.

All the above inferences are what Clark classifies as *authorised* inferences: speakers cannot know directly what is in hearers' minds, so they rely on the tacit agreement embodied in the given–new contract to assume that appropriate referents will be found. However, *unauthorised* inferences are also possible: these are made when there is a violation, or an absence, of a contract between speaker and hearer. Sometimes this happens deliberately, as we have hinted, but sometimes one party unwittingly fails to adhere to the contract intended by the other. Authorised and unauthorised inferences are quite distinct: for one thing, people tend to be aware of making unauthorised inferences, but not so aware of authorised inferences.

In his more recent work, Clark has expanded the ideas of bridging and the given–new contract and developed a more general *collaborative* theory of conversation. It is based on the notion of the *common ground* between speakers and hearers (Clark and Carlson 1981). Common ground includes not only the information that is objectively shared between the two parties, but also their knowledge, or supposition, that each has that information available to determine reference: thus, I am looking at a picture; you know that I am looking at the picture; I know that you know that I am looking at it, and so on.

This example portrays one of the proposed sources of common ground: 'physical co-presence', to use Clark's term. That is, the same information is in the perceptual experience of both conversants simultaneously. A second source is 'linguistic co-presence': what is currently being talked about. A third is 'community membership': knowledge that speaker and hearer are both members of some social or interest group. If you and I find out we are both Londoners, say, or Mozart enthusiasts, or alumni of the same school, then certain mutual knowledge becomes available which otherwise would not have been. This is a familiar experience when meeting new people. Community membership is a fairly enduring source of common ground, whereas physical and linguistic co-presence are more transient. The influence of common ground can extend to the level of single-word meanings, as well as to the kind of inferences which we have been considering: to a policeman, for instance, the word 'grass' can refer to different things depending on whether he is talking to an informer, a drug squad officer, or his lawn mower salesman.

This process of finding common ground is expanded upon by Clark and Wilkes-Gibbs (1986). They look at some of the conversational gambits revealed in naturalistic studies of people talking, in terms of their function in establishing and maintaining reference, and go on to test the resulting predictions, successfully, in an experiment.

The goal of conversation is, according to Clark and Wilkes-Gibbs, the establishment of understanding between the participants, and this itself entails that each must *mutually accept* each other's references before conversation can proceed. Common ground is established and augmented in an orderly way as mutual acceptance develops – indeed, this orderliness is taken by Clark to be a prerequisite for efficient conversation (Clark and Carlson 1981; Clark and Wilkes-Gibbs 1986). In principle, mutual acceptance is quite a simple matter: participant A presents some information, and if participant B signals acceptance, or at least the absence of rejection, the conversation can proceed.

Naturally there is more to it than this. Clark and Wilkes-Gibbs go on to specify the ways in which B can signal acceptance: simply by allowing A's statement without comment (presupposing acceptance), or by actually asserting acceptance by head-nods or comments such as 'yes', 'right', and so on. Similarly, A can present the initial statement in different ways depending on his or her assumptions about the current state of the common ground. For instance, the initial statement may consist of a trial or 'instalment' noun phrase, where the information is communicated in discrete portions, each of which B can only accept by overt assertion; or a self-corrected noun phrase, which B must only signal acceptance to after its correction. In some cases – and we all know people who overdo this – B actually supplies part of A's statement, usually when invited by A to do so by a pause or 'er ...', as in:

A: When you talk to Mike, he always completes your, er ...
B: Sentences.
A: Your sentences, yes.

Detailed examples of these and other conversational intricacies can be found in Clark and Wilkes-Gibbs (1986); so let us ask whether there is evidence for this collaborative theory of conversation. First, do people actually go through the iterative process of presentation, acceptance and modification? Clark and Wilkes-Gibbs cite numerous examples from their own work and that of others, such as social psychologists and ethno-methodologists, which convincingly substantiate this claim. Further predictions were tested in the more structured situation of their own experiment.

This involved two people, who could not see each other, communicating about the arrangement of Tangram figures. These are geometric shapes which, when put in certain patterns, can suggest silhouettes of people and other objects. One person had an ordered array of these and had to explain their arrangement to the other, so that he or she could reproduce the arrangement. Each pair did this six times. Clark and Wilkes-Gibbs's theory makes a simple initial prediction: that as common ground is established, the number of words used should decline. The reason for this is the principle of the *minimisation of collaborative effort*: people will generally not waste their breath, and the existence of common ground leaves less to be explicitly stated. There was ample confirmation of this: the number of words used per Tangram figure referred to fell from around 40 on the first trial to around ten on the last. Here is an example given by the authors of this process; this is how the speaker refers to one of the figures:

Trial 1: All right, the next one looks like a person who's ice skating, except they're sticking two arms out in front.
Trial 6: The ice skater.

A similar decline was observed in the number of conversational turns: clearly, the interchange becomes more economical as common ground is established.

Collaborative effort cannot be minimised by one participant alone: both must make contributions which indicate acceptance of each other's inputs to the conversation so that common ground can be quickly assured; once this has happened, common ground becomes built in to the conversation in a way that allows fewer and fewer turns with fewer and fewer words in them. Perhaps this is what lies behind the piece of folk wisdom about married people not saying a lot to each other.

Of course, it is possible that the very task used by Clark and Wilkes-Gibbs begs the questions they are asking: it is by design a highly collaborative task. Clark has found evidence of similar processes in another version of the task, where people talked about arrangements of postcards of New York City (Isaacs and Clark 1987). Here the object of interest was the development of common ground in the sense of expertise: some people were experts – they were New Yorkers – and some were novices, not having been to New York. It was predicted that conversants would assess, supply and acquire expertise in this situation. Thus, in the use of proper names to describe the postcard scenes, participants would establish whether each was or was not a New Yorker: if so, they would tend to use proper names; if not, they would use fewer proper names; and if one was an expert and one a novice, use of proper names would change.

These general predictions were borne out, along with the observation of an increase in the efficiency of the conversation, as measured by Clark and Wilkes-Gibbs. Thus, in conversations between two experts, proper names were used about 80 per cent of the time; between two novices, the figure was below 20 per cent; when an expert was talking to a novice, the number of proper names initially decreased as it became clear to the expert that the novice did not know what some of the names referred to; and when novices talked to experts, the number of proper names increased as some of the expertise 'rubbed off' and the names were learnt from the expert partners. Experts and novices seem to have discovered they were talking to other experts or novices by the way the conversations proceeded: in only six of 32 pairs did a participant actually ask or tell the other whether they were New Yorkers.

Again, one might object that this is still the same picture-arranging task, with collaboration designed in. However, these findings are consistent with those of research in other disciplines on conversation, and with one's intuitions too. It would be interesting, though, to apply this type of analysis to different sorts of conversation, perhaps where collaboration is a double-edged affair. We are thinking of argument, in the debating sense of the word, where the participants are trying to maintain their own position at the expense of that of their 'partners'. On one level, debaters are competing with each other; but on another, some sort of collaboration must be taking place for the interaction to qualify as a true debate and not a spate of name-calling. Many of the points we have made so far can be reinforced by taking a more general and philosophical look at pragmatics, and that is what we turn to now.

Speech acts

Consider the following sentence:

Can you tell me the time?

Speakers who used this sentence in some cases, such as when talking to a 4-year-old child or to someone trying on a new pair of glasses, would intend it to be taken literally: they would be asking listeners to indicate whether they were capable of telling the time, and a 'yes' answer would then be sufficient to satisfy the speakers. However, the sentence is probably more often uttered in a more familiar context: speakers do not know what time it is and are seeking that information from people whom the speakers believe may possess it. If the listeners were just to say 'yes', the speakers would not in this case be quite so content. In general, listeners will only be able to understand uses of this sentence if they can infer what speakers who utter it are trying to do.

Even more generally, listeners will be able to understand speakers only if they are able to perform the correct inferences about the actions of the speakers. Now, it is important to be clear about what an action is. A person who is pushed out of a window does not perform the action of falling through the air, no more than the sound the person's body makes when it hits the ground is an utterance. An *action*, properly speaking, is caused by the beliefs and desires of an agent and is done with a certain *intention* or goal in mind. An *utterance*, properly speaking, is a linguistic action of a speaker. For example, the utterance of the above sentence by a speaker in a particular context may be caused by a desire to learn the time and a belief that a listener has that information The intention of the speaker would then be simply to acquire this information, and not, say, to test the sight of the listener.

Austin (1962) recognised the great importance of studying the actions of speakers and developed his account of *speech acts* as a result. According to Austin, there are three different actions we can be said to perform when we utter some sentence, such as:

The heaviest politician is unhealthy.

First, there is the *locutionary act* of uttering words with certain senses and references. In this case, we have used 'the heaviest politician', which has a certain reference, rather than 'the tallest politician', which may possibly have the same reference (there could be one person who is both the heaviest and tallest politician) but which certainly has a different sense. This is a result of the fact that 'heaviest' and 'tallest' have different senses, in that these terms express different ways of identifying an object. Austin relied here on the fundamental semantic distinction between *sense* and *reference* introduced by Frege (1892), and it is at this point that pragmatics meets semantics in his account. The sense and reference of a sentence, as determined by the senses and references of the words within it, is its fixed semantic content, which does not vary as the sentence is used by different speakers, in a variety of contexts, in pragmatically different ways.

Second, there is what Austin called the *illocutionary act*, which he took to be the action we perform *in* saying something, such as informing, warning, questioning, and so on, someone. We might in our example simply be performing the illocutionary act of informing someone about the heaviest politician, but we also might be issuing a warning about the connection between weight and health. And third, Austin listed the *perlocutionary act*, which he held is the action we perform *by* uttering a sentence, such as making someone well informed, persuading someone to go on a diet, puzzling someone, and so on.

Austin concentrated his research on illocutionary acts and so have his many followers (for a review, see Levinson 1983). One of the important notions he introduced is that of *felicity conditions* for illocutionary acts. (See Searle (1969) for a discussion of this notion.) One of these conditions for a warning would be that the speaker has some reason to believe that the listener is at risk of being harmed by some possibility. Our supposed warning would be 'unhappy' or 'infelicitous', as Austin would say, if we did not believe that there is a connection between being overweight and being unhealthy. It is clearly important for speakers and listeners to understand such conditions for performing illocutionary acts successfully and happily; otherwise, they would not know when to attempt these acts or what to make of them when they occurred.

There is a problem in acquiring and applying knowledge of felicity conditions, since illocutionary acts can be performed in a great variety of ways. We have already seen that a warning does not have to begin with the phrase 'I warn you ...' Consider the following imperative:

Wash your hands.

Here are some examples of how this *direct* speech act of ordering someone to do something could be performed as an *indirect* speech act (see Searle (1975) for this distinction):

I'd like you to wash your hands.
Would you like to wash your hands?
Why haven't you washed your hands?
I think it would be a good idea if you washed your hands.
Your hands are rather dirty.
What do you normally do now?
Haven't you forgotten something?

If you were speaking to your own child, almost any of these could be used (they are arranged in rough order of indirectness), but when talking to other adults these apparent circumlocutions are highly likely to replace the direct imperative. Two general questions are raised by examples like this one. How does our understanding of indirect speech acts develop? And what allows the full use of indirect forms in adult discourse?

Children are exposed early to many indirect forms, as these are very common in the speech of adults to children. Clark and Clark (1977b: 364) cite findings that mothers used as many indirect as direct speech acts when talking to their children. Adults also provide many 'direct' interpretations of what children seem to be trying to say 'indirectly'. When an 18-month-old child at the single-word stage says 'coat', we can report its beliefs and desires in a number of ways: 'That's a coat', 'Where's my coat?', 'I want my coat', and so on. Of course, adults do not just go on the dictionary meaning of a single word in such a situation: they use other, contextual information to construct an interpretation of the child's utterance. The child's experience of this method of 'rich interpretation' seems to be an essential part of its acquisition of communicative competence from the very earliest stages.

According to Dore (1975), intonation is an important source of such contextual information. Children characteristically use a wider range of intonation than adults do, and when adults interpret the child's utterance they usually incorporate what the child has conveyed by intonation. The physical or social context is another powerful factor, as we saw in the section on normalisation above. Dore classifies a range of speech acts which can be ascribed at the one-word stage, including greeting, labelling, requesting and protesting.

Different types of speech acts tend to appear at different times in children's linguistic development. Among the first to appear are assertions or statements of fact, such as saying 'coat' when pointing at a coat or just pointing to one when asked 'Where's the coat?', and of course, expressions of emotion, requests and refusals. Then these are elaborated, and indirect modes of expression are intentionally used by the child, rather than just attributed by an adult. Some other illocutionary acts are still later developments: even 7- and 8-year-olds have trouble with the speech act of promising to do something (Chomsky 1969). But again, more elaborated forms of this type successfully appear as the child grows, and indirect expressions increasingly replace direct ones.

Eventually, we have a sophisticated ability to perform indirect speech acts ourselves and to interpret them in others. How is this possible? Speakers who perform indirect speech acts intend to convey something more than, or distinct from, what is expressed by the semantic content of the words they use, and they are often understood by good listeners, who do not need to hear a word like 'warn' to know that a speech act like a warning has been performed. This is, in fact, a special case of a more general phenomenon – good listeners, in many other types of case, are able to infer that speakers intend to convey something different from, or even inconsistent with, the semantic content of the sentences they use. How are such inferences possible? And how are they justified? We turn now to a general attempt to answer these questions.

Grice's conversational theory

Grice (1967, 1975, 1978, 1981) has been immensely influential by stressing the fundamental point that a rational conversation must have a goal or purpose, such as exchanging information about some topic of common interest. We have already seen earlier in this chapter how this point is acknowledged in work like that of Clark and Wilkes-Gibbs (1986). But Grice not only made the point, but also derived from it what he called the *co-operative principle*, which states that the utterances of participants in a conversation should help to achieve the goal or purpose of that conversation. He pointed out that this general principle can be adhered to by following a number of specific *maxims*, which he claimed fell into four categories: quantity, quality, relation, and manner. The maxims under these categories were the following (see particularly Grice 1975):

> *Quantity*: Speakers should try not to give too much or too little *information* for the purpose of the conversation.
> *Quality*: Speakers should try to say what is *true*, and should avoid saying anything for which they do not have adequate *evidence* or *justification*, given the purpose of the conversation.
> *Relation*: Speakers should try to be *relevant* to the goal of the conversation.
> *Manner*: Speakers should try to be *clear*, given the goal of the conversation.

Grice admitted that these maxims were not all of equal importance, that there could be other maxims – such as one requiring politeness – and that the above are designed for conversations in which the main goal is the exchange of information. (See Leech (1983) for an argument about the importance of politeness and Sperber and Wilson (1986, reviewed in Chapter 8) for one about the particular importance of relevance.) Nevertheless, the above maxims have far-reaching applications in pragmatics.

Let us illustrate this point by supposing that some students ask us whether there will be an assignment question on a certain topic. We might reply using this sentence:

It is an important topic.

If we utter this sentence and say no more, the students will justly infer that we have not already decided that there will be no assignment question on this topic. But what is the explanation of the fact that this inference is justified in this context? The students have clearly gone beyond the semantic content of this sentence. That content, as determined by the senses and references of the words in the sentence, is a proposition which has nothing to do with what we, as particular speakers, have or have not decided. Ordinary people would say that we, in using this sentence in this case, 'suggest' or 'imply' something about what we have decided. This ordinary notion of 'suggestion' or 'implication' cannot be accounted for in terms of semantic content. But Grice introduces a technical version of this notion – *conversational implicature* – and explains it in terms of his co-operative principle and associated maxims.

Grice would say that our utterance of the above sentence *implicates* something about what we have or have not decided. (Generally, speakers themselves or their utterances on specific occasions can be said to implicate things.) The students can infer what we are implicating in the following way. They know from experience that we try to co-operate with them in conversations. By the maxim of quantity, we should, in this case, give them information about any decisions on assignment questions we have made. In particular, we should report any decision on the topic they specifically ask about, and since we do not do this, they conclude that we have not decided, at least, to rule out that topic. They know us so well that their conclusion is likely to be true, and their inference is justified.

There are two further points about conversational implicature which must be stressed immediately. First, implicatures of this type vary from context to context. It is an utterance – the action of a speaker in uttering a sentence on a particular occasion – which has an implicature. Another utterance of the same sentence in another context may not have the same implicature.

Return again to the sentence above, but suppose this time that we utter it after the students ask us about examination questions during a revision class. Now we have quite a different context, one in which the purpose is not to give specific information about the questions, but only general information about important and unimportant topics. The students understand this, and so would hesitate to infer anything specific about what we did or did not decide to include in the examination. They certainly could not justly infer anything of this type from the utterance if, after it, we added the statement that there are a number of even more important topics. And this brings us to the second point about conversational implicatures: these implicatures are *cancellable*. We can cancel a conversational implicature of an utterance, and block or defeat an inference based on it, by other things we say or do in a particular context. We would, for example, cancel the implicature in our original example about the assignment question if we added, 'But there is an even more important topic we have already decided to set an assignment on.' (See also Gazdar (1979) and Levinson (1983) on these essential features of conversational implicature.)

An utterance of a sentence can even have an implicature which contradicts the semantic content of the sentence. As an example, suppose a man absent-mindedly forgets to return a pen he has borrowed to sign a document. Taken to task for this, he might say ironically:

Oh yes, I am a crook.

Here the speaker's utterance implicates that he is not a crook, and this is actually inconsistent with the semantic content of the sentence he uses. If we know that the speaker is an honest person, and take proper note of his tone of voice and non-verbal behaviour, then we should be able to see that he is openly *flouting* (as Grice would say) the maxim of quality by uttering a false sentence, which is, moreover, very poorly supported in this context by any evidence of criminality. Thus, we should have no difficulty inferring what the speaker really wants us to believe, which is the implicature and not the semantic content. Now this example should be compared to Nixon's utterance quoted in the section on plausible denial in Chapter 1:

I am not a crook.

What is the difficulty with this utterance? Nixon appears to be supposing that we have been given reason to doubt that he is an honest man. Why else should we not already possess the information that he is not a crook? It reflects badly on him if our observation of his public behaviour has not given us this information. So he apparently does not want his utterance to be taken as a simple statement of fact, but rather as a denial, which is only a felicitous illocutionary act if he has been accused of being a crook. But after we infer that there must have been such an accusation, we may want to know the details of it, and may then discover that it has a great deal of plausibility indeed. Perhaps Nixon should have tried to say ironically that he was a crook.

As we have just illustrated, Grice's conversational theory can be used to explain how an utterance can be seen as an indirect speech act of some type, such as a denial, rather than as a direct speech act of another type, such as a statement of fact. The theory implies that we can do this because we have the ability to infer the intentions of speakers, given the assumption that they are following the co-operative principle and related maxims. This ability seems to be quite a sophisticated one in its full development – a fact consistent with the evidence, reviewed briefly above, about the time it takes for children to understand indirect speech acts fully. The theory can also be used to explain Fillenbaum's observations of normalisation. Assuming the co-operative principle and maxims, listeners are able to recognise which utterances are uninformative, false, irrelevant or unclear, given certain conversational goals, and are able to correct those utterances in line with those goals. This is also a relatively sophisticated ability when fully developed, and it is again unsurprising that children differ from adults in this respect.

Pragmatic presupposition

Another concept which can be explained in terms of the goal or purpose of a conversation is that of the *pragmatic presuppositions* of speakers and their utterances. (See Levinson (1983), van der Sandt (1988) and Stalnaker (1972) for a range of views on presuppositions.) Presuppositions of this type are propositions which are taken for granted by a speaker in making an utterance, and which must be true if the utterance is to satisfy the goal of the speaker in a conversation. (Note either the speaker or, derivatively, the utterance may be said to have the presuppositions.) Suppose we have a conversation whose purpose is to convey information about the morality of politicians, and consider:

That politician is a crook.

This utterance will help to achieve the purpose of our conversation only if some politician has been specified, by the content of the sentence and its context of utterance, for us to talk about. In other words, the pragmatic presupposition of this utterance is that that politician exists. Note that the negation of this utterance would have the same presupposition in this conversation – we need an object to talk about before we can satisfy the goal of ascribing to it the positive or negative quality of being a crook or of not being a crook. Further presuppositions depend on whether our use of *that politician* is deictic or anaphoric. The use of this term would be deictic if, say, we were at a political meeting and wished to use it to help us to point out a certain individual whom we could see there. A further pragmatic presupposition of the utterance would then be that the listener could also observe and identify this individual. Alternatively, the use of *that politician* might be anaphoric, as it would be when we were discussing politicians we could not observe, and then it would have an antecedent earlier in the conversation. A pragmatic presupposition of the utterance, in this second case, would be that our listeners could also identify that antecedent.

We can, of course, describe both of these cases in the terms used by Clark and his colleagues, which we have already introduced. In the first case, we presuppose that our listeners possess the 'given' perceptual information which will help them to pick out and observe the politician we are talking about. This information will presumably concern, in part, the physical appearance of that person. But the 'new' information, that that person is a crook, will not be directly perceptual, and we could certainly have had good reason to believe that our listeners did not already possess it. In the second case, we presuppose that our listeners possess as 'given' the linguistic information necessary to identify the antecedent of *that politician*. Here our listeners may know little about any politician we are referring to beyond the 'new' information.

We can illustrate this last point in another example (inspired by Russell 1912: 57–8):

The longest-lived of men, whoever he was, must have been extremely old when he died. And that man must have had a healthy lifestyle.

Our listeners would have no difficulty in finding the antecedent of the anaphoric use of *that man* in the second sentence – it is *the longest-lived of men*, a *definite description* specifying a unique man in the first sentence. They would also understand, from the context and what we say, that we cannot perceptually identify this man, and that we do not take it for granted that they can do so. Thus, by using *that man* in this case, we presuppose that our listeners can find the antecedent, but not that they can perceptually identify its referent. The 'given' information that they need to understand our second utterance is merely that we are talking about a man who lived longer than any other. Our utterance presupposes that they possess this limited 'given' information because, if they did not, we would be unable to satisfy the goal of giving them the 'new' information that that man had a healthy lifestyle.

Our use of *the longest-lived of men* is an instance of what Donellan (1966) calls the *attributive* use of definite descriptions. We have used this description to talk about whichever man had the attribute of living longer than any other. Donellan would say that we have only general reasons, and not more specific perceptual grounds, for thinking that that man had a healthy lifestyle. In more technical terms, we can only satisfy Grice's maxim of quality in this case by having a *non-constructive justification* for what we say. That justification would depend on general scientific facts connecting longevity with certain lifestyles. In contrast, there are what Donellan calls *referential* uses of definite descriptions. An example would be our use of *the man sitting over there* in the following utterance at a party:

The man sitting over there is making a fool of himself.

We presuppose, in making this utterance, that our listeners will also be able

the hearer indicated by a 'truncator' utterance such as 'Yeah yeah' that the pair were on common ground. Once established, common ground sometimes led to some very arcane expressions. The record seems to have been what Clark and Schaefer call a 'level 7 key' – in other words, it was seven steps removed from being a clear reference at level 1. It was 'The name of a woman who had a friend whose home town was near a city that had the same name as a dormitory where a friend of theirs lived with the same last name as someone they thought was in the ... picture.'

This kind of work is only just beginning, but Clark and Schaefer point out that it is part of an evolutionary trend in language research which began by considering utterances only in terms of semantic content, developed by considering audience design at the level of a single hearer, and is now widening to consider the audience at a more general level. This trend has revealed a great variety of inferences which need to be made to understand discourse, as we will continue to illustrate. Real-life discourse can be very complex, and some researchers have wondered in the past whether the ways ordinary people talk to each other were too messy to be accounted for by elegant theories; the work we have reviewed in these chapters has, we hope, allowed one to be rather more optimistic.

Part 2
Thinking and reasoning

4 Logic and inference

Some inferences are justified, but others are not, and sometimes people make mistakes, or commit fallacies, in the inferences they perform. The question of which forms of inference are justified naturally arises. Logic is the subject which answers this question, and in the course of doing so, it reveals some fundamental facts about semantic content. It is our topic in this chapter because of its *normative* aspect, its concern with the way we ought to reason, and because of the connection with semantic content. Later in the book, we shall investigate to what extent, and in what sense, people follow the principles of logic in their reasoning. We shall be interested in whether logic can be used to describe the way people actually reason, and in whether much of people's reasoning is, in fact, logical or even rational. The notion of the semantic content of sentences has been, and will continue to be, an important one in the book, and we shall get a better understanding of it by having a look at logic. It will not, however, suit our purpose to give a formal or technical introduction to logic, which is beyond the scope of this book (Hodges (1977) is a good place to begin for that).

Sentential logic

The most elementary part of logic deals with negation, conjunction, disjunction and a special kind of conditional; it is called *sentential logic* (also propositional logic or the propositional calculus). The language of this logic may be taken to consist of some restricted aspect of natural language, but it may also be set up to consist of completely new symbols. Let us suppose that, in this language, *not-A* is the negation of some arbitrary sentence *A*, that *A and B* and *A or B* are the conjunction and disjunction of *A* and some other sentence *B*, and *if A then B* is the special kind of conditional. Then consider the inferences or arguments set out in Figure 4.1.

		if A then B
A and B	A	A
A	A or B	B

		if A then B
not-A	not-(A or B)	not-B
not-(A and B)	not-B	not-A

FIGURE 4.1

These six arguments or inferences consist of one or two premises or assumptions above the line, followed by a conclusion below the line. In an ordinary argument in natural language, the premises would generally give someone's reasons for asserting the conclusion, which would probably be preceded by such a word as 'thus' or 'therefore'. The ordinary premises and the conclusion would appear in place of the *metavariables* above, the A's and B's, and would, of course, have some specific content as used in natural language. But in logic there are reasons for using metavariables like these, and one is to give *rules of inference* in what is called an *axiomatisation* of the logic. These rules indicate which general forms of inference are justified, and the only expressions appearing above with specific content are the *logical constants: not, and, or* and *if-then*. With the exception of these constants, the rules of inference are given independent of content and may be applied to reasoning about any subject-matter.

Inferences of any form above, with ordinary sentences in place of the A's and B's, are completely justified, and in a moment we shall begin to explain why this is so. But the first row of rules above is particularly interesting. It consists of three inferences called, in order, *and-elimination, or-introduction* and *conditional-elimination* (more traditionally, *modus ponens*). These rules would be among those taken as basic in a type of axiomatisation of sentential logic known as *natural deduction*, and the rules in the second row above would be among those derived from these basic rules.

So natural have logical systems of this type seemed that some psychologists have claimed that there is just such a system naturally present in the mind. In later chapters, we shall have a great deal to say about claims that there is this or some other kind of 'mental logic'. (See Prawitz (1965) for a full account of natural deduction; Quine (1972) for an introductory account; and Johnson-Laird (1983: 29) on mental logic and natural deduction.)

Rules of inference are displayed, as we have done, using certain syntactic or grammatical forms, called *logical forms*. But what does it mean to say that these forms of inference are completely justified? And how can we know that they are so justified? The way to answer these questions is to turn to the semantic part of logic, *model theory*, where the concept of truth is all important.

Model theory

Let us take an artificially simple example, and suppose that there are only two sentences, C and W, which do not contain any logical constants in our version of the language of sentential logic. Such sentences are called *atomic sentences*, while those containing at least one logical constant in them are called *compound sentences*. We can imagine that these could be used to make statements about the weather, C stating that it is cold, and W that it is windy. These two sentences are true in some states of the weather and false in others, or, in technical words, C and W are true in some models and false in others.

A *model* for the sentences of sentential logic is nothing more than an *assignment* of one of the two *truth values*, truth and falsity, to the atomic sentences; and there are obviously just four such models in this case. Both C and W might have the assignment truth (it is cold and windy in the first model); C might have truth and W falsity (it is cold but not windy in the second model); C might have falsity and W truth (it is not cold but is windy in the third model); and finally C and W might have falsity (it is neither cold nor windy in the fourth model).

We can now give a *recursive definition* of the notion of being true in a model. An atomic sentence is true in a model if and only if that model gives it the assignment truth. *Not-A* is true in a model if and only if *A* is not true in the model. *A and B* is true in a model if and only if *A* is true in the model and *B* is true in the model. *A or B* is true in a model if and only if *A* is true in the model or *B* is true in the model. And the special conditional, *if A then B*, is true in the model if and only if *A* is not true in the model or *B* is true in the model. This definition can be thought of as extending the assignment of truth values from the atomic sentences to the compound sentence in sentential logic. We simply say that any sentence, no matter how many occurrences of the logical constants there are in it, has the assignment or the *extension* truth in a model if it is true in that model; otherwise, it is false in the model and has the assignment or extension falsity there.

The justification of inferences in sentential logic becomes possible at this point. Any form of inference is certainly justified if we can rely on it never to lead us from truth in its premises to falsity in its conclusion, and in that case we say that it is *truth preserving* – its conclusion is true if all its premises are true. In more technical terms, we say that such a form of inference is *sound* or *valid*, and that it has this property if and only if there is no model in which all its premises are true and its conclusion is false. Inspection of any of the above rules of inference will show that its premises are not all true while its conclusion is false in any model. These forms of inference are therefore completely justified – we can absolutely rely on them never to lead us from truth to falsity in our reasoning. Of course, inferences of those forms will sometimes have false conclusions when we use false premises or make false assumptions, but then the fault lies in the premises or assumptions and not in the forms of inference themselves.

The concept of *logical implication* is related to that of valid inference. A set of *declarative sentences* – that is, sentences which have a truth value – logically imply another sentence if and only if there is no model in which all sentences in the set are true and the other sentence is false. Thus, an inference is valid if and only if its premises logically imply its conclusion.

It is interesting and instructive to compare logical implication with Grice's notion of conversational implicature, which we covered in Chapter 3. The former is a semantic relation of sentences and meanings, while the latter is a pragmatic one of speakers and utterances. It is a semantic fact, for instance, that *A and B* logically implies *B*, a fact determined by the meaning of *and* as given in the recursive definition of truth. No mention is made there of speakers or their utterances, which are just the concepts required to explain conversational implicature. Speakers, moreover, can always cancel conversational implicatures, but the fact that *A and B* logically implies *B* cannot be 'cancelled' by any speaker who uses sentences of this form.

Logical implication and validity are defined by reference to all models, and so nothing can 'cancel' logical implications or the validity of inferences like and-elimination. In contrast, we cannot absolutely trust any pragmatic inferences we perform based only on a speaker's utterance and Gricean considerations. Such inferences can be justified to some extent; we have already shown how they can be founded on the co-operative principle, and we shall say more about their justification later. Still, these inferences can sometimes lead us from truth to falsity and so do not have the absolute or complete justification that valid inferences possess.

The recursive definition of truth in a model for sentential logic has the important semantic consequence that the truth value of any compound sentence, such as *A and B*, can be determined from the truth values of its component sentences, in this case *A and B*. In turn, the truth values of *A and B* in the model can be determined from the truth values of their components, and so on down to the level of atomic sentences, by means of the definition. The truth value in a model of any sentence in sentential logic is a *function*, in the mathematical sense, of the truth values in the model of the atomic sentences it contains, and consequently this is said to be an *extensional* logic, and its logical constants are said to be *truth functional* operators or connectives. As can be seen from the recursive definition of truth, this property is possessed even by the special conditional, which is sometimes just called the *truth functional conditional* (or, alternatively, the extensional or material conditional). We can think of the recursive definition as giving the *truth conditions* of at least the compound sentences: it specifies the conditions under which these sentences are true in terms of their component sentences. For example, it specifies that the truth functional conditional, *if A then B*, is true under the condition that A is not true and also under the condition that B is true, and that this conditional is not true when neither condition holds – that is, when A is true and B is not true.

There is a clear connection between understanding the truth conditions of a declarative sentence and understanding its meaning or semantic content. This point is most clearly illustrated by the sort of sentences we have used as examples in this section. To learn the meanings of the atomic sentences, C and W, it is necessary to learn to distinguish between states of the weather, and to grasp which of these states makes each of those sentences true and which false. And after that, learning the meanings of the logical constants and the compound sentences involves learning implicitly what the recursive definition of truth specifies.

In this way, truth conditions are involved in the meanings of declarative sentences, but do these meanings contain something more than truth conditions? Using the terminology of Frege (1892), let us associate the truth conditions of a sentence with its *sense*, and take its *reference* as its extension, as determined by the truth conditions, in some model. Then the question becomes whether meaning in declarative sentences is something more than sense and reference, or whether some additional notion is needed to account for full semantic content.

Frege held that some further notion was needed, which he called *tone*. (For a theory of Frege's original view of reference, sense and tone, see Dummett 1973.) He argued for the existence of tone by pointing out the contrast between *and* and *but*, which we can illustrate in the following sentences.

Russell was an aristocrat and he was a socialist.

Russell was an aristocrat but he was a socialist.

These sentences have the forms *A and B* and *A but B*, and they are both true if and only if A is true and B is true. In other words, these sentences have the same truth conditions and thus the same sense. But obviously the second sentence does differ from the first sentence in some aspect of meaning, and this is what Frege called tone. The second sentence, with its tone determined by the tone of *but*, would be used to suggest that there is some contrast between being an aristocrat and being a socialist.

Grice (1975) introduces a concept which is related to tone, and which he calls *conventional implicature*. One respect in which this concept differs from that of conversational implicature, according to Grice, is that conventional implicatures cannot be cancelled. The meaning of *but*, as fixed by a convention for its use, is such that any utterance of the second sentence conventionally implicates that there is an appropriate contrast. By knowing more about the context of any particular utterance, we might be able to infer, say, that the speaker thinks that being an aristocrat is a positive quality while being a socialist is a negative one, or vice versa. But if no such contrast exists, then the utterance is only inappropriate and not necessarily false, as it would be if the second sentence logically implied that a contrast existed. Conventional implicature is distinct from both conversational implicature and logical implication. Like tone, conventional implicature is not a purely pragmatic notion, but must be at least partly explained in terms of some aspect of meaning distinct from truth conditions.

First-order predicate logic

Many valid inferences in natural language involve the concept of *quantification*, as in the following examples.

> Duck-billed platypuses are mammals which lay eggs. Therefore, some mammals lay eggs.

> Every book on the list has been ordered by the library. Every book ordered by the library will be available soon. Therefore, every book on the list will be available soon.

The first inference above has one premise while the second has two, but the important point is that the validity of inferences like these depends on the way *quantifier phrases*, such as 'some mammals' or 'every book on the list', are used within them. *First-order predicate logic* is an extensional formal system which includes, as a proper part, sentential logic and its concepts of negation, conjunction, disjunction and the truth functional conditional. But predicate logic has, in addition, the means to express quantification, through the use of new logical constants known as *quantifiers*.

In a system based on English, the quantifiers could just be taken as the words 'something' and 'everything' followed by variables, such as 'x' and 'y'. Phrases of the form 'something x' and 'everything y' would be, respectively, *existential quantifiers* and *universal quantifiers*, and could be read as 'some object x is such that' and 'every object y is such that'. What are technically called *predicates* in this kind of system would be formed from *general terms*, such as 'mammal', and variables – an example of a predicate would be 'x is a mammal'. Then the quantifiers and the predicates could be used together to make precise statements, such as the following versions of the conclusions of the inferences above:

Something x (x is a mammal and x lays eggs).

Everything y (if y is a book on the list then y will be available soon).

Using quantifiers and variables in this way helps us to be as clear as possible about what we are trying to say. (Quine (1972) and Hodges (1977) show how to base a predicate logic on more or less modified or 'regimented' versions of English.) But this type of precision and clarity depends on the fact that there is a model theory for this logic, and that is also what we need in order to state exactly when its inferences are valid.

A model for the language of predicate logic must first of all supply a *domain* or *universe of discourse*, a set of objects for us to talk about. The examples we have used may suggest that we are interested in animals and books, but the domain can be any non-empty set of objects. The model must also specify extensions for any proper names or other singular terms in the language and for the general terms.

To simplify matters, let us use 'Black Beauty' (the character) as an example of a proper name in the language and continue to use 'mammal' as an example of a general term. The extension of 'Black Beauty', and we could also say its reference, in the model would simply be an individual object in the domain for it to name – this would be the particular object we could use 'Black Beauty' to talk about in that model. The extension in the model of 'mammal' would be a subset of the domain – the collection of objects taken as mammals in that model. If the model were determined by the actual world, then the extension of 'mammal' in that model would be, of course, the collection of actual mammals. But if the model was given by the merely possible state of affairs described in the book *Black Beauty*, then the extension of 'mammal' would include at least one literate horse capable of writing an autobiography.

We have only briefly illustrated some very elementary aspects of model theory for predicate logic. We shall not go further into the technical details, but on the basis of this approach, the concept of truth in a model for sentences in this logic can be given a recursive definition. (Chang and Keisler (1977) is a full introduction to model theory.) And then the definitions of valid inference, logical implication, and of other semantic notions can be the same as they were for sentential logic, only with the new, more complex definition of a model in place of the earlier one of a model for the language of sentential logic. Consider these sentences of the language of predicate logic:

Black Beauty is a mammal.

Something x (x is a mammal).

The first sentence above is true in a model if and only if the extension of 'Black Beauty' is a member of the extension of 'mammal' in that model. The second sentence is true in the model if and only if at least one object in the domain is a member of the extension of 'mammal' in that model. Now clearly there is no model in which the first sentence is true and the second is false, and thus the first logically implies the second, and the second may be validly inferred from the first. This is a simple example, but there are an infinite number of valid inferences in predicate logic, just as there were in sentential logic. The problem is to find a recursive way of discovering these – that is, a set of rules which can be applied over and over again to generate more and more valid inferences. This is the problem of axiomatising predicate logic, and by solving it, we have the means to put valid inferences together in derivations or deductions, leading to conclusions which we never would have imagined were logically implied by our premises.

One way to solve this problem is to extend the system of natural deduction from sentential logic to all of predicate logic. Again, we shall not go into anything like the full technical details. (These are best studied in Prawitz (1965) with Quine (1972) used as a more introductory work. Fine (1985) develops a very interesting new approach to natural deduction based on the notion of arbitrary objects.) But what needs to be done is to supply introduction and elimination rules for the existential and universal quantifiers, to go with the rules of this type for the other logical constants. Looked at as an inference, the example above is an instance of the rule for *existential introduction* – 'something x' has been introduced by inferring a sentence containing it from a sentence with a proper name in place of the variable in the predicate. These rules may have instances containing recognisable terms like 'mammal' with some informal content, but as we pointed out when discussing sentential logic above, the rules themselves are given in a formal, syntactic way and specify their instances through the use of general metavariables and the logical constants. In spite of the presence of logical constants, such rules are sometimes said to be *content-independent*.

Another way to axiomatise sentential logic and predicate logic is equally formal and content-independent (in the above sense), but is directly and explicitly related to model theory. With this method, we use what are called *semantic tableaux* to try to construct a model in which the premises of an inference are all true and the conclusion is false. If we succeed in doing this, then obviously the inference cannot be valid – its conclusion will not be true whenever its premises are true. But if every possible way of trying to construct such a model runs into a contradiction, then the inference is valid – there just cannot be a model in which its premises are true and its conclusion is false.

These tableaux are also to be constructed according to rules containing metavariables. If we applied these rules to our last example of an inference, we would try to construct, on paper or just mentally, a model in which the extension of 'Black Beauty' was a mammal, and yet in which it was false that . something was a mammal. The formal tableau rules for the quantifiers would then tell us that this model would have to be one in which the extension of 'Black Beauty' was not a mammal. In this way, we would contradict ourselves in trying to construct a model in which the premise of the inference was true and the conclusion false, and that would prove that this is a valid inference.

As in the case of the rules of natural deduction, we need to be able to recognise the logical form of sentences in order to apply the tableau rules, but we do not need to know the truth values of the sentences nor the informal content of terms like 'mammal'. Both types of rules give us the means to understand even what is logically implied by sentences about purely imaginary or possible states of affairs, such as those in books like *Black Beauty*. (The book we have recommended as an elementary introduction to logic (Hodges 1977) uses a tableau-like system. Beth was the originator of semantic tableaux, and Beth and Piaget (1966) contains an account of this system, with suggestions about how it might be relevant to the study of the mind.)

As we also indicated above, some psychologists have held that the mind naturally possesses a system like that of natural deduction for performing inferences. It might equally be held, as an alternative, that the mental system is like that of semantic tableaux. Indeed, Johnson-Laird (1983: ch. 5) seems to have based, to some extent, his theory of *mental models* for reasoning with quantifiers on semantic tableaux, although he denies that the mental system is sufficiently formal and rigorous, as a way of trying to determine whether inferences are valid, to be properly called a logic. However that may be, the notion of a mental model for a first-order language is of general interest. A model of this language can be any set-theoretic construction of the sort we have described. The domain of a model, for example, need not be a set of physical objects like mammals, but could be a set of mental representations of mammals or of anything else. A mental model could also be thought of as a way we have of representing, or at least partially representing, external objects like mammals and their properties, or even possible objects and their possible properties. Thus, model theory allows for the existence of mental models, which in the right mental system may constitute part of our knowledge and understanding of a first-order language.

The broad definition of a model, as any set-theoretic construction of a certain type, remains fundamental. An inference is valid if and only if there is no model, whether mental or of any other kind, in which the premises are true and the conclusion false. Moreover, the study of general model theory reveals deep semantic facts about *expressibility*. For example, it can be shown that there is no first-order sentence which expresses the proposition that the domain is finite, i.e. which is true if and only if the domain is finite. (This is one of the consequences of the compactness theorem; see Chang and Keisler 1977.)

There is much to learn in model theory about what can and cannot be expressed using just the first-order logical constants in an extensional language. But we should also study intensional logic and its model theory, as intensionality is a common feature of ordinary sentences and inferences.

Intensional logic

Necessity and possibility are examples of *intensional* notions. Consider these statements:

It is not the case that some chimpanzee understands English as well as a 3-year-old child.

It is possible that some chimpanzee understands English as well as a 3-year-old child.

The phrase *it is possible that* is grammatically a one-place sentential operator, like *it is not the case that*: both are used syntactically to construct a longer sentence from one shorter one. If we let E be the statement about what some chimpanzee understands, then the first example above can be represented by 'not-E' and the second by 'possibly-E'. The grammatical similarity is obvious, but there is an important semantic difference we mark by the distinction between extensionality and intensionality.

Since negation is an extensional concept, the truth value of 'not-E' (its extension) is totally determined by the truth value of E (the extension of E). If it is true that some chimpanzee understands English as well as a 3-year-old child, then 'not-E' must be false; and if it is false that some chimpanzee understands so much, then 'not-E' must be true. Of course, if E is true, then 'possibly-E' must also be true – the truth value of the latter is determined by the former in this case.

But as a result of the fact that possibility is an intensional concept, the matter is different when E happens to be false. In that case, the truth value of 'possibly-E' is not determined by the falsity of E alone. There are various ways of interpreting possibility, but thinking of it in one way, we would say that 'possibly-E' was false if we knew some physiological reason why chimpanzees were incapable of understanding English at all well. In a contrasting case, however, we might know that chimpanzees were capable of understanding English very well. We would then not only say that 'possibly-E' was true, but we would continue to think that it had been true even if we discovered that, in fact, no actual chimpanzee had ever had the opportunity to learn English.

This difference between negation and possibility can be further clarified by introducing the distinction between the *actual* state of affairs and a merely *possible* state of affairs. By saying that a sentence is true without qualification, we are saying that it is true in the actual state of affairs. What is actually or in fact true is obviously of great interest to us, and negation is important as an extensional notion because it helps us to talk about that. But we can also think and make comments about purely imaginary or conceivable states of affairs, and possibility helps us to do this as an intensional notion.

The sentence 'possibly-E' is true in the actual state of affairs if E is true in some relevant possible state of affairs. The actual state of affairs does count as such a possible state of affairs (though a special one), and so if E is actually true, then 'possibly-E' is actually true. But although E is false in the actual state of affairs, 'possibly-E' is true here if E is true in some other, merely possible state of affairs. To find the actual truth value of 'possibly-E', other relevant possibilities must be taken into account, and only when E is false in all of these, is 'possibly-E' false in the actual state of affairs.

It is easy to set up a *modal* sentential language by adding 'possibly' and its companion 'necessarily' as new one-place sentential operators to 'not' and the other logical constants in the sentential language we have already described. This was an extensional language, but it now contains two non-truth functional operators and becomes an intensional language which requires a new model theory. A model for the new language must contain a set of possibilities or possible states of affairs, usually called *possible worlds*, one of which may be specified as the actual world. The model may also distinguish between possibilities which are relevant or 'accessible' and those which are not; and different ways of doing this could be associated with different understandings of possibility and necessity. But given these possible worlds, truth is defined relative to them in the model.

The interesting new clauses in this definition state, for any sentence A, that 'possibly-A' is true in a possible world in the model if and only if A is true in some relevant possible world in the model, and that 'necessarily-A' is true in a possible world in the model if and only if A is true in all relevant possible worlds in the model. Then any inference in the new language is valid if and only if it preserves truth in a possible world in a model – there is no possible world in any model in which all its premises are true and its conclusion false. And logical implication can also be defined for this language in the obvious way.

The next step in a formal development would be for us to axiomatise these semantic concepts. One approach we could use would be to lay down valid introduction and elimination rules for the new logical constants, 'possibly' and 'necessarily', to be used together with the introduction and elimination rules for the extensional logical constants. The rule of necessity elimination is easy to give as an example: this tells us that we may always infer A from the single premise 'necessarily-A'. The result of all these rules would be a natural deduction system of *modal sentential logic*, which would help us to understand intensional sentences by showing us how to use them as premises, or derive them as conclusions, in valid inferences.

We can also have systems of *modal first-order predicate logic*. After adding 'possibly' and 'necessarily' to the language of predicate logic, we would extend the definition of a model by having, not only a set of possible worlds, but as well a way of specifying a domain for the variables to range over in each possible world. This would allow us to say what it was for predicates to be satisfied by objects in any possible world in any model, and then to define the concept of truth in a possible world in a model. Validity and logical implication would be defined here in the same way as in modal sentential logic, and this modal predicate logic could be axiomatised in different ways. We should just note that there are really distinct modal sentential and predicate logics of these broad types, depending, for example, on how the notion of 'accessible' possible worlds is defined, or on how exactly domains are assigned to possible worlds. But these different logics could help us to see the implications of the different ways of interpreting 'possibly' and 'necessarily', and to understand how they interact with other expressions, such as the quantifiers.

The model theory of modal logic gives us the means to define an intension for each expression in the language, in addition to its extension. Let us take some particular model with its set of possible worlds and use 'stallion' as an example of an expression. We can speak of the extension of 'stallion' in any possible world, and that would be the set of objects considered to be stallions in that possible world. The intension of 'stallion' could then be thought of as a function which, given any possible world, specified the extension of 'stallion' there. It may so happen that the intension of an expression in some model is related in some interesting way to the intension of some other expression in that model. For example, in a model which was the set theoretic representation of what we ordinarily take to be possible states of affairs, the intension of 'stallion' would be identical with that defined for 'male horse'. The result is that

All stallions are male horses

is necessarily true in that model, just as it is in ordinary affairs. What this special model reflects is the fact that 'stallion' is synonymous with 'male horse' in English, and that this English sentence is *analytically* true, true in virtue of its meaning. The intension of a sentence in a model can just be defined as the set of possible worlds in which it is true in that model; and this set is sometimes identified with the *proposition* expressed by the sentence in the model. The above sentence is true in every possible world in our example, and thus its intension, or proposition, in that model is the set of all possible worlds. Now consider:

There is a stallion on the farm.

There is a horse on the farm.

The intensions of these sentences are not identical in our example, but they are still related there in an interesting way. The second is true in any possible world in which the first is true – put more technically, the intension of the first is a subset of the intension of the second. In a case like this, we say that the first *strictly implies* the second. Strict implication is a weaker relation than that of logical implication, but that in itself makes it useful for justifying many more ordinary inferences. We are always justified in inferring the second sentence above from the first used as a premise, just as a result of what 'stallion' means in ordinary English. (See Hodges (1977) for an introductory section on intensionality, and Chellas (1980) for an introductory book on modal logic. Montague (1974) contains fundamental papers on intensional logic and applications of it to the study of natural language. Kripke (1972) is also a seminal but more philosophical work on necessity and possibility.)

Conditional logic

There are a number of different kinds of conditional in natural language, some of which at least have an intensional logic. Let us look at a standard example of two of these (from Adams 1970):

If Oswald did not kill Kennedy, then someone else did.

If Oswald had not killed Kennedy, then someone else would have.

The first of these examples is an *indicative conditional* while the second is a *counterfactual* or *subjunctive conditional*. There is an obvious difference between these two conditionals, and clearly they cannot have the same meaning, as the first is true and the second is false (on the assumption that there was not a general conspiracy to kill Kennedy). Both of these types are common in natural language, but it is hard to state precisely how they differ grammatically or logically and semantically. We will, of course, be concerned here with their basic logical and semantic properties. (See Dudman (1984) for grammatical as well as semantic points. Chellas (1980) includes a technical introduction to conditional logic, and Jackson (1987) is excellent as a more philosophical introduction. Traugott, ter Meulen, Reilly and Ferguson (1986) is a recent collection of papers on conditionals.)

So far in this chapter, our conditional *if A then B* has been extensional and logically equivalent to *not-A or B*. This conditional is true whenever its antecedent is false, no matter what the truth value of its consequent is, and independently of any other fact. It is also automatically true when its consequent is true, whatever else holds or does not hold. But at least the subjunctive conditional in natural language cannot have these properties, and there would have to be a separate logical constant for it in a conditional logic. In using a subjunctive conditional, we presuppose that we are not talking about the actual state of affairs, since our sole object is to talk about the purely hypothetical (which is sometimes very helpful, in spite of what slippery politicians say when they refuse to answer hypothetical questions). People who believe (as most of us do) that Oswald did kill Kennedy would accept this proposition in using the above subjunctive conditional. Their object would be to talk about hypothetical circumstances in which he did not do so, and their message might be that there was a general conspiracy to kill Kennedy. We would not immediately agree that their subjunctive conditional was true because we shared their belief in the falsity of its antecedent. In fact, we would say that their subjunctive conditional was false (on the assumption that we rejected any theory like the conspiracy one).

The subjunctive conditional does not have the same truth conditions as the extensional conditional. What then are the truth conditions of this intensional conditional? We may get some help in answering this question from a suggestion, which goes back to Ramsey (1931: ch. 9), about how we ordinarily try to decide whether to assert a subjunctive conditional.

The idea is that we take the antecedent of the subjunctive conditional we are considering and add it as a kind of supposition to what we believe. But to do this consistently and coherently, we must restrict our beliefs in some sense; after all, one of these beliefs in the standard case is that the antecedent of the subjunctive conditional is false. We proceed by temporarily 'suspending' or 'setting to one side' beliefs which would not be true together with the supposition; and then we assert the subjunctive conditional if its consequent appears likely to be true, given its antecedent as supposition and our restricted beliefs. (Ramsey may have meant something like this procedure to apply only to indicative conditionals. Stalnaker (1968) refines it, and Lewis (1973: ch. 3) criticises it as applied to subjunctive conditionals. It has inspired more detailed psychological theories of how the mind processes conditionals, as in Rips and Marcus (1977) and Johnson-Laird (1983, 1985).)

What are we trying to do when we apply this procedure to a subjunctive conditional? One answer is that we are trying to find out whether the consequent of the subjunctive conditional holds in a possible state of affairs in which the antecedent is true, but which is not radically different in other respects from the actual state of affairs. A model for a language containing the subjunctive conditional should, in light of this, contain a *selection function* which picks out such a possible world, given the antecedent. The possible world specified will be 'close to' or 'similar to' the actual world – it will not differ very greatly, though the antecedent will be true in it, from the actual world. The subjunctive conditional will then be true in the actual world in that model if and only if its consequent is true in that specified, similar possible world.

This type of semantics for subjunctive conditionals has been presented more generally and rigorously in various ways (one of the varieties is to have the selection function specify a range of similar possible worlds instead of just one), and the results have been axiomatised in different ways. (See Chellas (1980); Lewis (1973); Stalnaker (1968) and Thomason (1970).)

We must now return to indicative conditionals. The above examples showed that we evaluate these and subjunctive conditionals differently at some stage. However, we can describe a Ramsey-like procedure for indicative conditionals, one that is to some extent like that for subjunctive conditionals. We do not ordinarily presuppose that the antecedent of an indicative conditional is false, but perhaps we have other presuppositions in particular contexts.

When we use the first example above, for instance, we may presuppose that Kennedy has been shot, and may consequently not 'suspend' our belief that this is so when we consider the supposition that Oswald did not shoot him. From our beliefs, 'unrestricted' in this respect and this supposition, we would infer that someone else must have shot Kennedy, and be ready to assert our example. More formally in the semantics, the selection function could pick a possible world in which not only was the antecedent of the indicative conditional true, but also certain presuppositions held. Taking this approach, we could have essentially the same semantics and logic for the indicative and subjunctive conditionals, and put the difference between them down to different interpretations of the selection function. (See Stalnaker 1968, 1984.)

Some would argue against this that the indicative conditional is, in fact, the extensional conditional, and that the example we are using has the same truth conditions as the statement that either Oswald killed Kennedy or someone else did. This statement, as an extensional one, concerns only the actual world, and Jackson (1987) has a general argument against introducing other possible worlds in the semantics of the indicative conditional. He points out that, if we believe both an indicative conditional of the form 'B is the case if A is the case' and 'B is not the case', then we do not say, 'Things are different from the way they actually are if A is the case.'

What he wants to conclude is that we are concerned only with the actual world when we use indicative conditionals. But with those beliefs we would say, 'Things are different from the way we take them to be if A is the case.' By saying this, we would acknowledge that, if A is true, then some of our beliefs are not true in the actual world, but only in some other possible world. Our beliefs are an attempt to represent the actual world; if Oswald did not kill Kennedy, then one at least of our beliefs fails to represent actuality, and represents only some merely possible world. Thus, other possible worlds do come into the way we speak and think about indicative conditionals.

Jackson is correct that possible worlds are relevant in different ways to the evaluation of indicative and subjunctive conditionals, and that this is the real difference between these conditionals. (Any apparent grammatical difference is less significant, in spite of their different grammatical names.) When thinking about an indicative conditional, we are interested in the actual world, and we presuppose or 'hold constant' some firm beliefs we have about the actual world, such as that someone shot Kennedy. But when we consider a subjunctive conditional, we are prepared to give up such presuppositions, with the idea of trying to find out what is true in some other possible world.

The use of indicative and subjunctive conditionals in natural language is so subtle and complex that there are some problems with the semantics we have sketched for them. One difficulty is the use of conditionals embedded in other conditionals, and a good illustration of this has been presented by McGee (1985), who even claims that he has found a counter-example to modus ponens. His best example is given in the following way (with the numbering (1)–(3) added by us).

Opinion polls taken just before the 1980 election showed the Republican Ronald Reagan decisively ahead of the Democrat Jimmy Carter, with the other Republican in the race, John Anderson, a distant third. Those appraised of the poll believed, with good reason:
[1] If a Republican wins, then if it's not Reagan who wins it will be Anderson.

[2] A Republican will win.

Yet they did not have reason to believe

[3] If it's not Reagan who wins, it will be Anderson.

In our view, this inference only appears to be a counterexample to modus ponens because of an ambiguity in the use of (3). If we think of (3) as an isolated sentence, then (3) does not appear to be true. But if we look on (1)–(3) as an inference, then we have to see (1) and (2) as the assumptions on which (3) depends. (Let us take it for granted that (1) and (2) are not premises themselves dependent on assumptions in a longer derivation.) And under the *assumption* that a Republican will win and that (1) also holds, we can only say that (3) is true: that is all (3) can be, *given* those assumptions.

We explain the ambiguity in examples like this by pointing out that different possible states of affairs are relevant in these two cases. When (3) is thought of as an isolated sentence, a possible state of affairs is relevant in which Reagan does not win but Carter does. However, this possible state of affairs, in which (2) is false, is ruled out when (3) is taken as the conclusion of the inference (1)–(3). In that case, (3) turns out to be true because the assumptions restrict the relevant possible states of affairs to ones in which (2) is true. This restriction has to be the same as that which the antecedent of (1) places on the consequent of (1); for otherwise there would be equivocation in the inference, the interpretation of (3) would not be the same as that of the consequent of (1), and it would not really be an instance of modus ponens. An adequate theory of conditionals embedded in other conditionals must take account of the way in which antecedents and assumptions can perform this function. (McGee (1985) and Over (1987b) have more on this example and its significance.)

Deontic logic

Another special kind of logic is that for the *deontic* concepts of obligation and permission. Let us concentrate on obligation and this example:

It ought to be the case that you give up smoking.

We could express this more colloquially by saying that you ought to, should, or must (in one sense) give up smoking. But we wish to bring out that 'it ought to be the case that' is grammatically like 'it is not the case that': both are one-place sentential operators. On the other hand, the deontic operator is obviously an intensional one: the truth value of the above sentence is not at all determined by whether or not you give up smoking in the actual world. Deontic logic is a type of intensional logic in which this operator is a logical constant.

To explain what sentences like our example mean, we need possible states of affairs, and in addition we must make use of the idea that some of these possibilities are judged better, in some sense, than others. Using our example, we would probably have it in mind that you would be healthy in a possible state of affairs in which you gave up smoking, and unhealthy in one in which you did not. We think of our example as true, since the former would be a better state of affairs than the latter from our point of view; otherwise, we would think of it as false. It could be said that this is a subjective concept of truth, and that there may be hypochondriacs or masochists who think it is better to be unhealthy. However, the aim is not to try to establish that there are objective deontic facts, only to state the conditions under which deontic statements should be thought of as true, whether those conditions are objective or subjective.

Sometimes people do disagree strongly about which possibilities are better than others. But there are occasions when some of us at least agree with each other about this, and there can be very widespread agreement indeed, as there is about the value of health. Where there is agreement, we can communicate to some purpose using deontic statements.

The way we have explained our example has made it one of prudential obligation, but there are obligations of other types, as can be clear in context. Perhaps you have promised your friends to give up smoking, and then you have a moral obligation to do so. Perhaps tobacco will be outlawed as a dangerous drug, and then you will have a legal obligation to give up smoking. We can use deontic operators whenever we prefer some possibilities to others, on personal, moral, legal, or any other grounds.

There is also *conditional obligation*, which can be personal, moral, legal, or whatever, but expressed by a two-place operator in a conditional form:

If you decide to smoke, you ought to smoke cigars.

The antecedent of this conditional restricts the possibilities relevant for the evaluation of the consequent to those in which you decide to smoke. Suppose that in a particular context there are only two relevant possibilities of this kind: one in which you smoke cigars, and one in which you smoke cigarettes. Would the former be a better state of affairs, in some sense given by the context, than the latter? We should consider the conditional obligation true if and only if the correct answer to this question is 'yes'. When actually used in some context, the example might clearly be one of conditional prudential obligation. If we preferred being healthy to being unhealthy, then we would find it significant that cigar smoking is healthier than cigarette smoking, and we would rightly conclude that this example was true.

Some logicians have held that the form of modus ponens – or *detachment* as it is called – is not valid for conditional obligation. (The semantics of

Lewis (1973: ch.5) has this consequence; and see Jackson (1985).) They are thinking of examples like the following.

If you decide to smoke, you ought to smoke cigars.

You decide to smoke.

Therefore, you ought to smoke cigars.

We may know that the assumptions of this inference are true yet continue, quite rightly, to give you the advice that you ought not to smoke at all, not even cigars. Is this then a counterexample to modus ponens? The answer is again 'no', for reasons similar to those we gave above in the Reagan and Anderson example. In the context of this inference, the assumptions restrict the possibilities relevant for the evaluation of the conclusion to those in which you decide to smoke; and this must be so if the conclusion and the consequent of the first assumption are to have the same interpretation. Among *those* possibilities, the ones in which you smoke cigars would be better than any of the others in our eyes; and the conclusion above does validly follow from the assumptions.

But when we are giving you advice, should we assume, presuppose, or take it for granted, that you have decided to smoke and that is that? Perhaps we should if you are strongly addicted to tobacco. On the other hand, we may well feel that we should not do so if the decision is one which you can easily alter. We could then insist on considering a wider set of possibilities, including ones in which you do not smoke, and the last sentence above would be false relative to this wider set. This sentence has different interpretations in the different contexts we have described. What is conveyed in these contexts, without any invalid inference or inconsistency, is that cigar smoking is better than any other type of smoking and not smoking anything is best of all.

It would be out of place here to go further into the technical details of the semantics of deontic logic and its axiomatisation, but we shall say more about ordinary deontic reasoning later in the book. (Chellas (1980) has a formal introduction to deontic logic, and we have found Jackson (1985) very helpful and stimulating.)

The logic and semantics of natural language

The various logics we have introduced here, and many others, would have to be combined to get a logic and model theory for all of English or any other natural language. Attempts have been made, as in different ways in Montague (1974) and Barwise and Perry (1983), to specify models for parts of English. An agreed way of doing this for all of English seems to be a very distant goal, but it is one we must reach to get a full theory of truth, valid inference and expressibility in our language.

Parallel to the development of model theory for natural language must be work on how the mind contains or represents models, and on how it performs inferences which may or may not be justified by them. Craik (1943) suggested that the mind contains models of states of affairs, and this idea has been taken up by Johnson-Laird (1983) in his theory of mental models, which we have referred to here and elsewhere in the book. Constructing and manipulating these mental models may be our way of trying to discover which inferences are valid and which are invalid. We may also use them to represent external, non-mental models and actual or merely possible states of affairs. Psychologists have at least as far to go in the theory of mental models as logicians do in the model theory of natural language.

In addition to mental models and their construction, we have spoken of other kinds of mental processes and structures, and these must also be properly related to models and model theory. For example, we referred in Chapters 1 and 2 to bridging inferences and to mental structures like schemas as possible ways of understanding what a text or discourse is about. There must be some normative theory of when these inferences are justified or unjustified, and before that, some account of the truth conditions of any proposed mental structures for representing the content of discourse.

The latter problem is seriously addressed in the *discourse representation* theory of Kamp (1981). (A good introduction to Kamp's theory is Spencer-Smith (1987).) Suppose we hear the following:

Some mammal in the zoo is laying an egg. It is covered in spines.

We get a discourse representation of what is conveyed here by using the *reference markers*, x and y, in the following type of structure:

mammal-in-the-zoo(x)
egg(y)
lays(x,y)
spines(x)

With a mental structure of this type, we would have represented x as a mammal in the zoo and y as an egg laid by x, and performed the bridging inference to the representation of x as having the spines. The structure as a whole is true in a model if and only if x and y can be assigned to members of the domain in such a way that these individual representations of x and y come out as true in the model; in that case, the structure is said to be *embedded* in the model. Suppose that there actually is an echidna, a spiny anteater, in the zoo laying an egg. Then x can be assigned to this creature and y to its egg, and the above structure can be embedded in the actual world. Since that is so, we can say that the structure represents part of the actual world.

Once we know what it means to say that our discourse representation is true, we can ask what makes our bridging inference justified. Of course, it is not justified merely because its conclusion is true in the actual world. Nor can it have the absolute justification of a valid inference: there will be models in which its premises are true and its conclusion false. But at least we can ask whether there are good reasons for thinking that its conclusion is *probably* true, given its premises. Are we justified in believing that mammals are more likely than eggs to have spines? This is the type of question we shall take up in Chapter 7.

In the next two chapters, however, we shall be particularly concerned with what Johnson-Laird has aptly called the doctrine of *mental logic.* Psychologists who believe in the existence of a mental logic hold that 'an inference is made by translating its premises into a mental language ... and then applying formal rules of inference to these representations to derive a conclusion from them' (Johnson-Laird 1985: 154). The formal rules would, of course, contain logical constants, but would otherwise use metavariables to specify logical form in a syntactic way that was independent of semantic content. The translation process would have to reveal the logical forms of sentences in ordinary, natural language, before these formal rules could be applied correctly.

This translation process would be extremely difficult to describe in full detail – it is sometimes quite a problem to work out the logical form or forms of a sentence in natural language for the purpose of performing a useful inference. But leaving this difficulty aside, some psychologists have found the doctrine of mental logic very attractive. It always seems to be presupposed by these psychologists that mental logic would be a version of extensional sentential logic (the propositional calculus), or even of extensional first-order predicate logic. These logical systems are well understood, and can be axiomatised using natural deduction or semantic tableaux which arguably seem to describe the way we at least sometimes reason.

If they are descriptive as well as normative systems, telling us how we do reason as well as how we ought to reason, then the job of psychologists is much simplified. In that case, psychologists would not have to look for a variety of mental models, schemas, or other mental representations and processes, individually applied to some sentences and not others of the same logical form but different semantic contents. It is harder to describe ordinary reasoning if it is essentially content-dependent rather than content-independent, as it is if the presence or absence of a non-logical constant like 'horse' or 'mammal' in sentences determines what is ordinarily inferred.

We have seen in this chapter that more than just extensional logic is needed to give us a normative, let alone a descriptive, theory of ordinary reasoning. We shall therefore sometimes distinguish between the doctrines of mental extensional logic, mental modal logic, mental conditional logic, mental deontic logic, and so on for any other logic. Some supporters of mental logic may want to hold that the mind possesses all of these, while others may wish to be more modest and hold, say, that there is only a mental deontic logic. But any specific doctrine of mental logic has the empirical consequence that ordinary reasoning – whether extensional, deontic, or whatever – is content-independent and not content-dependent. In Chapter 6 we shall discuss experiments which attempt to show whether this consequence is true, but first, in Chapter 5, we shall consider the work of the most influential proponent of the doctrine of mental logic.

5 Mental logic

In Chapter 4 we referred to the claim, made by some psychologists, that people perform inferences by using a *mental logic*. We shall discuss in later chapters whether any theory of this type can be correct, but in this chapter we want to investigate, as an example, what appears to be a version of the theory: that found in the work of Piaget and his collaborators. Piaget has been one of the most influential figures in the history of psychology. In response to his work, some theorists have assumed the existence of some kind of mental logic, while others have reacted to the problems with his views by trying to find some alternative account of inference.

Piaget is not, unfortunately, as clear about mental logic as one would wish. As we indicated at the end of the last chapter, it is Johnson-Laird (1983, 1985, 1988) who has used the phrase *the doctrine of mental logic* most clearly to characterise a range of theories. It is easy to understand why such a doctrine has had a great attraction for many cognitive psychologists. If it is essentially correct, then they can interpret a ready-made normative system as an actual mental one, and in this way use it to explain actual reasoning. It is certainly not absurd, as MacNamara (1986) has charged, to hold that the mind contains a system like those found in books on formal logic. The symbols and rules of inference of such a system would not be 'inert' if the mind also contained the right kind of computational processes for operating on them. These natural processes might not themselves be *explicitly* represented in the mind, unlike the mental rules of inference, but could be said to follow certain rules *implicitly*. (In Manktelow and Over (in press a) we briefly explain how this type of system could be implemented on a computer. We say more about computational processes and the mind in Chapter 9.)

Johnson-Laird always cites Piaget as providing the prime example of the doctrine, pointing out that he says such things as 'reasoning is nothing more than the propositional calculus itself' (Inhelder and Piaget 1958: 305). At the beginning of Chapter 4, we preferred the phrase *sentential logic* to that of *propositional calculus* for the logic we presented there as part of a normative theory of how people *ought* to reason. But in contrast, Piaget seems to think that this logic is naturally acquired by people and used in their *actual* reasoning. In this respect at least, his approach is in line with the doctrine of mental logic, as we shall try to show in this chapter. As the above quote illustrates, Inhelder and Piaget seem to take the logic in question to be what we would call a *mental sentential logic*. (But see Beth and Piaget (1966) on first-order predicate logic.)

Piaget: thinking as mental operations

There is an interesting biological theme running through Piagetian theory: cognitive development is conceived of as a process of 'intellectual evolution', in Piaget's own phrase (Piaget 1977): that is, the role and purpose of cognitive development, like evolution itself, is the successful adaptation of the organism to the environment. According to Piaget, human cognitive development arises from the interaction of maturation, or the growth of mental processes, and experience.

The potential for more sophisticated thought thus expands as we grow through childhood, but this must be accompanied by the right sort of experience if it is to be realised. This interaction is characterised by the terms *assimilation, accommodation* and *equilibrium*. Assimilation is where we interpret experience using our existing thoughts or responses; accommodation is where our cognitions become altered as a consequence of experience, so that assimilation can be more effective; equilibrium is the state of balance between cognition and experience. Equilibrium is thus the engine of development: imbalance or disequilibrium is what promotes further development, as mental processes are changed so as to reduce it.

A further property of this process is *co-ordination*: cognitions do not develop piecemeal, any more than single aspects of physical growth occur in isolation from the rest of the body. Co-ordination is responsible for one of the most fundamental and controversial aspects of Piagetian theory: the idea that development occurs in qualitatively distinct *stages*. The characterisation of these differences leads to a second similarly fundamental and controversial aspect of the theory: that qualitatively different mental structures are acquired at each stage. We shall devote more space to this controversy later. To see how these processes culminate in mental logic, we shall take a brief look at Piaget's developmental stages and their general properties.

Stages of development

There are four developmental stages, some containing further substages. Each stage is unique in its properties, but each later stage depends on the previous one. So the first stage, the *sensorimotor* stage, is absolutely crucial because a person must pass through this before any further development is possible. The sensorimotor stage lasts from birth to roughly the second birthday, and contains six substages which involve the transition from 'circular reactions' – elementary sequences of behaviour which become more and more refined – to mental representations of the world, such as the concept of object permanence.

The next stage, lasting up to about age 7, is the *preoperational* stage. A major advance here over the sensorimotor stage is the ability to use symbols, and it is reflected in the onset of, among other things, make-believe play and language. The idea that something as important as language may be merely a particular aspect of some more general developmental process may be rather startling, but it follows directly from the theory: language is a symbol system based on vocal sounds rather than, for instance, the actions or objects used in make-believe play. It also follows that language does not itself produce thought, but it does enable the cultural transmission of thought, because it is a universal human symbol system, and hence it also enables the socialisation of the individual.

We can say, then, that true thought begins with the preoperational stage: the child is no longer tied to actions and goals in 'real time', but can represent whole sequences of experience and begin to think beyond the here and now. However, the preoperational child's thinking is, compared to an older child's or adult's, severely limited. The portrayal of these limitations, theoretically and methodologically, is a classic aspect of Piaget's work.

The best-known example of this, in both respects, is the phenomenon of conservation. In what is probably Piaget's most famous demonstration, a child is presented with two glasses of water, equally filled. One glassful is then poured into a taller, thinner glass, and the child is asked whether there is the same amount of water in the new glass or whether it has changed. Older children are well aware that the volume of a liquid does not depend on the shape of its container, hence that the quantity has not changed, but a preoperational child will say that there is more water in the taller, thinner glass. The same thing happens with other materials: a long line of coins is thought to contain more than a short line of the same number, for instance.

What is happening, according to Piaget, is that the child is *centring* on one perceptual feature and this dominates thinking. A similar property of this stage is the child's egocentrism: preoperational children seem unable to adopt another person's point of view. Again, children at this stage seem not to understand the concept of *reversibility*: they cannot appreciate that left and right for them are right and left for the person they are speaking to, or more generally that an event subjected to a transformation will be restored to its original state when the transformation is reversed. It is this lack of appreciation of logical operations that gives this stage its name.

Difficulties with tasks such as conservation and reversibility are resolved on progression to the next stage, that of *concrete operations*, which lasts up to about age 12. The advance which takes place here can be summed up as the ability to make certain inferences, such as those involving reversibility, addition and transitivity. Transitive reasoning provides a good example of this. Children are presented with two sticks, A and B, with A longer than B, followed by another pair, B and C, with B longer than C. When asked about the relation between A and C, preoperational children will either get it wrong, or answer by lining up the whole series and examining it. Concrete operational children do not need to do this because they can perform a simple transitive inference: from A is longer than B and B is longer than C, they infer that A is longer than C. This may seem like abstract thought, but it is not. Concrete operations are so called because Piaget observed that children at this stage are still tied in their thinking to the world of concrete experience: they cannot deal with apparent contradictions, or hypotheses about possible worlds. They have to have the materials they are dealing with there in front of them; in the example, they would have to have all the sticks in front of them.

The stage of *formal operations* is where the final, mature process of *formal thought*, detached from concrete experience, is said to be attained, at about the age of 12 onwards. From the point of view of this book, Piaget's proposals about formal operational thought are of the greatest interest, as it is here that he appears to posit nothing less than the acquisition of a mental logic. At this point, the child is said to leave behind the unsystematic thinking, tied to the real world, of the concrete operational child, in favour of mature, content-independent reasoning.

The theory of formal operations is expounded most extensively in Inhelder and Piaget (1958), but Gross (1985) is a good recent introduction to it. Besides setting out the constituents of the logic which is said to be held by the formal operational thinker, Inhelder and Piaget try to support their theory by presenting evidence in the shape of subject protocols, i.e. records of what subjects say and do while solving a problem.

Formal operational thought is supposed to be based on a *combinatorial system*. Consider *You smoke* and *You damage your health* as two atomic sentences. In formal thought, we could symbolise these as S and D, and we could ask abstractly how S and D might be combined using the truth functional connectives of sentential logic (which was introduced at the start of Chapter 4). One possibility is that *S and D* or *not-S and D* or *not-S and not-D* holds, but that *S and not-D* does not hold. From this we can validly infer that *not-S or D* holds, and that is just the truth functional (extensional or material) conditional, which can be symbolised in sentential logic as *D if S*. In that case, we have a good reason for not smoking. Of course, there are other possible combinations to consider, 16 in all, given in the following list (adapted from Gross 1985).

Conjunction	*S and D* holds and no other combination
Nonimplication	*S and not-D* and no other combination
Conjunctive negation	*not-S and not-D* and no other
Complete negation	no combination holds (this is actually a contradiction; see below under complete affirmation)
Negation of reciprocal implication	*not-S and D* and no other
Equivalence	*S and D* or *not-S and not-D*
Affirmation of S	*S and D* or *S and not-D*
Affirmation of D	*S and D* or *not-S and D*
Negation of S	*not-S and D* or *not-S and not-D*
Negation of D	*S and not-D* or *not-S and not-D*
Exclusive disjunction	*not-S and D* or *S and not-D*
Disjunction	*S and D* or *S and not-D* or *not-S and D*
Reciprocal conditional	*S and D* or *S and not-D* or *not-S and not-D*
Incompatibility	*S and not-D* or *not-S and D* or *not-S and not-D*
Complete affirmation	*S and D* or *S and not-D* or *not-S and D* or *not-S and not-D* (this is a tautology)

Thinkers who possessed the combinatorial system would be able to generate these abstract possibilities and to infer their formal consequences. There are other aspects to formal operational thought in Piaget's theory, but this system will illustrate the basic point. The possession of such a logical system would free thinkers from an exclusive reliance on particular experience, and enable them to think in an abstract, general, content-independent way. They could translate concrete problems into a kind of mental formal language, perform formal inferences to get a general solution, and then translate that back into ordinary, concrete experience.

Suppose such thinkers are asked whether you damage your health if you smoke. By translating this conditional into formal terms, these thinkers could discover that, if this conditional is true, the *S and not-D* combination cannot hold. Translating back into ordinary experience, they could then look for the falsifying case: that in which you smoke but do not damage your health. It is important to note that these thinkers would treat all similar questions about conditionals of this form in the same way. They would not approach this particular conditional in any special, individual way just because they had, or had not, some previous experience of doing research on health. (See Beth and Piaget (1966) for much more on how people are supposed to search for falsifying cases. As we pointed out in Chapter 4, that book uses semantic tableaux, which have some similarity with Johnson-Laird's mental models. The difference seems to be that the construction of mental models is taken by Johnson-Laird to be neither logically systematic nor content-independent; see Johnson-Laird (1983: 133).)

The general doctrine of mental logic, as well as what seems to be Piaget's version of it, has two highly significant consequences. First, people should tend to be correct in at least their elementary logical reasoning. This consequence follows from the fact that people are supposed to employ the normative theory of correct reasoning in their actual reasoning. They may fail to solve deep or difficult logical problems correctly, just because the number of inferences necessary might expand beyond their mental capacity, but a mental logic should be able to cope with the inferences required to solve an elementary problem. Second, people should tend to answer in the same way all problems requiring inferences of the same logical form. All conditionals of the form we have just used as an example should be translated into the same logical form in the hypothetical mental language, and the same logical processes should then be applied; the results should therefore be the same. Both these consequences open the doctrine to possible tests and criticisms. We shall review an experimental tradition which tests the general doctrine in the next chapter, but now we consider some particular criticisms of Piaget.

An outline critique

There are two broad classes of evidence which can be summoned in support or denial of Piaget's thesis. The first concerns the behaviour observed by Piaget and other researchers and whether it has been properly characterised by the Piagetian school. The second concerns the testing of people, both adults and children, specifically on logical problems, to see whether the results are consistent or inconsistent with Piagetian theory. These are, of course, two sides of the same empirical coin. In this section we shall concentrate on the first of these classes, and defer the second until later in this chapter.

Piaget was in many respects ahead of his time, and it took many years for mainstream psychological research to return to the study of mental processes after its spell of behaviourist austerity. It is therefore not surprising that the sorts of behaviour studied by Piaget did not attract the attention of non-Piagetian cognitive psychologists, those in the post-war human information-processing tradition, until comparatively recently. Once this did happen, critical research and theory started to accumulate.

Several summaries and collections of this research have appeared, such as Geber (1977), Gelman and Baillargeon (1983), Liben (1983), Modgil and Modgil (1982), Siegel and Brainerd (1978). We cannot hope to do justice to the entire range and complexity of these arguments; all we shall do here is give an account of some of those aspects of the critique which fit the purposes of this book.

One aspect of psychology's behaviourism which was inherited by cognitive researchers was a concern with rigorous experimental design and data analysis, and this in itself generated critical arguments. Piaget and his colleagues had not really done experiments at all, but had adopted what is known as the *clinical method*: observing and recording people's actions and sayings in more or less well-structured situations. Indeed, many of Piaget's own observations were of his own children. The controlled experiment and the clinical method both have to trade off rigour against reality. Experiments may be artificial, but they enable a fairly precise account of factors and their consequences; clinical observations seem more real-life-like, but contain many more unknown and uncontrolled factors and are therefore harder to interpret.

An example of a reassessment of Piaget's findings along these lines comes from Bynum, Thomas and Weitz (1972). They looked at the evidence offered by Inhelder and Piaget (1958) for the 16 binary operations said to be acquired at the attainment of the stage of formal operations. Somewhat disturbingly, they found that this evidence consisted of only a single protocol from one subject on a single problem. Moreover, Bynum *et al.* could find in this protocol definite evidence for only 6 of the 16 operations, suggestive evidence for 2 more, and no evidence at all for the other 8. This is not an isolated case: other researchers have also criticised the somewhat liberal evidential standards employed by Piagetian investigators (see e.g. Brainerd 1978; Donaldson 1978; Flavell 1963). It is sometimes hard to avoid the feeling that, to adapt the cynical journalist's dictum, the empirical facts have not been allowed to get in the way of a good theoretical story.

Besides methodology, modern cognitive psychology offers some general principles of its own which have enabled a critical reassessment of Piaget's account of mental function. Much of this argument centres on the role of memory and knowledge in accounting for characteristics of problem-solving performance which Piaget attributes to logical operations. As Carey (1985) states, 'no-one can doubt that a major source of the differences between children and adults is that young children know less.' The question is, can such differences in knowledge account for classic Piagetian findings, such as egocentrism and non-conservation?

An affirmative answer to this question is vigorously argued by Weisberg (1980). He poses the question directly: are the apparent differences between children's and adults' thinking the result of 'primitive modes of thought', or just ignorance? Ignorance alone, says Weisberg. Let us look at some of his arguments.

Weisberg examines some characteristic errors made by preoperational children, such as egocentrism, non-conservation and non-transitive comparisons. These traits, you will recall, arise from the young child's lack of the ability to decentre, and to perform logical operations such as reversibility and compensation; these are among the structural components acquired in the stage of concrete operations.

In the case of egocentrism, this results in children being incapable, according to Piagetian theory, of taking any point of view besides their own. Thus, a little girl will say 'no' when asked whether her sister has a sister, will say that a stone feels pain when you kick it, will think that people, often parents, do extraordinary things – such as make the rain or turn on the stars – and so on. Weisberg asks us to take the child's point of view: given what the child knows, what would we expect her to say? She will almost always have heard the word sister uttered with reference to her sister, not herself, have seen her parents water the garden and turn on other sorts of lights – she might have no idea that rain comes from thousands of feet in the air, or that stars are uncountable millions of miles away, and so not imagine that making rain or turning on stars would be in any way extraordinary. Weisberg argues that such a child's answers only look strange because we, as adults, have the knowledge which enables us to get closer to the right answers. A small child does not have this knowledge, and must depend on what she has. Thus, *sister* must mean her sister; people do things with water and lights, so why not these?

In the case of conservation, consider the preoperational child who says that there is more water when the contents of a glass are poured into a taller, thinner glass, and the concrete operational child who correctly denies that the quantity has changed. According to Piaget, transition from one stage to the next comes about via experience that dimensions compensate for one another but, as Weisberg demonstrates, this does not work in the case of cylindrical containers such as drinking glasses. If a 2cm-wide glass is filled to a height of 100cm, and its contents are poured into a glass 16cm wide, the height the water will reach will be decreased by a factor of 64, for an eight-fold increase in width. Thus, the two dimensions do not compensate for each other.

Weisberg therefore contends that for non-conservers to become conservers, they cannot go by this route: however, they need only to realise that quantities remain the same despite appearances, and this they can learn by analogy. They first learn to conserve number, which they do by counting and observing that numbers stay the same if nothing is added or taken away, and then transfer this knowledge to quantity. This explanation would require that number conservation be observed before the conservation of quantity, and that training on number conservation would itself lead to improved performance on tasks involving the conservation of quantity. Weisberg cites experimental evidence for just these predictions (Weisberg 1980: 363–5).

The introduction of evidence is welcome, because much of Weisberg's critique is conceptual. However, elsewhere in the literature there are similar arguments more firmly backed by empirical research. We shall briefly examine them, because they strengthen the case that much, perhaps most, of what changes in the development of thought (at least after the stage of infancy; Flavell 1985) has to do with quantitative, not qualitative, cognitive growth.

The contents of memory cannot be the only explanation for the observed differences between the cognitions of young children, older children and adults, any more than brute strength is the sole difference between boxers: it depends what you do with it. One factor which governs what you can do with the knowledge in your possession is the processing capacity of working memory: the smaller it is, the less you can do. There are two ways in which this capacity could be varied: young children could simply have less processing capacity available, or it could change with experience. There is evidence for both these possibilities.

The most well-known way to assess working memory capacity is the memory-span task devised originally by Ebbinghaus in the nineteenth century: you are given a series of random items to remember, usually numbers these days, and the length of list you can remember without error on repeated testing is your memory span. An adult's memory span, measured in this way, is usually of about six or seven items; a 4-year-old child's is, by contrast, probably only of about three or four items (Flavell 1985). There is more, incidentally, to working memory capacity than just storage space, which is why the term 'working memory' is used (see Baddeley (1987) for a general review, and Halliday and Hitch (1988) for developmental applications). Thus, a task which may be well within an adult's or older child's processing capacity may defeat a young child for this reason alone.

This factor interacts with knowledge, because the processing capacity an individual has available depends on practice and expertise. Very highly practised performances can make almost no demands on processing capacity: they run off automatically, like computer programs. Not only have young children not had the requisite number of hours of practice for fully automated performance in many instances, they have also not been around long enough to build the extensive library of such 'programs' which they will ultimately acquire. On this view, then, children are like novices at any stage of life: they do not know as much as experts in particular domains; neither have they perfected their performance by practice (Chi, Glaser and Rees 1982). Experts, of course, 'make it look easy'.

Some theorists working in the Piagetian tradition have incorporated processing capacity into *neo-Piagetian* explanations: Pascual-Leone (1970) introduced the idea of *M-Power*, which equates with working memory capacity, and proposed that at transitional points between developmental stages a further increment of M-Power is necessary for the attainment of the later structures. One is reminded of what sometimes happens in the learning of skills, such as riding a bicycle. You practise for hours without success and then, suddenly, you can do it: an increment of practice has led to a qualitative shift in performance. We use this example to raise the possibility that such effects may not be indicative of developmental stages in the Piagetian sense.

Another factor which is perhaps more in tune with the concerns of this book, and which may have occurred to some readers already, is what linguists might call the pragmatics of situations such as conservation and class-inclusion tasks (see Chapter 3). The conservation task is described above and again below; the class-inclusion task is similar, but the question behind it is different. In this case, to use an example from Gross (1985), a child might be presented with 10 wooden beads, 6 red and 4 blue. He is then asked whether there are more red beads, or more wooden beads. Of course, the answer is 'wooden', but the preoperational child says 'red'.

This task, and the conservation task, have struck many writers, including us, as pragmatically anomalous. In Chapter 3 we reported Fillenbaum's observations of *normalisation*: when the semantics and pragmatics of a situation conflict, people – not just children – operate according to what *should* have been said in the circumstances, even to the extent of incorrectly paraphrasing sentences. Perhaps something like this is going on in these tasks: the child 'hears' the question about beads as being about which colour is in the majority. Such considerations were put to the test in an extensive series of experiments by Donaldson and her colleagues, reported in Donaldson (1978).

In a standard conservation test, such as one involving number, two rows of items, equal in number, are arranged in front of a child. She agrees that they are equal. The experimenter usually says something like 'watch what I do', and then spreads one of the lines of items out so that, although it has the same number in it, it is now longer than the other. The child is asked again whether the two lines have the same number of items: if she is preoperational, she will say 'no'. Piagetians interpret this mistake as signalling a lack of the requisite logical structures necessary for the right conserving answer, but Donaldson, like Weisberg above, invites us to look at it from the child's angle. The experimenter has drawn attention to a change in the situation, then asked the child a question about it. What is she supposed to make of this state of affairs? Should she not suspect that the question and the change are in some way related, and respond accordingly? On this argument, what we have is a test of the child's pragmatics, not her class-inclusive reasoning, and she passes.

To test this idea, the experimental situation needs to be changed so that its pragmatics invite 'conserving' rather than 'non-conserving' responses. This was done by McGarrigle, reported by Donaldson (1978), in the delightful 'Naughty Teddy' version of the task. The aim here was to make it look as if the change in the perceptual properties of the array of items – where one row becomes longer than the other – occurred by accident, so as to break the link between this happening and the experimenter's question about whether there were still the same numbers of items in the rows. Naughty Teddy 'was liable to emerge from his box, swoop over the experimental material, disarrange it and thus "spoil the game"' (Donaldson 1978). When this version was used, significantly more 4- to 6-year-old children conserved number than in the standard version. As Donaldson remarks, Piagetian theory does not predict that a change of agent in the rearranging of the items will have this effect.

There is evidence, then, that children have failed to do themselves justice in certain standard Piagetian tests. This is a serious matter, because the results of these tests have been used as evidence for fundamental changes in cognitive development: the difference between children at different stages is held by the theory to be qualitative. If, on the other hand, we find that children's performance at what should be the preoperational stage is more in line with what we would expect at the concrete operational stage, then the theory has a problem. At the very least, the stage boundaries become blurred, and we have to ask how much they are left to explain; we may even ask, as a consequence, whether we need to posit such stages at all.

Tamburrini (1982) sums up the circumstances under which young children's performance exceeds what is observed in standard Piagetian tests: when the task materials are familiar; when the motives and intentions of other people match the child's; where the child's attention is directed to relevant features of the task; and where the child has an easy way of demonstrating understanding. These, of course, are not trick devices for outwitting Piaget, but are characteristic of children's everyday experiences.

There is one last point we would like to make before leaving this brief and somewhat negative assessment of Piagetian theory, and that is that there is often in the reports of this work a lack of attention to what adults actually do in comparable situations, compared to what it is assumed they will do. The reason for this is fairly straightforward: Piagetians assume that adults are in full possession of mental logic, and should therefore be fully logical in Piagetian reasoning tasks. However, adults and children are often not that different in what they do. For instance, we shall find in later chapters that it is not only preoperational children who tend to focus on salient perceptual features of logical problems, to the exclusion of a proper combinatorial analysis. Adults do it too, in certain reasoning tasks. They even do it when asked to judge simple properties such as weight: big containers are judged lighter, when lifted, than are small containers of equal weight (the size–weight illusion: see Ross 1969). It seems that Piagetians err in complementary directions: they underestimate children and overestimate adults.

Alternative accounts of intellectual development

If development in reasoning does not occur as Piaget supposes, by the attainment of qualitatively distinct logical structures in the mind, how does it occur? For information-processing theorists such as Weisberg (1980), the answer is simple: development is a quantitative increase in the contents of memory, cognitive processing itself remaining constant. Others such as Flavell (1985) distinguish between infant cognition, as non-symbolic, and the quantitative development of symbolic cognition which occurs afterwards (Flavell calls this transition 'miraculous'), and speak of 'trends' in general cognitive processes including working memory capacity, domain-specific knowledge and metacognition.

In this section we shall review some recent approaches which espouse a more structural view of the development of thought. We shall examine the arguments of Keil (1981, 1984), Carey (1985) and Campbell and Bickhard (1986).

Constraints

Keil has argued that there are inherent *constraints* which affect the way knowledge is acquired and represented in the mind. He holds that these are natural limits, specific to particular domains of cognition, on the possible forms mental representations may take. In addition, he adds one of the fundamental conclusions of modern cognitive psychology: that what we know now affects the way we take in information in the future. These two limiting factors – natural constraints and present knowledge – together imply, in his theory, that any structural changes in cognitive development will be *domain-specific*. This goes against Piagetian theory and the doctrine of mental logic, according to which we acquire *domain-general* ways of solving problems: ones which are based on the logical form of sentences and not on their particular content.

For Keil, a domain is not so specific that it is restricted to particular tasks. The domain of *metaphor* can be used to illustrate this point. Metaphorical reasoning is used by Keil (1984) to show how attention to existing knowledge is necessary to explain a piece of discontinuous development. He points out that the ability to use metaphors in general is not acquired in an all-or-none fashion – it is not as though children of a certain age cannot use any metaphors whereas a year later they have a complete mastery. But neither is it the case that use of metaphors increases gradually with age. Rather, whole classes of metaphors become available as *semantic fields* become elaborated. A semantic field, in this sense, consists of words which have related meanings, such as eating words or kinship words. Semantic fields can be juxtaposed, and when this happens metaphorical relations between fields become possible. Some juxtapositions occur before others, and this seems to predict the course of metaphor use by children. Thus, there is a discontinuous developmental process, with metaphors emerging in blocks, but not a wholesale discontinuity in metaphorical ability. In short, this ability cannot be explained without recourse to the contents of the knowledge (the semantic fields) in question.

For an example of the boundary conditions imposed by constraints, Keil uses ontological knowledge, which means knowledge of the basic concepts of existence. He argues that not only is ontological knowledge constrained to be represented hierarchically – i.e. as a sort of tree structure rather than, say, a network or a matrix – but that the hierarchies themselves are constrained to take certain forms. Violations of these universal constraints are noticed straight away by children, and cause knowledge to be restructured. The general notion of hierarchies in ontological knowledge has been argued elsewhere, for instance in the work of Rosch (e.g. 1978) on natural categories, but Keil is on shaky ground regarding the particular constraints he proposes: see Carey (1985). This is not the place for a technical debate on this question.

Keil is therefore arguing that human cognition is *structure-heavy* – that is, shifts in cognitive development are more to do with the organisation of knowledge than with changes in the processing operations which act on it. This is in many ways a restatement of the expert–novice position outlined above, with the child as novice and the adult as expert. Experts 'do not usually have a larger ... computational capacity; rather, they know a great deal more than most people about the domain involved' (Keil 1984: 96).

Conceptual change

Carey's (1985) work on *conceptual change* in cognitive development is in the same spirit as Keil's work on constraints and, like Keil, Carey backs up her theoretical claims with detailed empirical evidence. Her specific case study is of the child's developing concept of a biological domain of knowledge.

One of Piaget's earliest observations was of the young child's difficulties with distinguishing what is alive from what is not. As we saw when considering Weisberg's critique above, young children's explanations of the world around them are characterised by *animism*: the sun shines because it wants to keep us warm, rocks hurt when you kick them, and so on. Against the spirit of Piagetian theory, Carey's explanation of this is that 'the developments of explanatory frameworks ... are part and parcel of theory changes – they are not domain general' (Carey 1985: 194). Her research aims to explicate these theory changes.

No one doubts that a person's knowledge undergoes structural change: it is a familiar part even of our conscious experience, as, for instance, when you stay in a new town, learn your way around two sets of streets, and then discover the connection between these two bits of local knowledge and suddenly form a larger understanding of the spatial layout of the area. Carey distinguishes two sorts of knowledge restructuring. The first is the weak sort, of the kind portrayed in this example: the ability to make different relations between existing concepts. It is the kind of restructuring seen in novice–expert shifts (Chi, Glaser and Rees 1982). Restructuring of the stronger sort is what Carey refers to as *conceptual change*, which is said to be comparable to theory change and emergence in the history of science. She argues that children's knowledge is subject to changes of at least the weak sort, and probably of the strong sort too; it is these changes in knowledge which account for the observed changes in performance which Piagetians attribute to logical restructuring.

According to Carey, it is children's theories which change as they mature, not their ways of building them. She holds that children may only have two initial general theories about the world: a naive mechanics – i.e. a view of how things behave – and a naive psychology – i.e. a view of how people behave (p.201). This limits the distinctions children can make and the explanations they are able to produce, and means that other concepts must either be elaborations of these prototypes, or radical departures from them. Carey presents evidence for both these developments, and we shall provide a brief summary of it.

As we mentioned, Carey is concerned with the emergence of the concept of the biological world as a distinct domain of knowledge. She argues that this domain is absent at age 4, but present in an adult-like form by age 10, and that it emerges and then breaks off from the initial domain of naive psychology. This view was supported in an elegant series of experiments.

First, there is no dispute that young children (age 4–7) get it wrong when asked the simple question 'what is alive?'. They assert that cars and clocks are alive because they move or make noises by themselves; or that cars and clocks are not alive because people make them. Carey proposes two reasons for these errors: difficulty unpacking the semantics of *alive* (it can mean, in adult discourse, not dead, or animate, or, metaphorically, working, among other things); and a lack of a concept of living/not living on which the word *alive* can be mapped. Young children do not, in other words, know enough biology to know what *alive* really means.

Carey explored this by looking at how children of various ages handle properties of living things. What answers do they give when asked whether animals, plants and inanimate objects eat, breathe, have hearts, and so on? A clear pattern of responses emerged. All such properties were attributed to people, but not to all the animals, and there was an almost uniform ordering of attribution of all properties among animals: those animals most similar to people were most likely to be credited with the given properties. Furthermore, properties such as breathing and eating, which adults attribute to plants, were not extended to plants by the young children. It seems that children lack an appreciation of the idea that there is a common category of animals, of which humans are but one member, and that there is a superordinate category of living things to which animals and plants both belong.

Second, young children demonstrate the lack of these categories in their inferences from what they observe or are told. Children of various ages, and adults, were told about an unfamiliar part of the body (the spleen in the case of the younger groups, the omentum in the case of the older), including the information that people or dogs possessed it. They were then asked to judge whether other animals, plants and inanimate objects possessed this organ. Both children and adults, when told that the organ was possessed by people, exhibited the profile of attributions mentioned above: they were more likely to agree that a certain animal had it to the extent that that animal resembled humans. However, the youngest children (age 4) did not project the possession of the organ to other animals when told that dogs had it, whereas older children and adults did. Similarly, being told that both dogs and bees possessed the organ increased the likelihood of projection to other animals for older children and adults, but not for younger children. Young children seem to think of people as the only true exemplar of life, and judge other creatures by their resemblance to people. But by age 10, children know that *animal* refers to a wide category including people, and that it can be justifiably used in inferences about members of that category. (We say more about this type of inference in Chapter 7.)

Third, children grasp, between the ages of 4 and 10, that *animal* refers to an *ontological category*, one of the basic aspects of existence. They become able to see beyond surface features to the essence of what it means to be an animal. When 9-year-olds are shown a picture of an animal which looks like a skunk but are told its parents and offspring were racoons and that its internal organs were those of a racoon, they say that it is a racoon that looks like a skunk. Five-year-olds maintain that it is a skunk. The idea of something being essentially a racoon, then, is a property of ontological thinking. Animals have not emerged as an ontological category for young children, so they rely on appearance.

Carey's research sets out a clear picture of the difference between the thinking of young children, older children and adults. Young children lack completely any intuitive knowledge of a biological world. Four-year-olds have some idea of what animals are, as they attribute some properties only to animals and not to inanimate objects, but they do not use *animal* to refer to underlying properties which can be independent of behaviour and appearance. By age 10, a fundamental change has occurred: as Carey says (1985: 184) 'ten year olds resembled adults in every respect probed' in her research. Ten-year-olds reason about animals in the way they do, not because animals behave like people or have a certain shape and colour, but because, at 10, children possess the *concept* of an animal and so know what it is for something to *be* an animal. For these children, humans take their place in the biological world and are not the prototype for knowledge of life, which they are for the preschool child. This way of thinking is due to a reorganisation of knowledge in this domain. Ten-year-olds not only know more about the living world, this knowledge is differently structured: at 4, children say people eat 'because it's dinner time'; at 10, they know people eat for biological reasons. This is what is meant by conceptual change: at 4, children have available explanations based only on naive psychology; but at 10, they have a distinct theory of intuitive biology. Thus, the importance of studying the development of thought in particular domains is well illustrated by Carey's work.

Knowing levels

For our final look at alternative, non-Piagetian views of the development of thought, we turn to the work of Campbell and Bickhard (1986) on *knowing levels*. Campbell and Bickhard's scope is very wide, and we cannot do justice to their arguments in all their applications here. Instead, we shall keep to the themes of this chapter (but see also Bickhard and Richie 1983).

Some of the ideas of Campbell and Bickhard are redolent of those of Carey and Keil, reviewed above, though they do not cite these authors. However, there are other qualities in their approach which make it an interesting contribution. First, in a negative vein, they point out some shortcomings of Piagetian stage theory. They claim that the algebraic description of the operations said to characterise a person at a particular stage are merely descriptions of the formal properties of the tasks that can be performed at that stage, and are not really psychological explanations of how the tasks are accomplished. In addition, Piagetian theory has the property of 'structure of the whole'. Although in his late work Piaget stepped back from this, the classic version of his theory has to propose that the mental structures must be in place in an across-the-board fashion before tasks which depend on them can be performed. Furthermore, and as a consequence, Piagetian theory is rather quiet on the mechanisms of transition between stages, focusing instead on the 'finished articles', the logical structures.

Among the reasons Campbell and Bickhard give as to why Piagetian operations are abstract structures rather than actual mental processes is the following. If they are the latter, then the logical operations must match the contents of the person's mind when thinking about problems. Not only is there little evidence for this in Piaget's own work (recall the analysis of Bynum, Thomas and Weitz (1972), cited above), but there is a combinatorial explosion when problems more complicated than the binary ones considered by Inhelder and Piaget (1958) are involved: there are simply too many possible combinations of the atomic sentences for this to be a plausible account of mental processes.

The theory of knowing levels therefore attempts to get round such difficulties, as well as to give a more complete account than Piaget's. The idea of knowing levels rests on an hypothesised developmental process which Campbell and Bickhard call *reflective abstraction*: 'the process by which properties of the representations in one knowing level are abstracted at the next level' (1986: 81).

In this account, a child at knowing-level 1 (age 0–4) has acquired expertise in certain parts of the external environment. The knowledge here is implicit: it is not itself an object of knowledge. But at knowing-level 2 the child's knowledge about a part of the environment becomes itself an object of thought. Knowing-level 2 (from 4 to about age 9) is the stage at which the sophisticated inferences such as those involved in conservation become available. At knowing-level 3 a person can reflect on the knowledge possessed at the previous level, abstract the regularities in it, and use this knowledge as the object of thought, and this is where some of the high-level hypothetical reasoning associated with Piaget's formal operations becomes possible. Thus, class-inclusion reasoning is a level 2 ability, but the realisation that the relation between classes and subclasses holds for all classes and subclasses is a property of level 3.

Doubts could be raised about the theory of knowing levels and the clarity of its notion of abstraction, but there are two positive points worth making here. First, its focus is truly developmental: this theory concerns itself primarily with the means of transition between levels, not, as noted above, with the supposed finished products of given stages. This itself results in knowing levels being, as Campbell and Bickhard say, 'half a cycle advanced' on the Piagetian stages: the stages are where the abilities associated with a knowing level culminate, but the levels mark where the abilities begin to emerge.

Second, and this is where the theory is reminiscent of Keil and Carey, knowing levels in this theory develop with respect to particular domains. The stages in knowing-level theory are, like Piaget's, invariantly sequenced – one level must be completed before the next is possible – but one does not need to propose that all a person's knowledge is at a particular level at a particular time. To quote from Campbell and Bickhard, 'stage boundaries are drawn at the initial emergence of higher knowing-level thought in a specific domain' (1986: 60).

In conclusion

Our assessment of Piagetian theory has, on the whole, been negative, and we are forced to the conclusion that it can no longer be held as a plausible theory of thought, or of the development of thought, for the reasons we have put forward. However, that is not to deny the value of Piaget's work and that of his followers, nor its influence. The contemporary theorists we have highlighted in this chapter all give credit to the Piagetian programme for, at the very least, asking the right questions, and for taking a view larger than that commonly found in orthodox, information-processing psychology.

For instance, Carey (1985) draws attention to the price to be paid in abandoning the Piagetian scheme. Any parent or teacher knows that children develop rapidly and in unnumbered different ways: the stage theory offered the promise of bringing order to this chaos. If we abandon the stage theory, we are left again with the task of providing a framework which can make the understanding of the development of thought manageable. Moreover, Campbell and Bickhard (1986) point out that 'questions of development ... constrain possible models of adult cognition' – that is, one cannot just propose any old cognitive process or structure without considering at some stage how it could have been acquired. (They had cognitive development in mind in making this point, but we shall also be considering evolutionary development in Part 3 of this book.) This is as true of domain-specific processes and structures, such as abstraction itself or schemas, as it is of domain-general ones. Piaget at least emphasised the importance of developmental theory.

6 Logical reasoning: an experimental case study

The general doctrine of mental logic is not necessarily threatened by criticism of Piaget's particular version of it; some other version might appear more acceptable. But as we pointed out in the last chapter, there are testable consequences of the general doctrine. The two most important are, first, that people should tend to be correct in at least their elementary logical reasoning and, second, that they should tend to answer in the same way all problems requiring inferences of the same logical form. In this chapter, we introduce, as a case study, a famous experiment which has been used to test these consequences. This experiment is *Wason's selection task*. Like most of the best experiments, it is brilliantly simple, and yet there is much to learn from it. Since its appearance in 1966, it has stimulated a large body of work on the nature of human inference, and we shall also introduce some of this important new work in this chapter.

Wason's selection task

Writers on problem solving and thinking often ask their readers to attempt the problems concerned before reading on, more in hope than expectation, we suspect. If you have not met the selection task before, we would none the less urge you to have a go at it now: the effort really will pay off when you come to read about the research in the following pages. We shall present, in more or less their original form, three versions of the problem in the order in which they first appeared.

> *Task 1.* Drawn below are four cards. Each card has a letter on one side and a number on the other – you can only see one side here, of course. Here is a rule about these four cards:
>
> *If there is a vowel on one side, then there is an even number on the other side.*

Which of the cards must you turn over to decide whether the rule is true or false?

The cards:

A	M	2	7

Task 2. As above, assume that the four cards drawn below all have a letter on one side and a number on the other. This time the rule is:

If there is a D on one side, then there is not a 3 on the other side.

Which of the cards must you turn over to decide whether the rule is true or false?

The cards:

9	K	3	D

Task 3. Imagine that you are the manager of a large department store. You have to inspect sales receipts at the end of the day to ensure that they have been properly filled out. The rule is:

If any purchase exceeds £30, the receipt must have the signature of the department manager on the back.

Which of the receipts must you check?

Form 111 1 chair £75	Reverse of Form 111 Approved ..J. Jones..	Form 111 1 lamp £25	Reverse of Form 111 Approved ....

We have given these three versions of the problem because they will illustrate many of the points to be made later on: you will probably have got the first one wrong and the other two right; you were probably right on the last two for different reasons; and it would not have made any difference if you had received these three problems in any other order.

No doubt you now want to know what the right answers are. We shall first adopt the traditional way of explaining them, though as we shall see later there are very serious problems with this. In particular, we shall question, later in the chapter, the implicit assumption of the traditional analysis that any mental logic in question would be a sentential one – a mental formulation of the elementary extensional logic we introduced at the start of Chapter 4.

The right answer is supposed to be basically the same in all three cases because, it is traditionally held, these problems require inferences of essentially the same logical form. Each task contains a so-called 'rule' which can be written in the general form of a conditional, *if P then Q.* These rules are assumed to be truth functional conditionals, the truth values of which are decidable in the following way: they are false if the antecedent (*P*) is true and the consequent (*Q*) is false, otherwise they are true. In all three tasks above, you should be looking for cards which might make *P* true on one side (a *P* card) and *not-Q* true on the other (a *not-Q* card).

In Task 1, you should infer, by modus ponens, that the A card must have an even number on its back if the rule is true, and therefore that it should be chosen to test the rule. Again on the assumption that the rule is true, you should infer, by modus tollens, that the 7 card (which is a *not-Q* card) must not have a vowel on the back, and thus that it too should be chosen to test the rule. Finally, you should infer that there is no need to turn over either the M card or the 2 card, since no matter what was on their reverses, neither could establish the decisive combination of *P* and *not-Q* both true.

In Task 2, you should choose the D card for exactly the same logical reason that you should choose the A card in Task 1. The other correct card is the 3 one. Let us continue to think of the rule in Task 2 as of the form *if P then Q,* in which *Q* replaces *there is not a 3 on the other side.* Then the 3 card makes *Q* false and so *not-Q* true, from which you should infer that there must not be a D on the other side of this card if the rule is true, making it necessary to turn it over to test this rule. (Strictly speaking, we should take the logical form of this conditional to be *if P then not-Q,* and use the inference rule of double negation before we use modus tollens, but it is traditional to ignore this wrinkle as not affecting the essence of the matter.) It is unnecessary to turn over the K and 9 cards for the same logical reason as in Task 1.

In Task 3, the traditional view is that we simply have a more realistic version of Task 1, but that the logical form of the conditional is exactly the same. (We shall argue against this view below, but for now we assume that it is correct.) You should examine the receipt for £75 and the unsigned receipt, and not the receipt for £25 or the signed one.

As we mentioned above, you are highly unlikely to have chosen the right cards for Task 1, but much more likely to have done so for the other two. This should not be so, of course, if the doctrine of mental logic is correct. You should have been highly likely to get Task 1 right, by the first consequence of the doctrine we mentioned above; and also highly likely to do the three tasks in the same way, by the second consequence above (on the assumption that the logical form is essentially the same in all three cases). Some explanation is called for.

Initial findings and explanations: Task 1

The selection task was introduced informally by Wason in a British paperback called *New Horizons in Psychology* (Foss 1966). Task 1 above was modelled on its description there and in the first systematic experimental report (Wason 1968a). Wason nicely sums up the reason why this little problem should have excited so much interest, in the title of a later paper: 'Structural simplicity and psychological complexity' (Wason 1969). As you can see from the outline of the solution given above (especially if you did not actually try to solve it first), there really is not that much to it: a conditional, four cards, and a straightforward question that anyone can understand.

And yet, as Wason and his colleagues discovered, the vast majority of people fail to answer all three questions correctly (see the summary of all the early work reviewed in this section in Wason and Johnson-Laird 1972). In fact, if one surveys the research done with the versions similar to Task 1 above, one finds that, overall, fewer than 10 per cent of subjects in these experiments have produced the right answer (see also Evans 1982, 1989; Manktelow 1981). We can presume that it was not lack of general intelligence which was responsible: nearly all the subjects have been under-graduate students, as is the way with experimental psychology.

People's mistakes are almost always more interesting than their successes, and the early experiments were devoted almost entirely to the need to explain the large proportion of errors in the Task 1 version of the problem. The first thing to point out is that these errors are not random, i.e. people are not simply guessing. Most people (about two-thirds) choose the P and Q cards, or just the P card by itself. It is therefore necessary to explain not just why people do not choose the right answer, but why their wrong answers take the form that they do.

Wason and his colleagues proposed an explanation along the following lines. Bear in mind that the key to the right answer is to attempt to *falsify* the rule, i.e. to find the cards which make P true on one side and Q false on the other. Perhaps most people did not appreciate this, or did so but then did not realise which were the potentially falsifying cards, or even failed to understand which combination of values constituted the falsifying case. The latter can be ruled out straight away, since Wason himself (1968a) found that people readily recognised when a conditional of the form *if P then Q* was falsified: in a technical sense, they could *evaluate*, after the task was finished and all the cards were turned over, the semantic significance of a card which showed *P* true on one side and *Q* false on the other. Wason's own explanation of what happened in the task was that people were attempting to *verify* the rule, i.e. to find the cards which made *P* true on one side and *Q* true on the other, rather than falsify it. He held that they would choose *P* with *Q* or *P* alone, depending on whether or not they thought that the rule also implied its converse. And they ignore *not-P* because, as Wason (in Foss 1966) had previously claimed, people tend to regard the negated antecedent as irrelevant to the truth value of the conditional.

The assumption implicit in this analysis is that people do have an underlying mental sentential logic, but that something about the selection task prevents them from employing it. Following this idea, Wason set about giving people what he called 'therapeutic' sessions in which they had several attempts at the task, and were supplied with various sorts of hints if they kept failing to get it right. This procedure resulted in the appearance of an otherwise rare selection pattern of *P* together with *Q* and *not-Q*, and ultimately to a significantly higher proportion of choices of *P* along with *not-Q* (although still around half the subjects kept to their erroneous solutions).

The pattern of behaviour observed in these therapy experiments led to a formal information-processing model (see Johnson-Laird and Wason 1977: ch. 9), which we shall call the *Insight Model*. This specifies three states of insight into the selection task which determine the answers a person will produce. The state of *no insight* is the one we have been concerned with in this section: people in this state try to verify the rule and focus on the values named in it, and hence choose *P* alone or *P* along with *Q*, for the reasons given above. Following therapy, people begin to see the need to falsify the rule but continue to attempt to verify it: they are thus in a state of *partial insight*, and will select *P* along with *Q* and *not-Q* (*not-P* will still be seen as irrelevant). Finally, when people fully appreciate the need to falsify and not verify, they attain *complete insight* into how to translate the rule into their mental logic and how to use that to infer the correct selections: *P* along with *not-Q*. In this model, it is again assumed, without question, that the 'rule' in any version of the task is a truth functional conditional, and that the mental logic is sentential logic.

We now know that not only is the Insight Model deficient in certain technical aspects which we shall not deal with here (see Evans 1982;

Manktelow 1981), but that there are more serious problems with this attempt to explain, or explain away, performance on the selection task, while holding on to the doctrine of mental sentential logic. The shift away from the notion of insight and mental sentential logic is an important outcome of research on the selection task, and in the next three sections, we shall review the areas of experimental work which have led to other conceptions of reasoning.

Matching versus verifying: Task 2

In our brief look at Task 1 and the Insight Model above, we reported that the state of no insight was held to mean that people would try to verify the conditional or to focus on the values named in it, selecting P or P and Q. You may have noticed that either of these tendencies, verifying or focusing on named values, can account for P and Q choices by itself, because the verifying cards are also those named in the rule. The problem is to distinguish between them, since both result in the same observed behaviour. What is needed is a technique that will predict different selections depending on whether people are verifying or focusing. This is where Task 2 comes in, because that is what it does.

Task 2 was devised by Evans, who in an earlier investigation into conditional reasoning, using another sort of task, had detected a response he called a *matching bias* (Evans 1972), which is a tendency to regard as relevant only those terms used in a rule. Such a tendency would produce, except by accident, unjustified inferences, and that is just what a bias is. Evans predicted that this bias would also be observed in the selection task, and he was right.

He distinguished between the *matching value* of a card (i.e. whether or not it contained a term used in the rule) and its semantic value (i.e. whether it verified or falsified a rule component), by the ingenious but simple expedient of negating one or other of the parts of the conditional, its antecedent or its consequent. In Task 2 the consequent is negated: it says there is *not* a 3 on the back. So somebody who was trying to verify would select a card showing a value which was not a 3 (in this case, a 9), but someone who was matching would select the 3 card. In Task 2 the matching case is a card which makes the consequent false, whereas in Task 1 it is a card which makes the consequent true. It follows that while matching will result in a wrong answer in Task 1, it will produce the right answer, by accident as far as the subject is concerned, in Task 2.

When this technique was used in an experiment on the selection task (Evans and Lynch 1973), there was indeed a significant tendency for people to select cards according to their matching value, and there was no evidence at all that they were trying to verify. The matching effect was stronger for consequent selections: on the antecedent, people were much more likely to select a *P* card (one which made the antecedent true) whether or not it showed a matching term (one which was used in the antecedent). This cannot be taken as evidence for a tendency to verify, since both verifying and falsifying responses require the selection of the *P* card.

Evans (1983) has since argued that matching bias arises from linguistic and pragmatic sources. The antecedent of a conditional invites a supposition (see Chapter 4). When you say, 'If I go swimming ...' you are asking your listener to suppose you will go swimming, and when you say, 'If I don't go swimming ...' you ask them to suppose that you will not. Hence, people will tend to select the *P* card whether or not there is a match. On the other hand, the *not-Q* card will tend to be selected according to a bias to focus on the topic of the sentence. When you say, 'If I don't go swimming I don't take my towel', you are talking about swimming and towels, and not about not-swimming and not-towels.

Evans therefore concluded that people decide on a *non-logical* basis whether or not to select the *not-Q* card: they have a response bias which has nothing to do with the logic of the task. This is a conclusion which many people found hard to take at the time, and still do. Before returning to it, though, we shall pass on to a parallel and equally significant set of experiments.

Facilitation by realism: Task 3

We mentioned above the therapy experiments conducted by Wason in the initial assault on people's failure at the selection task. One radically different sort of therapy was devised after a while: to make the task more akin to the problems people might have encountered in real life. If you are feeling uneasy about the selection task as a useful instrument for probing the workings of the mind, it is probably mostly on account of its obvious artificiality. This occurred to Wason's research group too, and the solution is obvious: make it *realistic.* Hence the inclusion of Task 3 in this chapter.

In 1971 Wason and Shapiro reported a comparison between a standard so-called *abstract task*, like Task 1 here, and a *thematic task* which seemed to be more realistic. The latter concerned journeys, the rule being *Every time I go to Manchester I travel by train*, and the cards showing Manchester (*P*), Leeds (*not-P*), Train (*Q*) and Car (*not-Q*), with a destination referred to on one side and a means of transport on the other. Naturally, the claim made in the rule would be false if a journey to Manchester had not been made by train, so the correct solution is to examine the Manchester and Car cards. Ten out of 16 subjects chose this combination, compared with only two out of sixteen who chose *P* along with *not-Q* on an abstract task.

This effect was confirmed in a number of subsequent published experiments, most notably in the case of Johnson-Laird, Legrenzi and Legrenzi (1972). This experiment is worth picking out because we shall refer to aspects of it again. They used a task in which people were asked to imagine they were postal workers, sorting the mail. They were given the following postal regulation, actually in force at one time in Britain, as a rule: *If a letter is sealed then it has a 5d (or 50 lire) stamp on it.* (All the subjects were British.) The 'cards' were real envelopes either sealed (*P*), unsealed (*not-P*), bearing a 5d/50 lire stamp (*Q*) or a 4d/40 lire stamp (*not-Q*). A second *not-Q* item, a letter with no stamp, was also included, but this is of little consequence (it is not even referred to in the report of this experiment in Wason and Johnson-Laird 1972). In addition, each subject also performed an abstract task. Twenty-one out of 24 subjects were correct with the postal task compared with two correct with the abstract task – and remember that each subject did both.

The preferred interpretation of these results for several years was that casting the task in realistic terms *facilitated* translation of the problem into logical form in sentential logic and so led to successful performance. The existence of this *facilitation effect,* as a result of realism in the task, is a problem for Piagetian theory, of course, since it appears that formal operational thinking is only available in certain circumstances, not generally (see Chapter 5; also Wason 1977). But any supporters of the doctrine of mental sentential logic would have to explain why realism facilitates such translation, while they made sure, at the same time, that the doctrine remained testable. No such explanation has been forthcoming.

A problem with facilitation was reported by Manktelow and Evans (1979). They tried and failed to reproduce the facilitation effect with rules containing negations about *arbitrary* food and drink combinations, such as *If you eat fish then you do not drink tea.* They tried again with rules not containing negations about the same sort of thing, and yet again with a replication of the journeys task of Wason and Shapiro, and failed each time. Reluctant to blame themselves or their subjects, they proposed that reliable facilitation only occurred when tasks were so realistic that logical reasoning was circumvented and the correct solution was retrieved from memory.

In the postal task of Johnson-Laird *et al,* for example, the subjects were likely to have had actual experience of sending letters from when the postal regulation used was in force, and so could possibly remember how to operate under it. But no subjects were likely to have had experience of rules like the above about tea and fish, which might appear to be thematic or realistic in some sense. What was proposed, then, was an explanation of correct solutions which made no use of the doctrine of mental sentential logic. This could be set alongside the matching bias, as an account of incorrect solutions, to get a more satisfactory overall explanation of performance in the selection task than could be provided by that doctrine.

This explanation was dubbed the *memory-cueing* hypothesis by Griggs and his collaborators, and tested in an elegant series of experiments (see Griggs (1983) for a review). According to the memory-cueing hypothesis, the postal task should only produce a high proportion of correct solutions (a facilitation effect) among people who have had experience of the regulation conveyed in the rule; in a population without such experience, such an effect should not occur. Griggs and his collaborators duly ran the experiment in Florida, where there had never been a postal regulation of this kind, and sure enough, the facilitation effect was absent. They went on to do a positive test of the hypothesis, by surveying their subject population for a content with which people would be familiar, and then using this content in a selection task. The resulting task concerned drinking-age rules, such as *If a person is drinking beer then that person must be over 19 years old.* A facilitation effect was predicted and observed.

It has been pointed out by a number of authors, including Griggs (1983) and Johnson-Laird (1983), that a *strong* memory-cueing hypothesis must fail, because it is too restricting. Quite simply, one can readily demonstrate a facilitation effect when it is quite implausible to suppose, as a strong interpretation of the hypothesis would imply, that people have actual experience with the exact content of the task. In fact, in one version of the postal experiment devised by Johnson-Laird, Legrenzi and Legrenzi (1972), some British subjects were given the task with Italian units of currency. Surely they had not all remembered posting letters in Italy. Similarly, in a task recalling Fillenbaum's normalisation principle (see Chapter 3), Griggs and Cox (1983) observed a facilitation effect with drinking rules containing negations, of which the subjects did not have experience.

This feature of memory-cueing is characteristic of the most reliable facilitating content we know of: Task 3 in this chapter, based closely on the 'Sears' task devised by D'Andrade (see Rumelhart 1980b). Most people get this problem right, but hardly any would have had actual experience as department store managers.

Schemas and the selection task

The old consensus that realism facilitates translation into mental sentential logic has been overturned in favour of a new consensus, that reasoning is content-dependent: dependent, that is, on content which evokes relevant knowledge from memory. The most recent stage in this research effort, one that is still going on, has been the attempt to characterise the knowledge evoked, and that will be the problem we introduce in this section. We shall not spend a lot of time on it here because it bears directly on the question of human rationality. Rationality is an issue which we explore at length in Part 3, and we shall be returning to the reasoning literature there.

We have already rejected two ways of trying to characterise the knowledge which produces facilitation in the selection task. The first derives from the doctrine of mental sentential logic, and claims that realistic content evokes knowledge of extensional logical form and formal rules of inference in sentential logic. The second assumes the strong memory-cueing hypothesis, and claims that realistic content evokes knowledge of how to perform tasks which have been experienced and solved before by trial and error. These two possibilities represent the two extremes. In the first case, there is completely general, content-independent knowledge of formal sentential logic, while in the second, there is totally specific knowledge, dependent on previous experience with the content, of how to solve a problem worded in one particular way. Between these extremes are attempted characterisations based on frames, scripts, or broadly schemas, which are structures we met in Chapter 2. These extremes could also be thought of as limiting cases of the broad notion of a schema, and then one could speak, for example, of a schema, at the one extreme, for analysing the logical forms of sentences.

Schemas (whether called frames or scripts or whatever), you will remember, have been informally described as representations of stereotyped situations. They can be more or less general, and indeed are perhaps best thought of as representing what certain specific objects, events, or states of affairs have in common. There could be a schema for what it is like to order a meal in any restaurant, or just in a Japanese restaurant. There could be one for what it is like in general to give and take receipts, or just to give receipts in one particular department store. It is very natural to try to use this notion to explain facilitation, and the application of it to this topic was advocated, though not worked out in detail, by a number of authors (e.g. Evans 1986; Mandler 1983; Manktelow and Jones 1987; Rumelhart 1980b; Wason 1983).

Two detailed schema theories of performance in the selection task have now emerged: those of Cheng and her colleagues (Cheng and Holyoak 1985; Cheng, Holyoak, Nisbett and Oliver 1986) and Cosmides (1985, 1989). This work is some of the most significant in this area for many years. Both propose what we shall refer to as *deontic* schemas, by which we mean schemas which are about obligations and permissions (see Chapter 4 on deontic logic).

Cheng and Holyoak (1985) introduce what they call *pragmatic reasoning schemas* to try to explain the facilitation effect. These schemas are given by *production rules* which are 'generalized, context-sensitive rules ... defined in terms of classes of goals ... and relationships to those goals'. Cheng and Holyoak concern themselves mostly with a *permission schema*, which they say has been evoked in most of the reliable cases of facilitation.

Consider again the drinking-age rule: *If a person is drinking beer then that person must be over 19 years old.* According to Cheng and Holyoak, subjects who have experience of this sort of rule know that it states a *precondition* for drinking beer, and can apply the following permission schema containing four production rules:

1. If the action is to be taken, then the precondition must be satisfied.
2. If the action is not to be taken, then the precondition need not be satisfied.
3. If the precondition is satisfied, then the action may be taken.
4. If the precondition is not satisfied, then the action must not be taken.

The activation of this schema will lead, according to the proposal, to the selection of the correct cards: the *P* and *not-Q* cards will be chosen because rules 1 and 4 specify, in this case, what must hold when beer is to be drunk and what must not happen when a person is not over 19 years old. Rules 2 and 3 are used to try to explain why subjects with this schema do not choose the *not-P* and *Q* cards, respectively. In this way, the schema is supposed to specify what holds in states of affairs in which there is a precondition for action.

Cheng and Holyoak predicted that there would be a facilitation effect when subjects knew from previous experience that a given rule stated a precondition for permission to perform some action, and that this effect would also occur, without previous experience, when there was in the task a plausible *scenario* or *rationale*, explaining the point of the rule. These predictions were upheld. Subjects in Hong Kong tended to solve the postal form of the selection task correctly, with or without a rationale, and they had experience of the postal regulation in real life. American subjects, on the other hand, lacked this experience and only showed the facilitation effect when a rationale was given, explaining that the point of the regulation was to specify the extra money one had to pay in order to have permission to seal one's envelopes. Both sets of subjects showed the effect with a novel content outside their real-life experience only in the presence of a rationale. Cheng and Holyoak accordingly concluded that a permission schema could be evoked from memory, either by previous experience with a certain kind of rule or by a scenario of the right kind for it.

Recently, Girotto and his collaborators (Girotto 1988; Girotto, Light and Colbourn 1988) have done some interesting work under the influence of this approach. They have found that children as young as 7 correctly solved a reduced form of the selection task (in which only the consequent values are given) when scenarios about permission were used. These results support, we feel, the idea that deontic knowledge produces the facilitation effect.

If this is so, however, then we should take an even more radical view of the selection task than Cheng *et al.*, and call the traditional analysis of it very much into question. In that analysis, the conditionals in all versions of the task are said to be 'rules'. But it is no longer pedantic to point out that only in versions like Task 3 is the conditional really a rule in the proper, deontic sense. In fact, the rule in this version and its kindred is a conditional obligation (discussed in our section on deontic logic in Chapter 4), and that means that the conditionals in Task 1 and Task 2, on the one hand, and Task 3, on the other, are not of the same logical form. The subjects are not even asked to do the same thing in these different versions of the task. In Tasks 1 and 2, they are asked to decide whether an indicative conditional is true or false, while in Task 3 they are asked whether a conditional obligation has or has not been *violated*. A conditional obligation, of course, is not falsified when it is violated (as revealed by the truth conditions for conditional obligation given in Chapter 4).

Moreover, the question now arises whether there is a mental *deontic* logic, in a formulation which does not include an extensional sentential logic as a part. Such a mental deontic logic would not be applied to Tasks 1 or 2, but only to Task 3, which subjects tend to get right. A claim that this logic exists would not, therefore, face the objections we have so far considered in this chapter to the doctrine of mental sentential logic. This possibility should be discussed in connection with the work of Cosmides.

Cosmides's analysis shares some of the properties of Cheng and Holyoak's, but contains significant differences. Her underlying perspective comes from evolutionary theory, and she proposes that the facilitation effect is attributable to innate schemas, which she terms *Darwinian algorithms*. She holds that these schemas have evolved out of the dependence of the human species on social exchange as a means of survival. Fruitful social exchange depends on the effective understanding of the benefits and costs it incurs. At the foundation of this exchange are what Cosmides calls *social contracts*, which are expressed in conditionals to the effect that, if you take a benefit, then you must pay a cost.

Along with innate knowledge of the nature of these contracts comes the inherent ability to know what it means to violate one. This happens when you take your benefit without paying the required cost, and you are then, in a technical sense, a *cheater*. Cosmides argues that reliable facilitation is produced by the evocation of the innate schemas which embody algorithms for understanding social contracts. She claims that facilitation occurs in the selection task when the rule states a social contract. In that case, the combination of P (taking a benefit) and *not-Q* (not paying a cost) indicates the presence of a cheater. For example, a cheater under the old British postal regulations would be someone who had the benefit of privacy in a sealed letter without paying the extra cost for it. The facilitation effect is thus supposed to arise from an innate propensity to be on the look-out for cheaters.

This analysis is backed by striking empirical support. In one interesting type of experiment, Cosmides uses what she calls *switched* social contracts, in which the conditional states that, if you pay a cost, then you take a benefit. For example, this kind of conditional would state that, if you pay the extra cost for privacy, then you seal your letter. As with Evans's studies of matching bias, Cosmides makes this move to try to get a differential test of two predictions. She argues that, if the facilitation effect is due to an enhanced understanding of the conditional, then with the switched rules in a selection task, subjects should tend to choose the P and *not-Q* cards – cards which, in this case, would show a cost paid (extra money, say) and a benefit not taken (not sealing the letter). Alternatively, if the effect is due to a propensity to look for cheaters, then people should continue to do this irrespective of the conditionals they are given in a task with a switched social contract. In this type of task, to look for a cheater is to pick the *not-P* card (extra money not paid, say) along with the Q card (letter sealed). Needless to say, Cosmides did observe a tendency to choose *not-P* cards with Q cards in her versions of this type of task – the only time this combination has been predicted or found. We, however, are not convinced by her explanation of this result. She uses detailed scenarios in her experiments which could well suggest to the subjects that they are to look for cheaters, whatever the form of the conditional. In that case, the subjects would 'correct' or normalise, in Fillenbaum's sense (Chapter 3), the conditional to read that, if you have the benefit of privacy in sealing your letter, then you must pay the extra cost for it. With the normalised conditional in mind, the subjects in the switched social contracts would just be displaying the standard facilitation effect. (For more on these cases, see Manktelow and Over 1987, in press, a and b.)

Cosmides points out where she and Cheng *et al.* must make different empirical predictions. Not all preconditions for permission are social contracts; only ones which state a benefit/cost relationship of the right kind will do so. As it happens, the rules used by Cheng *et al.* in their experiments do so, but Cosmides compared preconditions for permissions which do have this property with those which do not. An example of a rule she used is, *If a student is to be assigned to Grover High School, then that student must live in Grover City*. In one version of the selection task, she made this conditional into a precondition for permission *and* a social contract by explaining, in a rationale, that Grover High was a better school than the alternative (attending it is a benefit) while Grover City was a rougher area than its neighbour (living there is a cost). In a second version, she restricted the conditional to a precondition for permission without a benefit/cost relationship by explaining, in another rationale, that this rule would allow the Board of Education to assign the proper numbers of teachers to each school. Her results showed that more than twice as many correct choices were made in the first version as compared with the second, apparently favouring her theory against that of Cheng *et al.*, who would have to predict that both versions would evoke the permission schema and tend to produce the same facilitation effect. However, there is evidence that something more general holds: that facilitation also occurs when there are other costs than being cheated in prospect. (See Chapter 8; Cheng and Holyoak, in press; Manktelow and Over in press, a and b)

We shall discuss the research of Cosmides and Cheng *et al.* further in Chapter 8. But we want to note here how important it is to develop the study of deontic inference. Human beings are surrounded by all sorts of rules and regulations which purport to tell them what they should and should not do, and may and may not do, and a significant part of their reasoning has to be devoted to understanding these. Human beings are even more concerned with what they should and should not do to get some benefit or avoid some cost, given their individual beliefs and desires; we shall be able to say more about this aspect of deontic reasoning after we introduce the concepts of subjective probability and utility in Chapter 7. Moreover, the point of any normative theory is to reach deontic conclusions, and in particular our reasoning *about* any logic has to be in part deontic. The point there is to distinguish justified from unjustified inferences – to distinguish, that is to say, what we may infer from what we may not infer, given certain assumptions. Thus, for more than one reason, we cannot discuss rationality in Chapter 8 without returning to this topic.

We have not, however, finished with the selection task just yet. It has inspired another important topic in the research. We shall address this in the next section and, once again, discuss its wider theoretical import in Part 3.

Dual processes

Look again at Tasks 1 and 2 at the start of this chapter (pp. 103–4). Why did you choose the cards you did? This question has been asked of subjects in several experiments over the years, and their answers have been both surprising and revealing.

At one time, people's explanations of their choices were taken as confirmation of the Insight Model. People in the state of no insight should talk about verification, while people in the state of complete insight should say they were trying to falsify. In general, people do change their talk of verification to that of falsification (Goodwin and Wason 1972), but for reasons which will shortly become apparent, this tendency does not really support the Insight Model.

More intriguingly, people's introspections were sought in the early days of selection task research in an attempt to cast light on a curious finding: a conflict between *selection* in the task and *evaluation* after it first observed by Wason (1968a). You will recall that in a standard abstract task, like Task 1, most people incorrectly choose the *P* card alone or just along with the *Q* card. But when they finish the task and the cards are turned over, they evaluate a *not-Q* card with a *P* on the other side as falsifying the conditional. They recognise a falsifying case when they see one.

When people are confronted with this inconsistency between their selections and evaluations, they sometimes display some extraordinary behaviour. Here is a famous example of an exchange between an experimenter and a subject about a selection task, taken from Wason (1983). The sentence to be tested was *Every card which has a red triangle on one side has a blue circle on the other side*; the cards had red or blue circles or triangles on either side; and the four test cards show a red triangle (*P*), a blue triangle (*not-P*), a blue circle (*Q*) and a red circle (*not-Q*). The subject chose just the *P* card and the *Q* card.

Experimenter: What could be on the other side of the red triangle?
Subject: A red circle or a blue circle.
E: If there were a red circle on the other side, could you say anything about the truth or falsity of the sentence?
S: It would be untrue.
E: And if there were a blue circle on the other side, could you say anything about the truth or falsity of the sentence?
S: It would be true.
E: By the way, what was your choice of cards to turn over in order to find out whether the sentence in front of you is true or false?
S: The red triangle and the blue circle.
E: Are you quite happy about this choice?
S: Quite happy, as the other two do not agree with the statement made.
E: What could be on the other side of the red circle?
S: A red triangle or a blue triangle.
E: If there were a red triangle on the other side, could you say anything about the truth or falsity of the sentence?
S: The statement would be meaningless because it doesn't apply.
E: In fact it would be false.
S: It could be true but you are not doing it that way round. The statement would be untrue in any case, no matter what is on the other side.
E: If there were a blue triangle on the other side, could you say anything about the truth or falsity of the sentence?
S: No.

E: Are you quite happy about needing to turn over just the red triangle and the blue circle in order to find out whether the sentence is true or false?

S: Yes.

E: Please turn over the red triangle and the blue circle and tell me whether the sentence is true or false. [blue circle (*Q*) on reverse of red triangle, red triangle (*P*) on reverse of blue circle]

S: The sentence is true.

E: I am now going to turn over the red circle [*not-Q*], and I want you to tell me whether you still think the sentence is true. [red triangle (*P*) on reverse]

S: Wait a minute. When it's put like that the sentence is not true. Either the sentence is true, or it is not true. You have just proved one thing and then you have proved the other. You've proved a theorem and then its contrary, so you don't know where you are. Don't ask me about the blue triangle [*not-P*] because that would be meaningless.

E: Are you quite happy about needing to turn over just the red triangle and the blue circle in order to find out whether the sentence is true or false?

S: There is only one card which needs to be turned over to prove the statement exactly: the red triangle. Strictly speaking, you don't need the blue circle. You must find every card with a red triangle on it and turn it over, but there is only one.

E: But you just said when the red circle was turned over the sentence was false.

S: That is doing it the other way round.

E: The problem is very difficult. Very few people get it right. What we are interested in is why they don't get it right.

S: I am a member of Mensa. I wasn't going to tell you that until afterwards.

Note: Mensa is a society for people who excel at IQ tests.

Some people find this protocol and others like it – it is merely a vivid example of a general type of performance – disturbing: it is difficult to conceive of more blatantly irrational behaviour, as Wason (1983) says. Others are interested not so much in its role as evidence for the prosecution in some sort of trial of human reason, but in what it shows us about mental processes. The one aspect of this subject's protocol which stands out is the utter division between his or her original selection, and the subsequent evaluation of the fully revealed cards. When what is revealed is consistent with the original selection of relevant cards, as when the *P* card is turned over, all is well. When an inconsistency arrives, like a policeman at the door, the shock is palpable, and the subject retreats behind a veil of denial and evasion – anything to justify the initial decision.

In fact, there are less spectacular pieces of evidence which point in the same direction. You will recall that Evans attributed performance in the abstract task to matching bias; however, subjects never explain their choices by saying, 'I chose those cards because they were named in the conditional.' They usually say they were trying to verify it. This seems to indicate that the value of people's self-reports is questionable, a matter explored in further research by Wason and Evans.

Think again about Tasks 1 and 2 in this chapter, and about what people typically do when given these versions of the selection task: they tend to choose the matching cards in both cases, which means they get Task 1 wrong, but Task 2 (with the negated consequent) right. What would these subjects say when asked to explain their choices? Wason and Evans (1975) gave both versions of the task to each subject and recorded both their choices and their stated reasons for making them.

The results were a problem for any lingering temptation to use the Insight Model to explain performance on the selection task. As expected, the most frequent performance, with both versions of the task, was to choose the matching cards. However, the subjects appeared to be completely unaware of this: in most cases, they explained their choices in the Task 1 cases in terms of verification and in Task 2 cases in terms of falsification. But how could they be in a state of no insight one minute and complete insight the next?

Not surprisingly, Wason and Evans do not interpret their subjects' behaviour in this way, but instead propose that the self-reports were justifications, or rationalisations, made after the fact, and not veridical reports of the causes of the subjects' choices at all. Wason and Evans went on to test this idea by giving subjects completed selection tasks and asking them to explain why the answers given were the correct ones. Some of these 'solutions' were in fact incorrect, but no matter, subjects readily gave justifications for them, and expressed a high degree of confidence in them (Evans and Wason 1976). Wason and Evans therefore suggest that subjects' performance in these experiments was mediated by *dual processes*: one for the selections in the task, and the other for explaining their selections afterwards. This proposal has deep theoretical consequences, as we shall elaborate in the next two sections and in Part 3.

Heuristic and analytic processes

There have been some reformulations of the theory of dual processes (see Evans 1982, 1984), and it has evolved recently into a theory of *heuristic and analytic processes* (Evans 1984, 1989). The distinction between these is set out by Evans (1989) in the following way:

reasoning proceeds in two stages: (i) a heuristic stage in which aspects
of the problem information are identified as 'relevant' and selected
for further processing and (ii) an analytic stage in which inferences
are drawn from the selected information.

For Evans, heuristic processes are pre-attentive ones largely to do with
trying to find what is relevant to a problem, while analytic processes are
higher-level ones – more attentive and verbal – which operate on the
results of the heuristic processes and generate inferences. In a realistic
version of the selection task, a heuristic process would be one which
selected a relevant schema for solving problems of that sort, and then this
schema would be used in an analytic process which would yield the
solution, by means of actual inference, to that particular problem. Evans
holds that, in an abstract selection task, subjects tend not to have a relevant
schema in their memories, and a heuristic process creates the matching
bias by selecting cards which are taken to be relevant to the topic of the
unusual, abstract conditional.

Evans (1984: 465) thinks that not even analytic processes produce
content-independent logical inference. But we would emphasise what we
reported in the last section: subjects can make content-independent
semantic evaluations. This does not mean that they can, after all, use formal,
syntactic rules of inference in a mental logic to solve problems. But what it
does mean is that they have some *semantic* knowledge about any
conditional of the indicative form, no matter what its content is. They can
even infer that an abstract indicative conditional is false when they see that
its antecedent is true and its consequent false. This knowledge enables
them to evaluate revealed cards correctly at the end of a selection task, and
the process which accomplishes this evaluation could be described as a
metalevel analytic one.

Mental models and semantic evaluation

Semantic knowledge of this general type must also be applied in the
processes which construct mental models, if the proposals of
Johnson-Laird (1983, 1988) are basically correct. As we explained in
Chapter 4, the point of using mental models to evaluate the validity of an
inference is to try to find out if there is a model in which the premises are
true and the conclusion false. People using this technique have to be able
to recognise that the inference is invalid when it has true premises and a
false conclusion, but is otherwise valid. Let us see in more detail how this
semantic knowledge is supposed to be used in practice.

Johnson-Laird (1983: 34) concludes that people get a realistic version of
the selection right because they have a pre-existing model of the type of

state of affairs described there. He says little about this sort of model, but concentrates instead on a theory of how models are constructed to evaluate *syllogisms*. These inferences with two premises have been studied since Aristotle, and are now embraced by first-order predicate logic. Johnson-Laird, of course, uses examples in natural language, like the following.

Premises: All German cars are reliable
All expensive cars are reliable

Conclusion: All German cars are expensive

We can easily work out that this example is invalid. But exactly how do we do this? In Johnson-Laird's view, we first of all construct a mental representation of the state of affairs described by each premise. For *All German cars are reliable*, our representation should be something like this.

g = r
g = r
(r)

The (r) indicates the possibility that there may or may not be reliable cars which are not German. The exact number of elements is unimportant. For the second premise, *All expensive cars are reliable*, we would construct something like this.

e = r
e = r
(r)

Now (r) indicates that there may be reliable cars which are not expensive. The next step is to combine the representation of the second premise with that of the first, in all the different ways this is possible. We would then get the following as one possibility:

g = r = e
g = r

This represents a state of affairs in which the two premises are true but the conclusion is false: in it all German cars and all expensive cars are reliable, but there is at least one German car which is reliable but not expensive. Our final step would be to grasp that this model demonstrates the invalidity of the original inference: that it is a *counterexample* to the claim that the inference is valid. In another case, we would conclude, according to

Johnson-Laird's theory, that an inference was valid if we could find no counterexample among the mental models we had constructed.

Johnson-Laird (1983: 133) holds that people are not always logically systematic in their construction of mental models, and on this basis he would deny that what he proposes is like a mental 'semantic tableaux' logic suggested by Beth and Piaget (1966), which we referred to in Chapter 4. There is similarity between looking for a counterexample to a claim that a conditional is true in the selection task, and looking for a counterexample to the claim that an inference is valid. (The connection between the logical truth of a conditional and the validity of an inference is expressed in the deduction theorem in logic; see Chang and Keisler 1977.) But Johnson-Laird could argue that people are generally unsystematic in looking for either type of counterexample when they are confronted by unusual or unrealistic problems. On the other hand, he does seem to think that people know the conditions under which any inference, whatever its content, is valid. This is the semantic or *metalogical* knowledge that any inference is valid if and only if there is no model in which all its premises are true and its conclusion false. This strong position is not strictly required by the theory of mental models, and may be a rather optimistic view: Evans (1989) reviews evidence that people tend to assess arguments differently, depending on whether or not they believe their conclusions.

People may use all sorts of unsystematic ways of trying to select which inferences are valid, and the results of these processes may sometimes be incorrect. But if they have a sound metalevel evaluative process, of the sort we have just described, then there are consequences for what we say about their rationality, which we shall explore in Part 3.

7 Probability and inference

In Chapter 4 we explained the distinction between valid and invalid inferences. Valid inferences are *completely reliable* and so absolutely justified – we would never be led in one of these inferences from true premises to a false conclusion. These are *demonstrative* inferences – their conclusions must be true, given that their premises are true. Invalid inferences are *non-demonstrative* – their conclusions may be false even though their premises are true.

We said very little about non-demonstrative inferences in Chapter 4, except to suggest at the end of the chapter that not all of these inferences are completely unjustified. It would, of course, be a fallacy to infer that an inference was absolutely unjustified merely because it could not be absolutely justified. Absolute certainty is hard to attain in ordinary affairs or even in empirical science, and we naturally feel that there are many intermediate stages between absolutely good inferences and absolutely bad ones. We express this feeling whenever we are impressed by a conclusion which seems to us to be probably, though not certainly, true, given its premises. But what does it mean to say that a non-demonstrative inference is justified to some extent? Which forms of inference are highly, though not absolutely, justified? Do the non-demonstrative inferences of ordinary people tend to be highly justified? These are the basic questions of this chapter. (We shall not go deeply into some very important technical topics which arise here, but Skyrms (1986) is a good introduction to those.)

Subjective probability

Outside mathematics and formal logic, most people believe few propositions with absolute certainty. They are more or less confident about much of what they believe, and they express this in their probability judgments. They are not certain, for example, what the weather will be like in detail tomorrow, but if they are fairly confident that rain is on the way, they will say, 'It will probably rain tomorrow.' When pressed, ordinary people may be more exact about a probability judgment of this type. They might say that it is highly likely to rain tomorrow, or only that it is slightly more likely than not to do so. Those who study the weather and weather forecasting tend to be more definite in their judgments. As trained forecasters, who had collected all the available data, some might even use precise numbers to express their probability judgments.

Let us suppose that we are told that the barometer is falling, and on that assumption, we infer that it will rain tomorrow. We believe our conclusion, are quite confident about it and are willing to say that it is probably true. Our inference then appears *strong* to us: its conclusion seems to us to be probably true, given its premise. But some other people may disagree. They may prefer the state of their bunions to that of a barometer as a way of predicting the weather. Perhaps they infer from the lack of pain in their bunions that it will not rain tomorrow. Their inference appears strong to them, because they are confident in their conclusion, given their premise. From their point of view, their conclusion is probably true, given the state of their bunions. We state that their inference is weak compared to ours, but they reply that theirs is strong and ours is weak.

The concept we have just introduced is that of *subjective probability*, which is explained in terms of the beliefs of individuals. We believe that it will rain tomorrow with a fair amount of confidence; in technical terms, we have a reasonably high *degree of belief* in this proposition. That being so, that it will rain tomorrow can be said to be probable from our point of view. But there are other points of view. Some other people are not at all confident, and so have a low degree of belief that it will rain tomorrow. From their point of view, this proposition can be said to be improbable. Here 'probable' and 'improbable' are used in the subjective sense and do not really conflict with each other. All that is really being said is that we are confident that it will rain tomorrow while some other people are not.

Subjective probability is a useful notion in ordinary affairs and in social science, particularly when combined with a measure of *subjective utility*, which specifies how much an individual desires some possibility. People's behaviour depends not just on what they believe and what they desire, but also on how confidently they believe and how intensely they desire. There are ways of trying to measure confidence in belief and intensity of desire, and when we do so, we can predict and explain behaviour to some extent. For example, we might be able to discover that most people confidently believe that just one candidate in an election will lower taxes if put into office, and that the only relevant desire of these people is a very strong one for lower taxes. Then we should be able to predict, with some confidence ourselves, that this candidate will win the election, and afterwards to give a reasonable explanation of why that has happened. (By speaking of degrees or levels of belief and desire, we do not mean to suggest that these are always very exact or can be precisely measured, nor that very confident prediction of action is always possible on this basis. An important additional factor is that of ability to perform an action, and of course, we need to know much more about the detailed workings of the mind to get fully scientific predictions and explanations of action. We take up these further points in Chapter 9.)

People make *decisions,* such as about whom to vote for, on the basis of how much confidence they have in, and how much utility they place on, certain possible outcomes, such as getting lower taxes. There is much to investigate empirically about how people make these decisions, and about how they get their judgments of subjective probability and utility in the first place. We shall return later in the chapter to the problem of discovering how ordinary people make probability judgments, but we now ask how these judgments ought to be made. This underlies the theory of how we ought to make decisions: normative *decision theory.* (Gärdenfors and Sahlin (1988) is a useful collection of important papers on subjective probability, utility and decisions.)

The probability calculus

The fundamental normative account of probability is given by a mathematical theory called the *probability calculus.* It has many important applications in science and, of course, is the basis of statistics. Without it, scientists themselves would never know what they ought to infer from their data. We shall not, however, go into the mathematical complexities of the subject, nor the subtleties of its scientific applications. (Skyrms (1986) contains a more technical introduction to the probability calculus and to the related topics we shall take up in this section.)

The probability calculus depends in turn on an even more fundamental subject, namely, logic. Let us suppose that we have assigned, by some means or other, numbers from 0 to 1 to some atomic sentences as a way of representing their probabilities. The probability calculus will then tell us how this assignment should be extended to compound sentences on the basis of certain logical properties and relationships. One rule for doing this concerns *tautologies.* These are sentences, such as *A or not-A,* which are true in all models of sentential logic. By this rule, the probability of any tautology ought to be equal to 1, and this informally means that it is certain to be true, just as it should be. Another rule is that, if the probability assigned to *A* is n, then the probability assigned to *not-A* should be 1 − n. More concretely, if the probability of *A* is $^1/_2$, then the probability of *not-A* should also be $^1/_2$; and this means that both *A* and *not-A* are as likely to be true as false. A rule that can be derived from these two is that the probability of the negation of a tautology should be 0, which means that it is certainly false.

The probability calculus can be formally axiomatised by taking certain rules as basic in axioms, and then using logic to derive further rules. We have already tried to give some indication how this might be done, and it would be out of place for us to do more in this line. It is, however, important to discuss some of the consequences of the basic rules. One of these is that, if A logically implies B, then the probability of A cannot exceed that of B. With just a little reflection, it is easy to argue that this must be so. If A is more probable than B, then A could turn out to be true while B turned out to be false. But that is impossible if A logically implies B, i.e. if B is true whenever A is true. Not much understanding of logic and probability is needed to follow this argument, and yet the rule tends to be violated, under certain conditions, in ordinary reasoning, as we shall discover below in this chapter when introducing the conjunction fallacy.

Other important consequences of the basic axioms concern what is called *conditional probability*. An example of this would be the probability that it will rain, given that – or on condition that – the barometer is falling, which might well differ from just the probability that it will rain (after all, the barometer might not actually be falling). As another example, let A express the proposition that some politicians say they will help education by putting money into it, and B the proposition that they really intend to do so. We are naturally interested in the probability of B *given* A and want to know what it is.

Suppose, as part of the example, that we already know another conditional probability, that of A *given* B, which is close to 1. We may have discovered that these politicians do tend to tell us that they will help education when they have definite plans for doing so. That does not necessarily mean, of course, that the probability of B *given* A is close to 1, that the politicians tend to have definite plans for helping education when they say they do. They could even have a tendency to break their promises of help for education. Perhaps they rarely have a real intention to put money into education, but whether they do or not, they are prepared to say they do.

How can we calculate the probability of B *given* A? *Bayes's Theorem* is relevant in cases like this one. It tells us that the additional information we need in our example is the probability of B and the probability of A *given not-B*. The latter may be high while the former is low. That would hold if, as we have just imagined, the politicians rarely had a sincere intention to help education, but often said they did when they did not. The theorem would then tell us that the probability of B *given* A was low. It might not seem that we need to appeal to a mathematical theorem to tell us to have no confidence in what is said by unprincipled and dishonest politicians. But the theorem is a general one, and does usefully show us how to calculate an exact numerical value for *B given A* in certain cases. We shall also see in the next section that people do not always appear to conform to this theorem in their probabilistic reasoning.

The question we should face in the rest of this section is why people should conform to the probability calculus at all. What does an abstract mathematical theory about numerical values and ratios have to do with the way they should arrange their degrees of belief or confidence? This is a good question, and the way we should try to answer it is by making some significant points about bets.

Most people have risked at least small amounts of money in more or less formally organised bets, as in horse-racing or lotteries. But bets do not have to be so public or so controlled by explicit law, nor do bets have to concern money. Most of us are introduced to informal bets as children, as in games in which marbles are won or lost. As adults, we continue to make such bets, and then some utility like prestige or reputation may be at risk and not money. We also tend to get some idea, from ordinary affairs, of how much to risk for some possible gain, and this is reflected by our behaviour when we agree the odds for a bet. Now this betting behaviour is obviously connected with how confident we are about certain outcomes and how much utility we attach to them, and indeed it can be used to measure subjective probability and utility under certain conditions.

Subjective probability may or may not conform to rules of the probability calculus. For example, people may or may not have the same confidence in *A* as in *not-A* when their degree of confidence in *A* is $1/2$. But if people do not conform to these rules, and still enter into bets in the natural way, then what is called a *Dutch Book* can be made against them. This is a range of bets which they can only lose overall – there is no other logical possibility. No matter what outcomes occur, their total losses would always be greater than their total gains. If we use the probability calculus as the basis of our non-demonstrative reasoning, attempting to infer conclusions we should be confident about, then we cannot be absolutely sure that these conclusions will be true if our premises are. But use of the probability calculus can be given a different justification in terms of what is certain. If we do not use it, and are drawn into a Dutch Book, then we are absolutely sure to come out losers.

The extent to which the Dutch Book argument justifies the use of the probability calculus is sometimes questioned. It has been said that the best way to avoid a Dutch Book is to refuse to bet. This might be easy for Robinson Crusoe, but may be more difficult for the rest of us. We are social animals, and we have an understandably strong reaction against *cheaters*. These are people who get something for nothing by breaking the understandings or agreements which are necessary in society; and those who would knowingly make a Dutch Book against us fall into this category. They would win what are supposed to be fair bets without paying the cost of running a risk themselves; and we would want to protect ourselves from even the possibility of dealing with them. (This issue does call for more discussion than we can give it here; see the end of this chapter on the problem of ultimately explaining even why truth is better than falsity and valid inference better than invalid inference.) The next question is, to what extent *do* we conform to the probability calculus in ordinary reasoning?

Actual probability judgments

It would be a mistake to think that the questions of subjective probability and utility are specialised topics which only affect scientists and gamblers. Much of our everyday thinking is pervaded by inferences in which they play a significant part. Why, for instance, are some people reluctant to walk the streets after dark or to travel by air rather than by car, and others affected by 'health scares' such as the one in Britain in 1988 about eggs and food poisoning? In all such cases, one makes a judgment of the likelihood (probability) of something happening, balanced against its desirability or undesirability (utility).

These judgments may be rational or irrational according to some normative theory, but let us now consider descriptions of what people actually do. There are then several issues to be tackled. How do people form and maintain their degrees or levels of belief? What sorts of strategies do they employ when they do so? What role, if any, does the probability calculus play in this process? These questions have been the subject of several decades of vigorous empirical research, and an important part of this has been on how subsequent experience affects beliefs we have already acquired.

The dominant psychological view of the effect of new experience on acquired belief is that people are prone to a *confirmation bias*, although, as we shall see, there is evidence of some dissent emerging. This bias exists when people tend to support, rather than to challenge, their existing beliefs. We shall deal with two 'families' of experiments which suggest the presence of the bias: those associated with Wason (1960, 1968b) and those with Nisbett and his colleagues (see Nisbett and Ross 1980).

Wason has a talent for devising intriguing experiments. The following is rather like the game of 20 questions. Subjects are given a sequence of numbers – 2, 4, 6 – and asked to discover the rule the experimenter has in mind for listing these. The unknown rule is simply to list numbers in increasing order of magnitude. The subjects are to try to infer this by generating further three-digit sequences, which the experimenter says are, or are not, consistent with it. Only when the subjects are convinced that they have inferred the rule can they announce what they think it is. The experimenter then says whether or not it is correct; if not, the process is repeated. The task is done with paper and pencil, so that memory load is minimised, and the subjects record comments alongside the number sequences they generate.

In Wason's original research (see also Wason and Johnson-Laird 1972), some strong behavioural tendencies were observed. Twenty-two of 29 subjects announced at least one incorrect rule; six announced the correct rule first go. From the recorded comments, it appeared that there were differences between these categories of subjects. First bear in mind what would be, normatively, the best way to go about this task. It is assumed that the original number series will cause subjects to think of a precise rule as their hypothesis, such as listing numbers separated by 2. But producing positive instance after positive instance, which are consistent with this rule – such as 4, 6, 8; 3, 5, 7 and so on – is not of much use. One can go on doing this indefinitely, and the hypothesis will never be proved true. One learns far more by attempting to *falsify* one's present hypothesis with a negative instance, and by varying hypotheses and testing them in this way. For example, subjects who used 3, 6, 9 as a test instance would learn from the experimenter's response that the correct rule does not specify that the numbers should be separated by 2.

Subjects all started off with over-specific hypotheses (as recorded in their written comments), but in the case of the first-time solvers, there was a tendency to try to falsify these initial hypotheses before announcing them. Here is an example of a protocol from such a subject (from Wason 1968b). The subject's comments are given alongside the sequences generated, together with a plus for a consistent case and a minus for an inconsistent one; the rule announced is given in italics.

12	24	36	(+)	unit figures are even and increase in twos
8	10	12	(+)	even numbers increasing in twos
2	6	10	(+)	even numbers increasing in fours
6	4	2	(–)	even numbers decreasing in twos
2	6	8	(+)	even numbers ascending
8	54	98	(+)	even numbers ascending
1	17	23	(+)	ascending numbers
1	18	23	(+)	ascending numbers
1	2	3	(+)	ascending numbers

The rule is ascending numbers (solution time: 9 minutes)

Here we can see both the normatively prescribed testing methods: the initial hypothesis is varied by the third sequence, and further negative testing takes place with the fourth and seventh. Now look at a protocol from a less successful subject.

8	10	12	(+)	step interval of two
7	9	11	(+)	with numbers not divisible by two
1	3	5	(+)	to see if rule may apply to numbers starting at two and upwards
3	5	1	(−)	the numbers do not necessarily have to be in ascending or descending order
5	3	1	(−)	could be in descending order

The rule is that the three numbers must be in ascending order separated by intervals of two. (wrong)

11	13	15	(+)	must have one number below ten in the series
1	6	11	(+)	ascending series with regular step interval

The rule is that the three numbers must be in ascending series and separated by regular step intervals. (wrong)

The rule is that the first number can be arbitrarily chosen; the second number must be greater than the first and can be arbitrarily chosen; the third number is larger than the second by the same amount as the second is larger than the first. (wrong)

1	3	13	(+)	any three numbers in ascending order

The rule is that the three numbers need have no relationship with each other, except that the second is larger than the first, and the third larger than the second. (38 minutes)

In both these protocols (and in others in Wason 1968b), one can see that, even in the case of the successful subjects, there is a tendency to generate positive instances: the difference between the successful and the unsuccessful subjects sometimes seems to consist in how quickly they stop doing this. In addition, the unsuccessful subjects have a tendency to cling on to their discredited hypotheses. This is particularly noticeable in the second protocol above: the second-announced rule is marked wrong, but the subject re-presents the same rule, worded differently, without generating any further instances.

Wason and his colleagues found that monetary rewards and penalties, replacing the numbers by objects in ordinary categories (e.g. lists of living things) and other variations did not affect these typical behaviours. In one version of the task in which subjects were given only one shot at the rule and, if wrong, asked how they would find out if they were wrong, only two out of 16 replied that they would try to generate cases inconsistent with their hypothesis. Three replied that no other rules were possible, one declaring, 'Rules are relative. If you were the subject and I were the experimenter then I should be right.'

In the face of this evidence, one might conclude that the case for confirmation bias is conclusive. However, we have to ask two further questions before returning the verdict: is this task representative of general hypothesis-testing behaviour? It is, after all, a novel and artificial procedure, although designed by Wason to mimic certain properties of this mode of thinking, such as the role of alternative plausible hypotheses with indefinitely many positive instances. Second, are there other possible interpretations of the observed effects besides a straightforward confirmation bias? We shall explore these two further questions in order, first by looking at the work of Nisbett and his colleagues, and then returning to the '2, 4, 6' task and its relatives to consider alternative explanations.

Not surprisingly, work on confirmation bias is not confined to a narrow set of researchers. A vivid account of such work, from the perspective of cognitive social psychology, is given by Nisbett and Ross (1980). A more philosophical discussion is contained in Baron (1985).

Nisbett and Ross link their consideration of confirmation bias to *theory maintenance*, the tendency to persist in one's beliefs, come what may. They offer three general and not very encouraging conclusions from their survey of this work. First, an existing theory (belief) will tend to be strengthened by exposure to any evidence, positive, negative, or neutral. Second, a new theory based on initial evidence will be resistant to subsequent evidence, even when the latter objectively cancels out the former. Third, when initial evidence is later shown to be worthless, a theory based on it still persists.

An example of empirical research on the first point will be sufficient to illustrate this line of enquiry. It is a well-known study by Lord, Ross and Lepper (1979) on the effects of evidence on people's beliefs about capital punishment. They surveyed the beliefs of students as to whether they considered capital punishment to be a deterrent to murder, and selected those who expressed a strong positive belief in this proposition, or who strongly disagreed with it. Each group of subjects was then presented with written accounts of supposedly genuine studies either confirming or disconfirming the deterrent effect of capital punishment. The task was to assess the studies; subjects' strength of belief was also measured after having done so. The study was carefully counterbalanced so that all subjects read both a positive and negative report, *vis-à-vis* their stated beliefs; half read the positive one before the negative one, the other half vice versa; and the design of experiment occupying either status was also systematically varied. These steps were taken to ensure an objectively equal weighting of evidence for and against either position.

Having already been given the conclusions of this body of research, you will not be surprised at the outcome of this experiment. As Nisbett and

Ross put it, 'supporting evidence was handled with kid gloves; opposing evidence was mauled.' In other words, subjects were more highly critical of whichever study opposed their prior beliefs. This is not necessarily irrational, as Nisbett and Ross point out, as long as that belief is well justified. However, it was also found that after reading both a positive and a negative report, subjects' beliefs were strengthened. This should not have happened: the weight of evidence on either side was equal.

Clearly, the treatment of confirming and disconfirming evidence differs in domains outside the artificial one of number series, but are we still entitled to view this as confirmation bias? Some claim that we are not. For instance, Baron (1985) argues that these subjects could be acting rationally: they might be looking at the opposing evidence precisely because it could cause them to change their beliefs. Having examined it closely and found fault, they conclude that their beliefs must be all the more justified for having stood up to such a test. Baron suggests other plausible reasons for theory maintenance, the overall point being that one must determine precisely what normative standards are appropriate, and what sort of judgment the subject is making. If someone favours capital punishment for purely moral reasons, this belief can only be positively affected by arguments about deterrence: if capital punishment does not deter, then so what? The belief is a moral one anyway. If it does, then the believer has all the more reason to support it: it is both morally and practically justified (a similar argument could be applied for an opposing belief).

More recently, some theorists have questioned whether confirmation bias, in the sense of seeking out and treating more favourably evidence in line with one's beliefs, really exists at all. Perhaps what is happening is that people tend to think in terms of *positive* instances: positive, confirming instances of the hypothesis and positive instances of the correct rule are not always the same. This view can be found in Evans (1989) and Klayman and Ha (1987).

Consider Klayman and Ha's discussion of the '2, 4, 6' task. They point out that the subject's problem, in the standard version of the task, is that the correct rule (ascending numbers) covers all cases of the likely initial hypothesis (numbers increasing by 2s), in that any positive, confirming instance of the latter – such as 3, 5, 7 – will be a positive instance of the former. That is why one needs falsifying instances of the initial hypothesis: a sequence such as 2, 5, 8 will be inconsistent with it but consistent with the correct rule. However, this is not the only relationship possible between an initial hypothesis and a correct rule. Another possibility is that the correct rule is to list three even numbers. Here the initial hypothesis *overlaps* with it, i.e. some positive, confirming instances of the initial hypotheses will not be positive instances of the correct rule. The series 3, 5, 7 is an example. In this case, generating positive instances of the initial hypothesis will lead to negative instances of the correct rule.

On this basis, and following a detailed analysis of other paradigms, Klayman and Ha argue that the utility of positive testing depends on the nature of the task in hand. Evans (1989) performs a similar theoretical analysis. Their two conclusions are different in that they attribute looking for positive instances, on the one hand, to an over-generalised problem-solving strategy (Klayman and Ha), and on the other, to a pre-attentive heuristic process (Evans). But one prediction to be made from their joint approach, for which there is some support, concerns what happens when the task is changed so that all instances will be positive: in that case, performance should improve. An experiment of this type can ask subjects to classify sequences as members of two (or more) complementary classes, rather than as members or non-members of one, as in the original '2, 4, 6' task. This was done by Tweney, Doherty, Warner and Pliske (1980). These authors have published a series of studies in which the essential methodology of the '2, 4, 6' task was adapted to make it more like real scientific hypothesis-testing: see Tweney, Doherty and Mynatt (1981) for a review.

In one experiment reported by Tweney, Doherty, Warner and Pliske (1980), subjects were told that the number series were classified according to two rules rather than one, both of which the subject had to determine in the usual way. The sequences would be either *dax* or *med* but not both. The correct rules specified that *dax* sequences were to be all ascending ones (i.e. the usual 2, 4, 6 rule) and that *med* sequences were to be all others. When the subjects produced a sequence, they were told whether it was a *dax* or a *med*, rather than whether it was right or wrong. Under these conditions, in which all the sequences were positive instances of *dax* ones or of *med* ones, most subjects announced the correct rules first go. This good performance, when positive instances of the one sort or the other decide the matter, is evidence that these instances do play an important part in ordinary inference.

The notion that people's non-demonstrative inferences may be prone to certain biases, such as that of only looking for positive instances, has been explored in another highly influential body of research, which we shall take up next.

Heuristics and biases

Of all the work on thinking which we review in this book, probably only Piaget's exceeds that of Tversky and Kahneman and their associates in its impact. Tversky and Kahneman were responsible for introducing the idea of *heuristics and biases* into the explanation of ordinary non-demonstrative inference. The best source of readings about their work is still the collection of papers in Kahneman, Slovic and Tversky (1982), though

Nisbett and Ross (1980) is also heavily influenced by it. The core of this approach is that ordinary inference is sometimes mediated by general mental strategies – the heuristics – which may have utility in some domains, but which in others create tendencies to error – the biases. We shall focus on the most extensively studied of these supposed heuristics.

Why are people seemingly convinced that we live in more violent times these days, that children are not safe on the streets, or that there is more reason to fear a plane journey than a car ride? Recently, the British Home Secretary was quoted in the newspapers as saying, 'In general, the fear of becoming a victim of crime increases with age, while the risk of becoming such a victim actually diminishes' (*Guardian* 7.3.1989). Tversky and Kahneman's work attempts to account for such phenomena.

In the case of these examples, the heuristic proposed is that of *availability*, which was introduced by Tversky and Kahneman (1973), and is defined in the following way: 'A person is said to employ the availability heuristic whenever he estimates frequency or probability by the ease with which instances or associations could be brought to mind.' Tversky and Kahneman point out that this is in many cases a quite legitimate technique: for instance, frequent events are generally more recallable, so an impression of recallability will often give a reasonable estimate of frequently occurring events (and be easy to perform). However, availability judgments are affected by factors which are not related to objective frequency, and hence will tend to lead at times to biased and inaccurate inferences.

One such factor is *vividness*. (See also Nisbett and Ross 1980.) This is sometimes a property of unique events, which by definition are not frequent. Particularly striking stories in the mass media are, of course, highly recallable, but vividness in itself is not necessarily indicative of frequency. This is supposedly the problem in the examples above: on this account, people are more afraid of plane journeys than car journeys because of the vividness of the reports of air crashes compared with car crashes. In fact, far more people are killed and injured on the roads. The problem is compounded by actual frequency: incident-free car and plane journeys do not figure greatly in the news bulletins. Advertisers, newspaper editors and political campaign managers are well aware of this: a single vivid instance will make a point far better than a mountain of dry statistics.

Another heuristic *representativeness* has been even more extensively researched. According to Kahneman and Tversky (1972), people use this heuristic when

> the probability of an uncertain event, or a sample, [is judged] by the degree to which it is (i) similar in essential properties to its parent population; and (ii) reflects the salient features of the process by which it is generated.

Several well-known experiments have been reported which illustrate these effects, and form the basis for the claim that people commit characteristic fallacies in their non-demonstrative inferences. Here are some examples from Kahneman and Tversky's work which illustrate their case.

1. Which of these birth orders is more likely in families of six children?

G B G B B G

B G B B B B

If you said that the first is more likely, you have fallen prey to the supposed bias: both sequences are equally likely, since what determines the sex of each child is essentially random, and the sex of a previous child does not affect the sex of a subsequent child.

2. Linda is 31 years old, single, outspoken, and very bright. She majored in philosophy. As a student, she was deeply concerned with issues of discrimination and social justice, and also participated in anti-nuclear demonstrations. Which is more likely:

Linda is a bank clerk

Linda is a bank clerk who is active in the feminist movement

Perhaps you judged, as did a large number of subjects in the research of Kahneman and Tversky (1982), that the second is more likely. If so, you have committed the *conjunction fallacy*: a conjunction cannot be more probable than one of its conjuncts, since the conjunction logically implies its conjuncts. In this particular case, there are lots of bank clerks, only some of whom are feminists. (The very most that is possible is that all bank clerks are feminists.)

3. Eighty-five per cent of the taxis in a particular city are green and the rest are blue. A witness claims that a taxi in an accident was blue. Under tests, the witness correctly identifies both blue and green taxis on 80 per cent of occasions. What is the probability that the taxi was, in fact, blue?

The answer is about 41 per cent. In other words, it is more likely (59 per cent) that the witness was *wrong*. This is why. Assuming each kind of taxi is equally likely to be in accidents, we can say that, for every 100 crashes, 85 will tend to be of green taxis and 15 of blue ones. The witness will wrongly identify 20 per cent of the former (i.e. 17) and correctly identify 80 per cent of the latter (i.e. 12) as blue. Thus, he would report blue 29 times, but only be correct on 12 of them, which is approximately 41 per cent. Most people estimate that the witness is about 80 per cent likely to be right, i.e. somewhere near the estimate of his accuracy, ignoring the *base rate* statistic. A full account of this case calls on Bayes's Theorem, which tells us how to calculate, from the information above, the conditional probability that the taxi was blue given that the witness said it was blue. (See Pollard and Evans (1983) for the more intuitive analysis we give here.)

> 4. A certain town is served by two hospitals. In the larger hospital about 45 babies are born each day, and in the smaller hospital about 15 babies are born each day. As you know, about 50 per cent of all babies are boys. The exact percentage of baby boys, however, varies from day to day. Sometimes it may be higher than 50 per cent, sometimes lower.
>
> For a period of one year, each hospital recorded the days on which more than 60 per cent of the babies born were boys. Which hospital do you think recorded more such days?

Most people reckon that the figure will be about the same for each hospital (Kahneman and Tversky 1972). In fact, the smaller hospital will be more likely to record such days: freak values are more likely with small samples (think of opinion polls).

In each case, it is proposed that people base their judgments on how *representative* each case is of its category, and ignore or violate relevant statistical principles. In the first case, there appears to be a misunderstanding of the nature of randomness. In the second, there is a tendency to match salient information about the person described (her radical politics) to a stereotypical category (feminists), leading to the conjunction fallacy. In the third, people ignore base-rate probability. In the fourth, people seem unaware of the law of large numbers, which states that larger samples provide better estimates of population characteristics than do smaller samples.

Problems with heuristics and biases

The ideas of Tversky and Kahneman and their colleagues have not been accepted without question. Most critical attention has concentrated on what appears to be their rather pessimistic assessment of the ability of people to make accurate judgments under uncertainty, and recently, some attention has been directed not only at alternative explanations of the findings of heuristics and biases research, but also at the good statistical intuitions which people *do* exhibit.

Writing on the former count has ranged from the merely critical to the openly hostile. For example, Evans (e.g. 1989; Evans and Dusoir 1977; Pollard and Evans 1983) has proposed that Kahneman and Tversky have underestimated people's knowledge of the law of large numbers and hence overestimated the prevalence of the representativeness heuristic. In the case of the hospital problem (above), for instance, subjects do appear to abide by the law of large numbers when the problem is simplified by asking which hospitals had more days when *all* the babies born were boys (see also Bar-Hillel 1979).

Evidence which confirms that people have, after all, some reasonable appreciation of statistical principles such as the law of large numbers comes from the work of Nisbett and his colleagues (see Fong, Krantz and Nisbett 1986; Nisbett, Krantz, Jepson and Kunda 1983; and a summary of this research in Holland, Holyoak, Nisbett and Thagard 1986). These researchers have found that this apparently general understanding can be triggered – and, conversely, inhibited – by the way the problem is framed, and its relation to a person's existing knowledge.

An example of a triggering condition is that of perceived variability. Some events and objects in the world are known, or believed, to be more variable than others, and this affects the degree to which people appeal to the law of large numbers. Nisbett, Krantz, Jepson and Kunda (1983) tested this by giving subjects problems concerning an imaginary newly discovered island. They were asked to estimate the likelihood of general classes of objects exhibiting certain properties on the basis of samples of varying sizes. These objects were a new species of bird, a new tribe of people and a new mineral. In the case of items which are usually invariant (the mineral), the size of sample did not matter: people were equally willing to generalise from a small one as from a large one. However, for more variant categories (birds and people), there was a greater tendency to generalise from larger samples, which is consistent with the law of large numbers. This effect was observed within categories too: judgments about variant properties of people (stature) were more affected by sample size than were judgments about invariant properties (skin colour).

There is a parallel here with social stereotyping. People generally believe that the group of which they are a member (the in-group) is more varied than a group of which they are not members (the out-group), perhaps because of the greater *availability* of varied examples of the former. It follows that there will be a greater tendency to generalise from small samples (individuals, say) to the group as a whole when people are thinking about the out-group than when they are thinking about the in-group. All is not lost, though: prompting people to consider the variability in each group reduces this effect (Holland, Holyoak, Nisbett and Thagard 1986).

Fong, Krantz and Nisbett (1986) pursue some interesting educational implications of these findings. It appears that training in statistics affects the degree to which people exhibit a general understanding of statistical principles, and that it does not matter much whether this training uses examples, or is purely formal. Psychology and social science graduates are, as a consequence, much more likely to give statistical answers on these probabilistic problems than are 'hard' scientists or humanities graduates: in neither of these other fields is the same use made of the norms of probabilistic inference.

Whether people can rightly be characterised as using heuristics and exhibiting biases has been questioned by several authors, e.g. Cohen (1981) and MacDonald (1986). Cohen's attack stems from his commitment to a highly general argument for human rationality, which we shall consider in more detail in Part 3. Put briefly, his position is that since people must be rational in order to communicate, experiments which demonstrate otherwise do so either because they require knowledge outside the subjects' experience, or because they have tricked the subjects into mistakes. This forces him to defend subjects' behaviour in dubious ways which we cannot consider here; see the commentaries to his paper by Evans and Pollard (1981), Griggs (1981) and Kahneman (1981).

MacDonald (1986) is sympathetic to Cohen's point of view and tries to offer additional points in its support. One interesting argument he uses concerns the subjective weighting of the information presented in the kind of problems devised by researchers in heuristics and biases. In general, he argues, communication and its contents are motivated: they occur for a reason. That is, people assume a reason for information being communicated. (See the extension of this argument in Sperber and Wilson's relevance theory in Chapter 8.) The case of Linda will serve as an example. According to MacDonald, presenting the idea of Linda's being a bank clerk in the conjunction question is to invite one to *assume* it to be true – otherwise, why mention it at all? If this is so, then subjects are judging how likely it is that Linda is active in the feminist movement given that she is as described *and* is a bank clerk. This may well be greater than just the probability that she is a bank clerk. MacDonald claims that this factor has been ignored in heuristics and biases research, and in this respect, he supports the view, which we would also press, that the pragmatic context always has to be carefully taken into account in experiments on reasoning.

We thus have evidence that people are neither wholly at the mercy of irrational heuristics, nor naturally gifted naive statisticians. There seems to be no useful general description of their competence which can be applied in advance of a detailed empirical investigation of the mechanisms of ordinary inference and its dependence on context and content. This is a point we shall enlarge on in Part 3, but to conclude this chapter, we should say more about normative theories of non-demonstrative inference.

Induction

We must be more explicit about two notions of probability we have used up to this point. There is subjective probability, varying from person to person, and measured by individual degrees of belief. We have pointed out that these subjective, individual probabilities should conform to the normative principles of the probability calculus, although we also found that people may have a systematic tendency to violate some of these, as in the conjunction fallacy. Some researchers, such as Kahneman and Tversky, would say that subjective probabilities which do conform to the probability calculus are objective to this extent. But if we speak in this way, we must be careful to distinguish this from another objective notion of probability, that of *physical probability*, which is an objective physical tendency or frequency. For example, there is such a tendency for people who smoke heavily to have poor health, and this is an objective fact about the world, independent of how intensely they, or anybody else, *believes* that they will have poor health.

By the scientific study of the frequency with which heavy smokers have poor health, we hope to get a good measure of the physical probability that they will have poor health. But what are the correct normative principles for scientific research? Here we reach a deep controversy about normative matters. Many argue that we need for this research more principles than just those given to us by the probability calculus. Some follow Popper (1959) and hold that we ought to try to falsify scientific hypotheses and theories, and accept them provisionally if they survive these attempts at falsification. (See also the collection in Schillp (1974) on this point of view.) Many others argue that, in addition to attempts at falsification, we require some notion of *confirmation*, which they may identify with what can be called *inductive* or *epistemic probability*. (See Carnap and Jeffrey 1971.) Consider the hypothesis that all mammals give birth to live young. We find a number of positive instances of this – that cats give birth to live young, that bats give birth to live young and that porpoises give birth to live young. These positive instances are said to confirm the hypothesis, making it more probable in the inductive or epistemic sense. In other words, we infer by *induction* that all mammals have a certain property because we have seen that cats, bats and porpoises are mammals which have that property. We can as well confirm hypotheses about physical probabilities, such as that there is a 25 per cent chance that smokers will damage their health, by examining the frequency of this in relatively small samples of smokers. This sort of reasoning can lead us from truth to falsity, as when we infer our hypothesis about all mammals from what we know about cats, bats and porpoises; and this failure of induction to be absolutely truth-preserving is the starting point for the classical philosophical problem of justifying it. (See Skyrms (1986) on this problem.)

Attempts at falsification make use of *deductive logic*, the general type of logic we have referred to up to this point, in which the conclusions of valid inferences must be true if the premises are true. For example, from our hypothesis about mammals and the observation that echidnas are mammals, we would infer by deductive logic that echidnas give birth to live young. This conclusion turns out to be false, and we have a negative instance of our hypothesis – a mammal which does not give birth to live young. We therefore infer that our hypothesis has been falsified. As we have said, many scientists and philosophers of science hold that there are also principles of confirmation. The possible codification of these principles, added to those fundamental ones of the probability calculus, has been called *inductive logic*; its point would be to specify formal rules for strong inferences, in which the conclusion would be probable in the inductive or epistemic sense, given the premises. If these rules were justified, then they would give us some objective normative standard, in addition to the probability calculus, for our judgments about when inferences were strong. We could develop some objective notion of evidence, and appeal to that to establish that barometers supply better evidence about what the weather will be than bunions do. However, justifying the rules of such an inductive logic would apparently be to solve the problem of justifying induction. (We may not need the type of inductive logic found in Carnap and Jeffrey (1971) to get a good concept of evidence; see Achinstein (1983).)

Some psychologists might suggest that we already have a *mental* inductive logic, i.e. a set of rules represented in the mind and used for performing strong inferences in our ordinary non-demonstrative reasoning. There appears, however, to be even less evidence for this doctrine than for that of mental deductive logic, which we have already examined, and which would anyway have to be included in a mental inductive logic. There is no agreed normative system of inductive logic, beyond the probability calculus, and the experimental evidence against its existence in a mental form are the results, reviewed above, which seem to show that people tend to commit definite fallacies in their non-demonstrative reasoning. People are not quite so irrational in this respect as some researchers have claimed, and there are grounds for saying that they do well at it when the content and context are right, as in the experiments of Nisbett, Krantz, Jepson and Kunda (1983).

The importance of content and context itself suggests that there are schemas for this sort of inference which, though relatively general, could not be said to constitute a mental inductive logic. Such schemas for learning about the world could be what enables us to acquire the general knowledge we considered in Chapter 2, embodied in the more specialised frames and scripts discussed there, and might help to explain certain results in, for example, non-deontic versions of the selection task, which we introduced in the last chapter. In these cases, subjects often choose the Q card, and that may mean that they are trying to confirm the conditional by finding positive instances of it, with P true and Q true. (They might even have some intuitive grasp of Bayes's Theorem and be trying to work out the conditional probability that Q holds given that P does.) This is a far-reaching topic which we cannot discuss further here, but see Holland, Holyoak, Nisbett and Thagard (1986) on schemas for induction in general and on this aspect of the selection task in particular.

What constitutes good non-demonstrative reasoning is an extremely difficult problem, and because we do not have a full answer to it, we can be unsure whether some tendencies in ordinary inference are rational or irrational. We have the Dutch Book argument for the limited aim of justifying the use of the probability calculus, but we must accept that justifying additional rules of inductive inference, in the attempt to lay down further objective standards for strong inference, is a formidable task. If we ought to follow some such rules, then by the semantics for deontic terms described in Chapter 4, it is better, in some sense, for us to do so than not to do so. Admittedly, it is not even easy to explain, at the deepest philosophical level, why it is better for us to speak the truth and perform absolutely reliable, valid inferences. Not doing either seems to be personally advantageous at times. (These may not only be trivial social occasions when a white lie is useful – think of an Orwellian world in which speaking the truth brings people to the attention of the Thought Police, although even there people have to know the truth about what Big Brother wants them to believe.) But it is a much greater challenge still to explain fully why we ought to conform to the standard normative methodology of science, which does give us some notion of probable truth and strong inference. Perhaps our species would be in less danger if we had never developed science. Of course, it could be said that what is valuable is not simply what makes us successful, in some simple way, as individuals or as a species. We cannot, however, go further into these questions here, and will continue to assume, as we have up to this point, that truth is better than falsity and well-confirmed hypotheses better than disconfirmed ones!

Part 3

Theoretical issues

8 Rationality

In Part 1 we saw that justified inference was often necessary for under-standing utterances and for successful communication. But in Part 2 we also learned that people sometimes fail to live up to the highest standards laid down by the normative theories of how they ought to reason. People seem to be prone to a number of *biases*: they have tendencies to perform various types of unjustified inference. Now, people can be called *rational* only if they have a general tendency to perform justified inferences. So which tendencies are the more marked? The ones to perform justified inferences, or the ones to perform unjustified inferences? Are human beings primarily rational or primarily biased and irrational?

These questions would be easy to answer if people possessed the full range of mental deductive logics and some mental inductive logic. But as we have argued, they would then be so rational that it would be hard to account for the irrational tendencies they undoubtedly exhibit. At the other extreme, we could not conclude that people were essentially irrational just because they did not have any sort of mental logic. The doctrine of mental logic is one about *how* people perform inferences. It states that people have explicit mental representations of rules of inference and employ these when they perform inferences. However, people do not have to use rules of inference *explicitly* in order to conform to them. Schemas and mental models can produce results which *implicitly* conform to at least some of these rules. If people use schemas, mental models or the like in their reasoning, then the question becomes whether these structures or processes generally produce justified inferences.

Broadly, there have been two ways of trying to assess human rationality. One of these has been the attempt to discover, through psychological experiments, detailed information about the structures and processes actually used by people in their reasoning. We have already said a great deal about this kind of research, and we shall say more later in this chapter. But the other way has been to argue, on more general grounds, the pros and cons of the view that human beings are essentially rational. Of course, these two approaches should not be completely unrelated to each other. The former has to be used to inform and test the latter, which might in turn suggest the sort of thing the former should be looking for. We shall begin this chapter by considering the general approach.

Relevance theory

The work of Sperber and Wilson (1986, 1987) has been called 'the first account of pragmatics which has been grounded in psychology' (Carston 1987), presumably as opposed to accounts like those of Austin and Grice (see Chapter 3) which originated in the philosophy of language. But Sperber and Wilson acknowledge the debt they owe particularly to Grice and to his maxim of relevance, which their *relevance theory* is an attempt to clarify and extend. They aim to state such a wide-ranging theory of cognition and communication that it cannot be fully described here, and we shall concentrate on what they have to say about human rationality.

Sperber and Wilson describe two basic models of what happens when people exchange verbal messages. In the *code model*, the thoughts of speakers are converted, or 'coded', into the physical signals of spoken or written language, and these are then 'decoded' into thoughts by the audience. There is much that is unclear in this simple model, and a great deal has to be said about the nature of thought and of the coding and decoding process before it can be called a theory of communication. But even if it is stated as a clear theory, it can be criticised for leaving out the pragmatics of communication.

For this reason, Sperber and Wilson want to go beyond the code model, and adopt what they call the *inferential model*, which is what is founded on Grice's pragmatics. This model takes speakers' utterances not just as coded signals, but as a form of evidence which the audience can use in justified inferences about the speakers' communicative intentions. In the model, an audience asks (in effect and unconsciously in the normal run of things), 'What, given this context, must this message mean?' Sperber and Wilson do not deny that verbal messages are decoded; rather they see these decoded signals as 'a source of hypotheses and evidence for the second communication process, the inferential one' (1987: 705).

Sperber and Wilson introduce a large number of their own technical terms, but we shall begin by trying to present their basic point of view more informally. When someone tells us something, our beliefs can be changed in various ways. We may give up some of our old beliefs, as when the speaker succeeds in convincing us that we are wrong about something; or we may acquire new beliefs, as when the speaker tells us something we did not already know. There are also an unlimited number of ways in which we might modify the degree of confidence we have in our beliefs; we might, for example, become much more confident about some proposition we believe – think it much more likely to be true – if the speaker testifies under oath that it is true. Sperber and Wilson take the extent to which an utterance modifies an audience's beliefs in all these ways as one measure of its relevance. More controversially, they also claim that another measure of the relevance of an utterance is the amount of work, or cognitive processing, the audience must do in order to understand how it should affect their beliefs.

We can describe the theory in more of its own technical vocabulary in the following way. Every message takes place against a contextual background supplied by the participants' beliefs, desires, expectations, and so on, including the content of previous messages in a dialogue; and a message is said to have a contextual effect if it changes that context after it has been processed. The greater this contextual effect, and the less processing required, the more relevance the message has in the context. Sperber and Wilson attempt to define a notion of optimal relevance on this basis, and then give their *principle of relevance*, which is that every message 'communicates the presumption of its own optimal relevance' (1986: 158). They hold that an audience attempts to infer the significance of a message on the assumption that it satisfies this principle.

Let us briefly consider in these terms an example used by Sperber and Wilson (1986: 71).

Peter: According to the weather forecast, it's going to rain.
Mary (standing at the window): It certainly looks like it.

What Mary says in this dialogue has relevance. Peter will have increased confidence that it will rain because of her remark; this will be a contextual effect of her message. By the principle of relevance, her message creates the presumption that it is optimally relevant, and so Peter assumes that he will not have to go to a great deal of trouble to infer some change in his beliefs as a result of it. He will assume that she sees something like very dark clouds in the sky, since it is easy for him, given his background knowledge, to infer from this that the probability of rain is increased.

Inference has thus an essential role to play in this account of relevance. How do people perform inferences, according to Sperber and Wilson? Their answer is that people use a restricted kind of mental logic (although they do not actually use this term). In their view, *some* deductive inference rules are explicitly represented in a mental language and used to generate inferences. The point of restricting the rules is to explain the inferences people do not make, as well as those they do. People are economical in the inferences they perform, inferring only what is necessary in a given context or indeed relevant. We have also seen that people tend to make mistakes by performing certain unjustified inferences. These may be, it might be argued, just the cases in which they do not have the appropriate rules to tell what they ought to do.

Sperber and Wilson suggest that mental logic is restricted by having elimination inference rules but no introduction inference rules. (These different kinds of rule were illustrated in Chapter 4; see Prawitz (1965) for an extended account of them.) Compare these rules:

A and B	A and B
A	B

A	B
A or B	A or B

The first row above gives the rules of and-elimination, and the second gives those of or-introduction. What they display are characteristics of all elimination and introduction rules. The former *eliminate* a logical constant and allow us to infer a relatively simple sentence from a relatively compound one, while the latter enable us to *introduce* a logical constant and to infer a relatively compound sentence from a simpler one. Obviously, if we use only elimination rules, what we infer will get simpler and simpler until we reach atomic sentences, when we will have to stop. We are restricted in this way if our mental logic contains only elimination rules, and we have no other means of performing inferences, as Sperber and Wilson suppose.

Gazdar and Good (1982) have pointed out that this suggestion is too restrictive. We may know that our insurance company will pay up if our car has been stolen or it has been damaged. What we know is a conditional with a disjunctive antecedent, and when we hear that our car has been stolen, we must use or-introduction before we can use modus ponens to infer the consequent. Sperber and Wilson (1986: 98–100) reply to this sort of point by suggesting some new, non-standard 'elimination' rules, which would allow us to avoid or-introduction in this particular case. But this is an *ad hoc* step that does not solve the general problem. Many ordinary conditionals have a variety of compound antecedents. For example, we may know that we are running a risk if we have not locked our car or parked it in a safe place. Here the antecedent of the conditional is the negation of a disjunction. One general way to cover examples like this would be to suppose that there are some introduction rules in mental logic for inferring compound antecedents and other purposes. But it is unclear how Sperber and Wilson would solve the general problem except in an *ad hoc* manner.

The problem of accounting for the economical and efficient nature of much human inference is a very serious one. It is so serious that we do not think it can be solved merely by holding that there is a mental logic containing only (standard or non-standard) elimination inference rules. However, the very existence of this problem is an argument for a high standard of human rationality, at least in certain areas. Sperber and Wilson and other researchers in pragmatics have shown how communication depends on economical, efficient and justified inference. Therefore one could argue, on general grounds, that human beings must be logical and rational to some extent, since they are fairly good at the pragmatics of communication.

Of course, this argument does not necessarily lead to the existence of even a restricted mental logic. Sperber and Wilson themselves quote Johnson-Laird's (1982) comment that 'a system of inference may perform in an entirely logical way even though it does not employ rules of inference.' They prefer to postulate a mixed system, with a restricted mental logic, as we have described, and some other procedures like those favoured by Johnson-Laird. In the end, experimental research must decide whether there is some kind of mental logic, a system of schemas or mental models, or some combination of all of these. However, there is a general argument that experiments, whatever their outcome, can never demonstrate that human beings are irrational.

Can human irrationality be experimentally demonstrated?

In posing this question, Cohen (1981, 1986) means you to stress the first word, and in doing so, be prepared for his answer: 'no'. Cohen has an uncompromising argument: he contends not so much that psychological research has not shown people to be less than rational, but that, no matter what its findings, it could not. Within this general argument, there are several strands. One is similar to that outlined in our discussion of relevance theory. Human beings must be rational for communication to be possible. Speakers must be rational to couch messages in the right way for their hearers, who must be rational to get the message; otherwise, there will be no communication. Cohen might say that communication carries not only a guarantee of relevance, but also a presumption of shared rationality.

Cohen goes further than this with a more sweeping argument. He points out that all normative systems of thought, inductive and deductive, ultimately appeal for their justification to human intuitions: they are, as it were, codified systems of intuitions of validity and invalidity. It is ultimately down to the intuitions of people when a logical inference is taken as valid, or a proof accepted as sound. That being so, the rationality of intuitions must be assumed: there is no other test of validity. From this extension of the argument about communication in the previous paragraph, Cohen infers that no matter what people do in experiments on reasoning, they must still be deemed to be rational.

Of course, as we have seen in previous chapters, people do not always behave in the way that logicians and mathematicians would like them to when they are tested. Cohen accounts for this in the same way that Chomsky (e.g. 1965) accounts for the fact that people do not always produce grammatically faultless sentences: by proposing a distinction between *competence* and *performance.* Competence refers to what you could do, under ideal conditions. Performance refers to what you do do on some occasion, affected by limitations of your attention and memory, by your motivation, by social factors, and so on. In this way, errors and biases are ascribed to performance, leaving the underlying competence unscathed.

Cohen suggests a number of reasons why people appear irrational in some experiments. One of these is that experimental devices, such as the selection task, create 'cognitive illusions', which induce experimental subjects 'to indulge in a form of reasoning that on a few moments' prompted reflection they would be willing to admit is invalid' (1981: 323). We shall return to this quotation shortly: Cohen is just mistaken about what people say on prompted reflection, as is clear from the 'Mensa' protocol in Chapter 6. The rest of these reasons are extensively discussed in the critiques which accompany Cohen (1981), to which he replies in the same article. (See also the 'Continuing commentaries' in *Behavioral and Brain Sciences* (vol. 6, 1983; vol. 10, 1987); and Kyburg (1983).) Our concern here is with his more general arguments.

Cohen has an epistemological problem which arises whenever the competence–performance distinction is invoked. Competence is that of which people are capable, but which they may fail to show owing to extraneous performance factors. To test whether people do have such a general competence would appear to be a fairly straightforward matter: one might, for instance, look for individual differences in behaviour in the same set-up, or look for inconsistent behaviour by the same person in different ones. The trouble is, any such inter- or intra-personal differences could always be put down to the fact that people vary in their educational or more general learning histories, or just to the fact that the circumstances are different. Indeed, Cohen tries to explain away some reasoning errors by appealing to factors such as these: a prime case is when he dismisses some experiments because of the mysterious cognitive illusions they supposedly depend on. Whatever errors or biases people exhibit, Cohen could always try to file them under 'performance'. Until he specifies the ideal conditions under which logical competence will reliably be exhibited, his competence theory is empirically untestable.

Cohen's underlying general argument about intuition is summarised when he says (1986: 154) that it is impossible 'to achieve some firm determination of how a person *understands* occurrences of logical particles that is quite independent of determining what his singular *intuitions* are about logical contradiction and deducibility' (his emphasis). This is a good point, as far as it goes. Subjects who do not understand *if*, because they are not native speakers of English or for any other reason, cannot be used to find significant results in the selection task. But we can test their understanding of this logical constant or particle by using semantic evaluation studies. The point against Cohen is that intuitions about truth conditions or truth preservation are *semantic*. Whether these semantic intuitions can be translated into an ability to deduce the right conclusions from premises using *syntactic* rules of inference is another matter. Expert logicians are usually needed to axiomatise semantic intuitions by setting up syntactic rules of valid inference. Cohen makes the logical competence he ascribes to ordinary people so extensive and content-independent that apparently only the possession of a full mental logic could account for it. But his argument does not really support the conclusion that there is this degree of competence, and experiments go against it.

Evans has said, 'If rational reasoning entails the possession and application of formal logical rules, then I do not believe people to be rational' (1984: 465). Note that this quote is a conditional. We have already quoted in this chapter Johnson-Laird's point that a system of inference can be logical without using rules of inference. Cohen presents us with far too stark a choice: his claim is that we must judge people either completely logical or totally unable to understand language. Common sense alone suggests that there are many possibilities between his alternatives. A full mental logic might be the only system which would make us completely logical, but some other system might be logical in much of its operation, while still prone at times to bias and error. We can possess this kind of system and still understand what we are saying, even when we fall into error. Of course, linguistic understanding is not itself an all or nothing affair, and people can grasp the meaning of a logical constant to some extent and yet have a tendency to use it in invalid inferences. This leaves open the possibility we now consider: that human reasoning is so highly prone to bias that human beings should really be called irrational.

Could man be an irrational animal?

This is the title of another theoretical paper, Stich (1985), and again there is a hidden invitation in it to favour one particular answer, in this case, 'yes'. Stich's position is the polar opposite of Cohen's, and we shall reject it as going to the other extreme. (Stich (1983) states his doubts about human rationality at greater length.)

Stich rightly criticises Cohen, but we feel he goes too far when attacking another general argument for human rationality. He calls it *the argument from natural selection*, and neatly summarises it in the following way (1985: 123):

1) Natural selection will favour (i.e. select for) inferential strategies which generally yield true beliefs ...
2) An inferential strategy which generally yields true beliefs is a rational inferential strategy. Therefore,
3) Natural selection will favour rational inferential strategies.

This argument seeks to establish that evolution by natural selection guarantees the rationality of our system of reasoning. Stich attacks – too strongly, in our view – both of its premises. (He refers to Dennett (1978: ch. 1) for this argument, but Dennett (1969, 1987) also have interesting discussions of evolution and cognitive science.)

He argues against the first premise by referring to an experiment in which rats are made ill by doses of radiation after they had been given some food or water with a distinctive flavour. The result was that the rats tended to avoid in the future food or water with that flavour. Stich speaks as if the rats had acquired the firm but false belief that the flavour caused the sickness, and he points out that flavours, or whatever is responsible for them, would not usually cause sickness in rats in the wild. Then he concludes that this is a case of an inference strategy, favoured by natural selection, which does not generally yield true beliefs.

We may or may not agree with Stich that the rats in this experiment are properly said to have any beliefs. But if we do talk about belief and related notions here, then we must distinguish rational belief from rational *action* or *behaviour*, which is determined by both belief and desire. We imply that the avoidance action of the rats is rational merely by supposing that they have associated to some degree the flavour and their sickness *and* have a strong drive to avoid sickness. And using in Stich's way terms more suitable for human beings, who could deny that the rats have some reasonable grounds for being suspicious of the novel (as it has to be in the experiment) flavour? We would consider ourselves rational to be suspicious of food with a novel flavour if we were sick after eating it, and rational to avoid it unless we got very hungry, or until we discovered that something else caused our sickness. Stich's essential point is that, when something as important as health is at stake, 'natural selection may prefer an extremely cautious inference strategy which is very often wrong, to a less cautious one which more often gets the right answer' (1985: 125). Against this, we would argue that evolution favours, in the first instance, types of behaviour. Such behaviour will tend to ensure good health in an animal, and it can be said to be rational if the animal can be said to have a desire to have good health. Stich has certainly failed to show that evolution will not favour behaviour which is rational in the sense that it tends to satisfy animals' survival needs.

Rationality as applied to beliefs and inference strategies is another matter. It is not always possible to say that there is a belief and an inference strategy behind the behaviour of an animal. Under what conditions we may say that there are beliefs and inference strategies in an organism is a deep problem (one we shall refer to again in the next chapter). But the evolutionary function of beliefs and inference strategies must be to satisfy our survival needs (in so far as this helps us to reproduce effectively). It would seem that this goal is best attained by inference procedures yielding more or less firm beliefs in propositions which are more or less probable, in some objective sense. A cautious inference strategy would lead people to be suspicious of an unfamiliar food if they became ill after eating it, and an even more cautious one would not give them the unshakable conviction that the food caused their illness – that might not be useful later when they were getting weak from hunger. Evolution might have brought about a strategy of this kind in human beings or even in rats, and Stich has not demonstrated that it is anything but rational.

Stich also contends that the second premise of the argument from natural selection is false. His claim is that 'inference strategies which generally get the right answer may nevertheless be irrational or normatively inappropriate when applied outside the problem domain for which they were shaped by natural selection' (1985: 127). As an illustration of this point, he considers what has been discovered about the behaviour of a particular kind of toad. Under natural conditions, these toads have an 'inference strategy' which leads them to reject as food a kind of unpleasant-tasting millipede after only a single experience of trying to eat one. In an experiment, however, the toads continued indefinitely to consume bland but inedible items, such as small steel balls. The vast majority of toads, Stich accepts, generally acquire true 'beliefs' about what they eat, but the 'inference strategy' which leads to these is irrational, he holds, in the experimental setting.

Let us take an example of a human way of acquiring beliefs. If we have normal sight, our eyes are a generally reliable way of getting true beliefs about the world. There are optical illusions, and we can be fooled in striking ways by these, especially under experimental conditions, but our eyes are generally reliable under normal conditions. The obvious way to take account of this legitimate point is to define rationality relative to these conditions, and to state that an inference strategy which generally yields true beliefs under certain conditions is rational under those conditions. After all, evolution does not guarantee that what it gives us will work outside a relatively fixed environment. There are problems with holding that rationality is relative to conditions, one of which is that a highly artificial notion of conditions could make almost any inference strategy appear rational. But the notion of the proper conditions or context for the application of an inference strategy is itself a reasonable and familiar one, which we should certainly introduce into the argument from natural selection. Stich gives us no reason for thinking that this notion cannot be clarified in a satisfactory way, and that weakens his attack on the second premise of the argument.

There is more than one reason why our reply to Stich does not mean that the argument from natural selection can be accepted as it stands. Further distinctions would have to be made, notions clarified, and special cases investigated before it could be more than the sketch of a good argument. The key reference to 'generally true beliefs' should in itself start a long discussion of concepts of objective probability. Our visual representation of what is immediately in front of us under normal conditions is probably accurate, partly as a result of the high *physical* probability that our visual equipment is working properly. Thanks to evolution by natural selection, there is an objective tendency for this equipment to work well under normal conditions. But what of inference? Our non-demonstrative reasoning ought to be based on the probability calculus and, it would generally be held, some further principles of inductive logic, such as that of induction itself.

It is easy to see how one could argue that simple induction, inferring the properties of everything of some kind from the observation of those properties in some things of that kind, was adaptive and helped the evolutionary success of our species under primitive conditions. But would it have been to our evolutionary disadvantage to deviate from the principles of the probability calculus under primitive conditions? Would there have been Dutch Books in some sense under those conditions? The argument from natural selection falls within the subjects of *evolutionary epistemology* and *evolutionary psychology*, where these and other difficult questions must be answered before it can be fully assessed. (See Quine (1969: chs. 3 and 5) on simple induction and evolution; Campbell (1974) and Radnitzky and Bartley (1987) on evolutionary epistemology; and Cosmides and Tooby (1986) on evolutionary psychology. Von Schilcher and Tennant (1984) is a general introduction to evolutionary arguments in philosophy.)

Stich relies heavily on the selection task in his suggestion that human beings are irrational. But the very latest experimental research undermines Stich's arguments at just this point. We shall therefore return to this research, which will help us to say more about the argument from natural selection.

The rationality of deontic reasoning in the selection task

In Chapter 6 we described how Cheng and Holyoak (1985) broke new ground in their account of deontic reasoning in the selection task. However, as we reported, there is a dispute between them and Cosmides (1989) about what produces facilitation in a deontic selection task. Cosmides claims that facilitation occurs when the subjects are on the lookout for cheaters in the task, but we shall say in a moment why we think that this is too restrictive. At the same time, merely couching a selection task in deontic terms is unlikely to have much effect in itself. Even the conditional in an abstract task could be made a conditional obligation, by stating, for example, that there *ought to be* an even number on one side of a card if a vowel is to be placed on the other side; and it seems unlikely that this alone would help the subjects. The crucial question is what type of deontic scenario or rationale produces the facilitation effect.

Cosmides's claim is that the effect is produced by a conditional of the form, *If you take a benefit then you must pay a cost*, backed by a scenario which describes the benefit, the cost, and the relation between them. She has found a facilitation effect in many experiments in which the conditional and the scenario are of this type. In these experiments, the *P* and *not-Q* combination is one in which there is a cheater, who takes the benefit without paying the cost. She argues that our great ability to recognise cheaters is only to be expected on evolutionary grounds, since an increasing ability to do this would have been adaptive for our early human ancestors, living in small groups in which co-operation was essential. Modifying the argument Stich wants to reject, she could contend that natural selection favoured inference strategies for recognising cheaters, and as these are rational strategies, natural selection favoured rational strategies at least to this extent. She does not actually use this argument, but it seems very much in the spirit of her thought.

It is hard to deny that a good inference strategy for recognising cheaters is a rational one. Any strategy of this kind would depend on valid inferences and strong inferences, but could be especially beneficial to us. And as we pointed out in Chapter 7, the concept of cheating is central to the justification of the probability calculus itself by means of the Dutch Book argument. What this shows is that, if we violate the rules of the probability calculus, then we leave ourselves open to cheaters, who can take benefits from us in bets without paying the cost of running any risk themselves. Whether or not there were anything like Dutch Books under primitive conditions, it would have been as beneficial to our early ancestors to be able to recognise cheaters in general as it is for us. We may not have evolved to have a full mental probability calculus, but to possess general inference strategies for recognising cheaters, which can only be called rational.

We ourselves have found, however, that the facilitation effect is not only produced by conditionals relating benefits and costs as Cosmides describes. We used in a selection task the conditional, *If you clean up spilt blood then you must wear rubber gloves*, along with a rationale which explained that the point of the rule was to prevent serious diseases, like AIDS. This is a conditional prudential obligation with the characteristic that the cost of violating it, the *P* and *not-Q* combination, might be very high: cleaning up blood without wearing rubber gloves could even mean contracting a fatal disease. Additionally, this combination is not one in which there is a cheater: cleaning up blood is not a benefit for which one should pay the cost of wearing rubber gloves. The result of the experiment was a strong facilitation effect, which is what we predicted. We thought that subjects would be good at recognising potentially disastrous outcomes if they were good at spotting cheaters, on evolutionary or any other grounds. (See Manktelow and Over (in press, a and b); Cheng and Holyoak (in press).)

We predict that facilitation will occur in deontic selection tasks whenever subjects recognise that conforming to the rule, the *P* and *Q* combination, is far better than violating it, the *P* and *not-Q* combination: that the utility of the former is significantly greater than that of the latter. (Cheng and Holyoak (1985 and in press) have found facilitation in fairly abstract tasks, but even the limited content of these suggests differences in utilities.) Further investigation of this claim should include some attempt to measure properly not only benefits and costs, but also *expected* benefits and costs, as some of these – such as catching a disease – will be perceived by subjects to be more or less likely to follow in different scenarios. This means, of course, that the concepts of subjective probability and utility are important for deontic selection tasks. We discussed these concepts and some research on them in Chapter 7, but what is now needed is to combine that work with a general study of deontic reasoning in the selection task and other experiments. Possibly another important factor is a dynamic one: by spotting a potentially disastrous outcome one may be able to take steps to avoid it, say, by wearing gloves. The effect of the presence of this factor in the selection task also needs to be investigated. (There has been research in computer science, at a high theoretical level, on deontic and dynamic logic, and this could be of use to cognitive psychology. See Maibaum (1987) and Meyer (1988).)

One object of this new research should be to assess how rational people are when their inferences make a real difference to them in benefits and costs. The work so far of Cheng and Holyoak, Cosmides, and ourselves suggests that people will be very rational in these circumstances: they will have rational inference strategies and display rational behaviour. Stich cites the results of abstract selection tasks as evidence of people's supposed irrationality, and criticises the argument from natural selection as an attempt to establish that people are bound to be rational in such cases. But it is not in these abstract tasks that this argument should lead us to expect that people will be rational. It does not seem to be a good argument for supposing that a full mental sentential logic would have developed by natural selection. It has not been established that formal, content-independent reasoning would have been adaptive in itself or connected with some adaptive property. Where we should expect people to be rational in the selection task, by this argument, is where we do seem to find that they are: in those cases in which they perceive that there are serious losses to be avoided.

Evaluations and rationality

We must remember yet again that people do have an ability to make content-independent semantic evaluations. Wason found, in his earliest research with the selection task, that people could make accurate semantic evaluations of the four cards, but did not appear to use this ability in the task itself. This sometimes led to inconsistencies between selection and evaluation and to some extraordinary behaviour when people were faced with these, as in the case of the 'Mensa' protocol described in Chapter 6.

It is tempting to take this kind of inconsistent response as *prima facie* evidence of extensive human irrationality. In light of our discussion, however, this is really more like evidence for the division between two thinking processes: one as the basis for the decision of which cards to select initially, and one as the basis for the semantic evaluations of the fully revealed cards. We make no apology for returning to this point again and again, as its significance has not been sufficiently taken into account in the literature on rationality. If it had been, then extreme Cohen-type arguments for the existence of unrestricted or unqualified human rationality could not have been advanced, nor could Stich have used the selection task uncritically to try to justify his stand at the opposite extreme. Subjects' semantic evaluations show that they are sufficiently logical and rational to understand even abstract conditionals in the selection task; and yet they do not seem to have a mental logic, in the form of a mental axiomatisation of these evaluations, which enables them to make the right selections in the abstract task.

In Chapter 6 we introduced the dual process theory of Wason and Evans and Evans's distinction between heuristic and analytic processes. Much more research needs to be done on these proposals. Our own feeling is that their binary contrasts are too simple for the complexity of human thought and reasoning. There certainly seem to be some processes for making decisions which we have little, if any, awareness of. Our later semantic evaluations of these decisions, and our verbal reports of how and why we have taken them, do sometimes appear to have little relation to what must be the real basis of them. But there does not seem to us to be a sharp break here between the unconscious and the conscious, the pre-verbal and the verbal, or even the implicit conformity to rules and the explicit appeal to them. We can be partially aware of what we are doing, partly able to put it into words, and more or less able to specify clearly the rules we are conforming to.

There is also the problem of explaining how our semantic evaluations and explicit appeal to rules can affect our more or less automatic decision-making. By noticing the mistakes we make and formulating rules for avoiding them in the future, we seem to be able to improve our decisions and actions. We can improve our tennis by formulating rules for when we should go to the net, or our reasoning by reflecting on our semantic evaluations and setting up rules of inference. Yet we must guard against assuming that this improvement occurs because these very rules are stored in a mental language and explicitly used without the delay of going through consciousness. Whether this always happens, sometimes happens, or never happens is something we must discover and not assume.

Finally, it is necessary to investigate to what extent semantic evaluation and its effect on decision and action was adaptive and directly selected for under primitive conditions. Our ability to communicate has been highly advantageous to us, and it depends on our ability to evaluate the truth conditions of statements. Our ability to learn from experience has been equally advantageous, and it depends on our ability to evaluate, for example, when a conditional prediction has been falsified. It looks as though there should be a good argument from natural selection for our rationality at the level of semantic evaluation. But detailed assessment of this argument, and the one for rationality in prudential deontic reasoning sketched above, depends on the work of evolutionary psychologists, who should ultimately be able to tell us what really was selected directly under primitive conditions, and what appeared as the indirect product of selection working on other factors.

Evolution by natural selection has to work by stages, which it cannot jump over to the best solution for all times and places or for new circumstances which suddenly develop. What is beneficial to us now, in our rapidly changing world, might not have been so before, and what served us well under primitive conditions might sometimes cause trouble for us now. We may have some mental structures or processes, vestigial or otherwise, which tend at times to produce irrational inferences in certain contexts in which we find ourselves today. The exact extent to which we are rational is not something which can be decided by general, almost a priori arguments, but only by detailed investigation of the mental structures and processes we actually possess.

9 Natural and artificial inference

In the last chapter we contrasted two extreme views of human rationality, that represented by Cohen and that by Stich, and argued for taking a position between them. We held that the exact degree of rationality ascribed to people must depend on a detailed investigation of how they perform inferences. We need to be able to explain and predict people's inferences on the basis of a theory of the mental structures and processes they possess. Precisely how these structures and processes evolved by natural selection is a problem for evolutionary psychologists, but it is also necessary to determine exactly how rational people are in present circumstances. Our purpose in this final chapter will be to say more about the study of inference and this difficult problem. We begin with an account of the ordinary way in which everyone tries to explain and predict human action.

Intentionality and folk psychology

We ordinarily try to understand people by ascribing mental states to them, as in the following examples of propositional attitudes:

Odysseus wanted to punish the suitors.

Odysseus believed that the suitors were at his mercy.

What did Odysseus want to do? What did Odysseus believe? We could use the above sentences to answer these questions, and in doing so we would be specifying the *content* of the desire and of the belief of Odysseus. In a technical sense, these mental states have *intentionality*, and in general, to say that a mental state has intentionality is just to say that it has a content. The fact that beliefs and desires have this property is fundamental to our ordinary way of understanding people. We use the contents of people's beliefs and desires to try to explain what they have done and to predict what they will do.

Why did Odysseus kill the suitors? Suppose this is a request for an ordinary explanation of what Odysseus did. We might be satisfied just by hearing of the above belief and desire, but we might want to know more. We could then be told how much Odysseus hated the suitors because of the way they had treated his wife and his household, and how he believed he could kill them with a bow and arrows at a banquet. With more detail, it can be seen that this type of explanation not only ascribes mental states to Odysseus, but also reasoning processes. The extended explanation implies that Odysseus is able to infer that the suitors are at his mercy because he is armed with a bow and arrows at a banquet and they are not.

The kind of ordinary explanation we have been describing is based on a common-sense view of how people acquire beliefs and desires. The contents of a belief are thought to arise from processes like perception and inference, and those of desires from whatever has been informally observed to affect human beings. This may not seem to be a very bold or exciting view, but perhaps that is because it is so familiar to us. Some philosophers and psychologists have called it *folk psychology* and others *belief/desire psychology*. The former term expresses the fact that it has been the ordinary view of ordinary people for presumably as long as *Homo sapiens* has existed, if it was not present in earlier hominids. But the latter term allows for the fact that it is the type of psychology taken for granted by most other social sciences. Archaeologists, historians and anthropologists are interested, unlike ordinary folk, in exactly how the culture and society of an archaic Greek warrior would have affected his beliefs and desires, but an essential part of their research is to find more precise contents for these beliefs and desires, the better to explain archaic Greek action.

Dennett (1978: ch. 1) speaks of the *intentional stance* we take to people when we ascribe beliefs and desires to them, and points out how in doing this we assume that people are, at least to some extent, rational. Our object in ascribing contents to people is to use logical and evidential relations between contents to explain and predict what they will do. Another example would be one in which we want to predict whether a nurse will clean up spilt blood. She believes, we know, that she will risk getting a serious disease if she does this without gloves. We reason in the following way:

> If she cleans up spilt blood without wearing gloves, then she will risk getting a serious disease.
> She will not risk getting a serious disease.
> Therefore, she will not clean up spilt blood without wearing gloves.

Our conclusion in this inference is a prediction about what the nurse will do. The first premise is the content of her belief which we have already mentioned, and we may know that the second premise is true, and that she herself believes it, because she does not want to get a serious disease. Our knowledge that these premises are true comes from justified non-demonstrative reasoning, but then we notice that they logically imply the above conclusion, and consequently that is what we predict she will do. Our underlying assumption is that her mental processes will be rational in this sense: that they will cause her to act in a way consistent with this prediction, inferred by such logical means from the contents of her beliefs and desires. We have used modus tollens to infer our prediction, but it is very important *not* to assume that this inference rule will be explicitly represented in the mental processes leading to her action. We should not even assume this if she uses modus tollens herself, after the event, to explain why she did not clean up spilt blood without gloves.

The nurse may not know any better than we do, before we investigate her scientifically, the cognitive nature of the mental processes which led to her decision to act as she did. She assumes that these are rational in the same sense in which we do. But certainly none of us needs to assume that she has a mental logic in which to perform modus tollens, nor even that she performed a particular instance of it in the process of making her decision in the first place. We must only assume that she conformed to modus tollens implicitly (or in the terminology of Dennett (1987: ch. 6) *tacitly*). She may have used particular schemas or mental models to make the original decision, or some unknown type of structure in an undiscovered mental process. These other structures may have conformed in this sense to modus tollens only by leading to a decision consistent with our prediction and the conclusion of the nurse's later explanation. As we indicated in Chapter 6, this explanation may be the result of the second part of distinct dual processes, the first part of which produced the nurse's original decision, or the result of a different analytic process from the analytic one which produced this decision.

The core of ordinary belief/desire psychology has been isolated and made more rigorous in normative decision theory, which we introduced in Chapter 7. The confidence we have in the contents of our beliefs and the intensity of our desires can be used in ideal cases to measure subjective probability and utility. Normative decision theory can then be used to tell us what we ought to do; and as an account of a kind of rational action, it can also predict what we will do, on the assumption that we are rational in this sense. Suppose, for example, that we are trying to choose between courses of action which lead to something having utility for us (we desire it to some degree), like good health. Then provided that we are rational, the prediction would be that we will take that course of action which has the greatest subjective probability of giving us good health (which we are most confident will give us good health). That course of action is just the one the theory tells us that we ought to take, from our own point of view. This may seem just common sense, but that is to be expected in a theory based on folk psychology. And not all the recommendations and predictions of the theory seem quite so trivial, as its wide use in economics and business indicates.

Pragmatics is another subject which makes essential use of belief/desire psychology. Grice's maxims, for instance, can be used to explain and predict how people will understand each other by rationally inferring beliefs and desires from utterances; and these ideal maxims also have a contribution to make to the normative theory of just what it means to be rational in these cases. To grasp that speakers are being ironical, for example, we must infer that they do not believe the literal content of what they utter, and that they do not want to deceive us. We should again not assume that we perform such inferences, or produce ironical utterances ourselves, by using explicit mental representations of Grice's maxims. We might follow these implicitly, just as we might conform to the principles of decision theory or modus tollens implicitly.

How much of our ordinary reasoning makes use of explicit mental rules or other representations is still primarily an open question, as is the question of how general or specific, content-independent or content-dependent, any such representations are. We have seen good evidence for doubting, in particular, that there is a full, or in the technical sense complete, mental sentential logic for inferring what to do in cases like that of the selection task. Yet we must also keep in mind the point that people have a high-level logical ability to evaluate when conditionals, or other logical forms, are true or false. This ability must be closely related to their ability to communicate with each other and to explain and predict each others' behaviour by using belief/desire psychology. The nurse's example above shows how natural it is to predict her behaviour by using modus tollens. Ordinary people's understanding of this type of prediction should certainly be further investigated. It would be very surprising if they did not understand the conditions under which predictions like that are successful or not; and part of that would be understanding inferences of this type and knowing, in general, when conditionals like that used there are true or false.

Propositional attitudes and processes

Belief/desire psychology calls for some ordinary understanding of the semantics of *believes that* and *desires to* themselves, and, of course, we want to understand this semantics theoretically. It helps to unify these terms grammatically, changing the latter to *desires to bring it about that*, allowing us to say that Odysseus desired to bring it about that the suitors were punished. When these expressions are prefaced with a term like *Odysseus*, they become one-place sentential operators grammatically like *it is not the case that*: they are applied to a relatively simple sentence to form a relatively compound sentence. But they are semantically unlike negation in being intensional operators. Consider the following:

Penelope believed that the beggar was in front of her.

Penelope believed that Odysseus was in front of her.

In the story the beggar is Odysseus – *the beggar* and *Odysseus* refer to the same man, have the same extension. Yet the above sentences do not have the same truth value, the same extension, as the first is true and the second is false. This means that *Penelope believes that* is an intensional operator, unlike the extensional *it is not the case that*, which does not have this effect when it is applied to the sentences contained in the above. (In that case, the resulting compound sentences are false when *her* refers to Penelope. See Chapter 4 for more on this distinction.) To avoid confusion between two closely related notions, it is best to say that the compound sentences above are inten*s*ional, but the mental states they are used to ascribe to Penelope are inten*t*ional.

In Chapter 4 we explained intensional concepts by using possible states of affairs, and identified the intension of a sentence with the set of these states of affairs in which it is true. Taking the same approach here, we would think of the content of a propositional attitude as a set of possible states of affairs. The content of Penelope's belief would be the set of these states in which there is a beggar in front of her; and this would not be the same proposition as the set of these states in which Odysseus is in front of her. Although Odysseus is the beggar in front of her in the actual state of affairs, there are other possible states of affairs in which different beggars are in front of her. The propositions are not the same, permitting Penelope to have an attitude to the first of them which she does not have to the second.

This view of the content of the propositional attitudes coheres well with what we have already said about intensionality in Chapter 4, but Stalnaker (1984) provides further support for it. He describes what he calls the *pragmatic picture* of intentionality, in which people are primarily seen as rational agents who act on the basis of their beliefs and desires. Such agents take themselves to be faced by a range of possible actions which have as outcomes possible states of affairs. Some of these outcomes are what the agents desire and some are not, and they have beliefs about which possible actions will lead to which outcomes. Those outcomes desired by Odysseus are ones in which the suitors are punished; those in which they are not punished are not desired by him. Possible states of affairs are also divided by his beliefs into those in which his beliefs are true and those in which they are false. According to his beliefs, states of affairs in which he uses his bow and arrows to attack the suitors at the banquet are ones in which the suitors are punished, and his action of killing them, by those means and in that place, follows as a result. In this way, the pragmatic picture also commits us to taking sets of possible states of affairs as the contents of the propositional attitudes.

The pragmatic picture itself fits well with the intentional stance. In belief/desire psychology we see people as agents, as in the example of the nurse above. What action will she perform? We tried to answer this question in belief/desire psychology by validly inferring a conclusion from the contents of some of her beliefs expressed as premises. By doing this we assumed that the contents of her beliefs were propositions, and that she was a rational agent, in that she would do something which is logically implied by these propositions. The sentences in our inference have as their intensions propositions which are sets of possible states of affairs, and any possible state of affairs in which both our premises are true must be one in which the conclusion is true. This conclusion will then be true in all possible states of affairs which make the nurse's beliefs true, and in this case, it is reasonable to conclude that she will herself state that she believes the conclusion: that she will not clean up spilt blood without gloves.

However, people do not always profess to believe the content of a sentence which is logically implied by what they do say they believe. How could they? An infinite number of sentences are logically implied by any set of sentences, and finite creatures, no matter how rational, cannot infer all of these. Moreover, it is not even rational to waste time inferring a fairly immediate consequence of some premises if it is not relevant or appropriate to do so. Human inference has to be efficient and useful to be rational, and for this purpose it has to be restricted. To account for human belief, we need more than propositions interpreted as sets of states of affairs – we need to consider also how these propositions are represented in the mind.

The beliefs of rational people are generated by some efficient and useful process of justified inference. Not any mental processes can count as inference; for it to be such, it must be what we shall call a *propositional process*. That is, it must consist of propositional representations, mental states which represent propositions, interpreted here as sets of possible states of affairs. What is the nature of these mental representations? And how are they processed by the mind? Stalnaker (1984: 22) says the following:

> These representations could conceivably take the form of a language of thought written in the belief centre of the brain, but they could also take the form of pictures, maps, charts, or graphs, or (most plausibly) a diversity of redundant forms ...

We agree with Stalnaker's plausible speculation, although other theorists have wanted to insist strongly that a language of thought does exist. Fodor (1987) broadly supports the view of belief/desire psychology and intentionality we have sketched, and takes propositions as essentially sets of possible states of affairs (though he calls them *contexts*). But he argues that propositional representations must be formed and processed in a mental system which is a language in the true sense. Why this has not persuaded us will come out below. (Salmon and Soames (1989) is a good collection of papers with different views on the propositional attitudes, and Schiffer (1987) is a recent book which criticises some of the ideas we have expressed here.)

Artificial intelligence

One way to try to answer the questions we have just asked about mental representation is to adopt the doctrine of mental logic. As we explained in previous chapters, this doctrine states that we perform inferences by translating premises into a mental language and applying formal, content-independent inference rules. We have distinguished various types of mental logic, such as mental sentential logic, mental deontic logic and mental inductive logic. A very strong doctrine of mental logic would state that there is an extensive range of mental logics in the mind, which has the capacity, when an inference is called for in a public language like English, to translate the premises into the right logical form for the application of some set of rules from one of these logics. It is difficult to describe how this translation process would work, as the logical forms of sentences in English, or any other public natural language, are not always clear, even to expert logicians. But this doctrine has one great advantage: it is possible for it to explain how the propositional process of inference in the mental language would take place.

A scientific or naturalistic account of the mind must ultimately explain how it is related to the brain. But how can a physical process in the brain have anything to do, in particular, with a propositional process in the mind? How can an apparently effective procedure of following rules to perform inferences also be a physical process? This is where *artificial intelligence* and computers come in. Computers are physical entities with physical processes; they are also artifacts we have expressly designed to carry out recursive procedures. In fact, the concept of a computer can be used to define what a recursive procedure is, and we have no better interpretation of what we mean by saying that a procedure is effective than that it is recursive in this sense. Since the axioms and rules of inference for a logic specify a recursive procedure for generating inferences, a computer with the right program will do this. The axioms and rules of the logic can be explicitly expressed in a programming language, as can premises representing propositions.

The programming language and the computer can be so designed that automatic procedures, following other rules implicitly, will be applied to these representations to generate inferences. We can explain fully how the computer works when it does this, from its *software*, its program, to its *hardware*, its physical structure. The ultimate aim of artificial intelligence is to design and program computers to have all cognitive states, like knowledge, and execute all cognitive processes, like justified inference. (Garnham (1988) is an introduction to artificial intelligence accessible to philosophers and psychologists. See Johnson-Laird (1983, 1988) on the importance of effective procedures in psychology, and Turing (1936, 1950) for classic papers on computation and what came to be known as artificial intelligence. See Searle (1980) for scepticism about artificial intelligence, and the reply by Dennett (1987: ch. 9).)

It was reasonable, at one time, for psychologists to hope that we have at least a mental sentential logic. For then a computer programmed to follow the rules of sentential logic would be doing what we do when we perform certain inferences: the computer's artificial inference would be functionally the same as our natural inference. The rules we followed in our mental logic would be the same as the computer's program, and could be thought of as our natural software. From this perspective, it would not matter if the computer's hardware was very different from the physical structure of our brains, as long as we could assume that our brains were some type of natural computer which could run the software. Of course, there always were serious questions to be asked about the doctrine of mental logic. How are we supposed to translate ordinary sentences into their logical forms in a mental language? And how do we efficiently perform appropriate or relevant inferences? These questions have proved difficult to answer, and on top of that, experiments like the selection task have cast serious doubt on the doctrine.

But all is not lost. There may not be a full mental sentential logic, with explicit representations of all the inference rules of the logic, but some of these rules could still be explicitly represented, such as modus ponens, to mention the most likely candidate. There might further be a mental deontic logic or other mental intensional logics, or at least some explicit inference rules from some of these, in the mind. More radically, cognitive psychologists can take over the concepts of frames and scripts from artificial intelligence, where they originally came from, and see if these are explicitly represented in the mind. Starting in Chapter 2, we indicated how these structures and the computational processes which go with them have been used to try to give computational accounts of our content-dependent reasoning. Johnson-Laird's theory of mental models is also an attempt to describe this reasoning in computational terms. Some explicit formal rules, some scripts, frames, mental models and other structures could all be part of a Stalnaker-type miscellany of mental representations, manipulated in a computational system for performing all sorts of inferences. There is indeed no reason to assume, particularly after giving up the full doctrine of mental logic, that evolution has settled on just one type of representation in the mind.

By studying explicit representations in computational systems, we might hope to discover how people, at their best, perform efficient inferences, neither inferring too much nor too little in context. But an even more radical proposal has been that there may be no explicit representations, at least of rules, in the mind. This idea extrapolates to an extreme the work on what is called *connectionism* or *parallel distributed processing*, and one reason it is so interesting is that it is based, more or less closely, on what is known of the nature and structure of the brain. (P.S. Churchland (1986) is an introduction to this with a discussion of its possible philosophical and psychological significance.) An older-style, standard computer with *serial processing* has a single processing unit, which operates on one representation after another sequentially drawn from memory, but computers capable of parallel processing have more than one processing unit and can perform many such operations at a time.

For a parallel computer to be much like the brain it must have a very fine processing structure. The basic units in the brain are its billions of cells, its *neurons*, which are connected to each other in an immense *neural network*. It would be far too difficult to design and build, in the near future, a neural network parallel computer which was anything like as complex as the brain, with its sort of fine processing structure. But modest artificial neural networks can be constructed, and the operation of more complex ones can be simulated on standard computers; in this way we can try to discover what these networks are capable of. These systems are capable of learning how to do certain things without being given a standard program with explicit rules. For instance, one of these could be set up to learn how to recognise a number of different faces by establishing, through trial and error, connections between its basic units. We could help it to do this, as we help a child, by telling it when it had named a face correctly and when incorrectly.

Different groups of units in this kind of connectionist system might respond, more or less vigorously, to the length of the nose, the width of the eyes, the size of the ears, and so on. Presented with a face on some occasion, the system would not, like a serial computer, examine these parts of the face one after another; rather, it would simultaneously produce a pattern of responses from its various groups of units. If the face had a big nose, wide eyes, large ears, and so on, the pattern would be one of a very vigorous response from all the groups; if the face were less grotesque, with more mixed features, the characteristic pattern would be more varied. And if we have corrected the system sufficiently in the past, it would be able to match any of these patterns with one it had stored in its memory and name the face correctly. The system would be said to *converge* on a solution when it came up with an answer in this way, and we might say that to do this it used a new kind of schema, a *distributed representation*, to recognise a face.

Schemas of this sort would not be explicitly represented rules for recognising particular faces, as there might be in a serial computer with a sequential program. These new, distributed schemas would be simply patterns of responses stored in the memory. Having no explicit rules, the system could not be said to perform any explicit inferences. But we could say that it tried to compare and match patterns of responses, and that by doing this it was following certain rules implicitly. (On this kind of account and this sort of schema, see especially Paper 14 in Rumelhart and McClelland (1986), an important collection of papers on parallel distributed processing.)

How far can connectionist accounts of this particular type be extended? The extreme view of P.M. Churchland (1986, 1988a,b) suggests that all cognitive states and processes might be accounted for in this way. He even suggests that the proper way to explain an action might not be by deduction from rules, as in belief/desire psychology, but by the use of a neural network to fit it somehow to a pattern of action, and that this latter type of explanation might completely replace the former, just as scientific medicine has replaced folk medicine. The scepticism of Stich (1983, 1985) about human rationality would, if legitimate, support this view. If human beings were as irrational as Stich charges, then perhaps human reasoning and behaviour could not generally be subsumed under justified rules of inference, explicit or implicit, and we would be forced, by the advance of science, to give up assigning intentional contents to mental states. We would not have good grounds for using these contents in belief/desire psychology to predict and explain behaviour, which would be too irrational for that, and the only alternative might be to talk about patterns of responses in neural networks. But we have rejected the claim that human beings are this irrational, and there seems little else to be said for the extreme view.

In fact, we are in great need of a good deductive theory of connectionist systems, so that we can infer when these will or will not converge, and what they will converge on. A special case would be when there was an attempt to get one of these systems to perform inferences (as in the work of Touretsky and Hinton 1985), and we asked whether it converged on valid ones. If it were properly said to perform an inference, it would have to contain a propositional process: one with representations of some type to which we could assign propositional contents. Some of these representations would be the premises and one the conclusion in the inference, and we would have to deduce whether the former logically implied the latter.

The need to find out how reliable the system was would lead us to view it as we view ourselves, as having states with intentional contents, and this would be just as well if it were designed to be at all like ourselves.

A less extreme form of connectionism does have much to say, we are sure, about many cognitive states and processes, such as the recognition of everyday objects, which human beings are much faster and better at than present serial computers. But consider how even our basic recognition abilities can be affected by our conscious use of rules. These abilities do not always work instantly – they may not, for example, when we are trying to recognise an object in a field on a foggy evening. In that case, we may be able to infer, consciously using justified rules, that the object is most likely to be a scarecrow, and that might help us to recognise it as a scarecrow. This suggests that the use of rules at a high level may get a neural network at a relatively low level to converge on a solution. And even if it does not, we can use rules consciously to evaluate our failure, and this may affect the future performance of the recognition ability. It is a common experience to begin to improve performance by the conscious use of rules, and then to find that an automatic ability to do this emerges later, apparently as a result. (Johnson-Laird (1988) and Boden (1988) are good introductions to computational accounts of the mind with comments on connectionism. Pinker and Mehler (1989) is a recent collection of papers on connectionism, and Clark (1987) discusses connectionism and cognitive science.)

The origin of intentionality

It is interesting to compare the scepticism of Churchland about human intentionality with that of Quine (1974) about dispositional operators, as in:

This piece of salt has the disposition to dissolve in water.

The operator, *has the disposition to,* has been used to construct this sentence, and can be used to construct indefinitely many more. In itself it is an extensional operator, but Quine was worried about the close connection between it and counterfactual or subjunctive conditionals (which we discussed in Chapter 4). He found it a problem that the above sentence seems to be equivalent in meaning to:

If this piece of salt were immersed in water, then it would dissolve.

This conditional is an intensional one, and as Quine doubted that its meaning could be fully clarified, he wanted to restrict himself to the extensional conditional, with its simple truth functional semantics.

Consistent with this, he did not think that a proper scientific language should contain dispositional operators, which can be freely used to assign dispositional contents to physical objects, since these uses would bring with them a free use of intensional conditionals. For him dispositional operators could have only a heuristic role as science develops: their use would eventually help scientists to discover the physical mechanisms which are responsible for processes like the dissolving of salt in water. Once these mechanisms are known, Quine argued, scientists should use descriptions of them in place of the dispositional operators in a scientific language for stating their theories.

Churchland similarly suggests that ascribing intentional contents to mental states may have only a heuristic value in a developing scientific theory of the mind and brain. It has been used for a long time as the basis of folk psychology, but only because, in his view, there has been nothing better to put in its place. His claim is that it, and all the rest of folk psychology, could be replaced by descriptions of the mechanisms of neural networks in the brain. In more Quinean terms, the result would be that unclear intensional expressions would be replaced by clear extensional ones, the use of which to predict and explain our behaviour did not require us to be rational.

The link between these positions is especially interesting because, by finding positive grounds for rejecting the first, we would make a start on finding those for rejecting the second. The operator *has the ability to* is broadly of the dispositional type, and to say, for example, that Odysseus had the ability to punish the suitors is to say something about what he would have successfully done (and did in fact do) if certain conditions held, particularly if he had the belief and desire we have already ascribed to him. (See Dennett (1984: ch. 6) for an introduction to the complexity of the semantic relation between statements about abilities and subjunctive conditionals.) The truth of statements like this about abilities is crucial for belief/desire psychology, since people, no matter what their beliefs and desires are, do not successfully do what they do not have the ability to do. Among these statements are some which are intensional, such as:

Penelope had the ability to point out the beggar.

This sentence is true at one point in the story, but the result of replacing *the beggar* in it with *Odysseus* is not, though (unknown to Penelope at that point) Odysseus is the beggar. What is ascribed to Penelope here would not normally be considered a propositional attitude; even so, it is closely related to recognition abilities and some very simple or elementary attitudes, particularly perceptual ones. To say that Penelope had this general ability in some context is to say something about what she would have reliably done, in the way of pointing out the beggar, if certain conditions had held. These must also concern her possible beliefs and desires, but what more can be said about conditions of this type? As Quine would remind us, there is a great deal that could be said about these if we understood fully the mechanisms which constitute abilities, which in turn depend on those to do with our beliefs and desires.

For this and other reasons, such as explaining the efficiency of much of our reasoning, we need to understand much more about the mechanisms which form and transform our beliefs. Consider the account in Stalnaker (1984) of what it means to have a belief rather than a desire or some other type of state. He holds (p.18):

> We believe that P just because we are in a state that, under optimal conditions, we are in only if P, and under optimal conditions, we are in that state because of P or something that entails P.

Consider a sensory cognitive state, such as what Penelope had when she was looking at the beggar. Did she believe, by Stalnaker's account, that the beggar was in front of her? That depends on whether she is in a state which, under optimal conditions, she would be in only if the beggar was in front of her and as a causal effect of the fact that he was in front of her. This particular account seems to have its best application to perceptual beliefs. However, speaking vaguely, we agree that people can be properly said to have beliefs if and only if they have, under optimal conditions, generally reliable mechanisms for getting and processing information about what is the case. It is just that this sort of statement has to be made much more concrete by discovering the detailed mental representations and processes which produce beliefs by perception and by inference. Only in this way can we uncover the optimal conditions under which our inferential mechanisms are reliable. We have criticised extreme scepticism about this reliability, and with our general reliability comes belief and inference.

To be completely clear about reliability, we must distinguish two notions of it: *hardware reliability* and *software reliability*. In a computational system, the former concerns the physical structure and the latter the rules followed explicitly or implicitly. The physical structure of the brain or a silicon chip may or may not have a tendency to break down or burn out after a certain amount of use, and the greater this tendency, which may be expressible as a physical probability, the less hardware reliability the system has. Software reliability, on the other hand, directly relates to what makes the mechanism a computational one: the rules it follows explicitly or implicitly. When we want a computer to do something for us, we are interested in whether its program has been correctly designed or written to achieve that goal. If it has been, then we consider its software reliable; otherwise we find it unreliable, with faults or 'bugs'. We may try to program a computer to perform reliable inferences, and then we want to know whether we have successfully given it software, which when running, explicitly uses or implicitly follows justified inference rules. We may have mistakenly used or relied on some invalid or otherwise unjustified inference rules, or made an error in translating valid and strong ones into the programming language. If we have slipped up in one of these ways, the software is unreliable; but if there are no mistakes of this type, then it is reliable. (Goldman (1986) discusses reliability and justification in cognitive science and epistemology, but he does not distinguish hardware and software reliability.)

We can leave the study of the hardware reliability of the human brain and sense organs to physiologists. What we are interested in is the software reliability of the mind – the mind being taken as the brain with the software evolution has given it. We want to ask whether this software achieves certain epistemological goals we have, such as yielding justified inferences, ones which are valid or at least strong. It is just that we do not yet know what the fundamental software of the mind is, underlying whatever we have consciously learned, and we have to discover it. Evolution has given us the means to process information about the world, and our aim is to find out what enables us to do this. What are our internal representations? Are they mental models, schemas of some other type, or of various types? Are some of these distributed representations while others are sentences in a mental language? What sort of computational processes operate on these internal representations? Do we have sequential software like that in a serial computer? Is our software simply the set-up of a great neural network which only follows rules implicitly as the connections between its parts are modified by its performance? Or do we have both types of software for different purposes, such as the conscious use of rules and automatic recognition? How does our software enable us to perform appropriate and efficient inferences?

Unless ordinary, sane people turn out, against the present evidence, to be very irrational indeed, we should not take the extreme step suggested by Churchland. We should not deny that their computational processes contain mental representations, with intentional contents, and explicitly use, or implicitly follow, justified inference rules. If people are generally rational and reliable, then we must find out how this comes about, and why it is so. This will mean ascribing propositional contents to some of their mental states and showing that, under certain conditions, these states are parts of efficient propositional processes which can be properly called valid or strong inferences. We cannot do this if we restrict ourselves to physical, non-intentional descriptions of great neural networks. At the very least, we must show that some input states and some output states represent propositions, and that what goes on in between sometimes makes the output content true or probable, given the input content.

The importance of intentionality can be further brought out by distinguishing between *narrow* and *wide* content. Compare the case of abilities, including recognition abilities. We need not have Quine's goal of replacing ascriptions of content to these once we have described their internal hardware and software. If we are confident that the semantics introduced in Chapter 4 will be the basis of a good explanation of subjunctive conditionals, we are free to ascribe the contents. And in fact, the more we find out about the internal nature of the abilities, the more we can say about the relationship between ascriptions of contents to them and subjunctive conditionals.

But if we focus only on the strictly internal nature of an ability, the content will be a narrow one. For instance, it might be an ability to exert a certain amount of force through the muscles of an arm. To put the matter in terms of a subjunctive conditional, we could say that this force would raise a free arm if it were in some gravitational fields but not others. However, in ordinary affairs – and for some scientific purposes – we are primarily interested in a wide notion of content. This is what we are trying to find out when we ask whether this is an ability to raise the arm here and now, in the actual, present state of affairs (with the gravitational field as it really is), or an ability to serve well in tennis in the same circumstances. Knowing the answer to these questions may help us to predict whether the arm will be raised in the near future, or who will win a tennis match.

It is also this wide notion of content we need to explain scientifically how the ability could have evolved in our species by natural selection, or why some methods of coaching in tennis develop better players than others. For this purpose, we must look at the wider world outside the body and ask how an increasing ability to use the arm in certain ways was adaptive there, or why certain types of coaching developed good co-ordination in it.

For like reasons, we must distinguish between narrow and wide contents for mental representations. Consider a mental schema of some type. This could represent, in the narrow sense, structurally similar aspects of many possible states of affairs, and its narrow content could be taken as a function which picks out these aspects in any given state of affairs. We may wish to study the internal aspects of the schema, its relation to other schemas, and the internal computational procedures which operate on it, and then we need no more than narrow content, which may be required to show that this whole internal system preserves truth. But again phylogenetic and ontogenetic questions would lead us to the wide notion of content for all such schemas. In the wide sense, our example might represent, in the real state of affairs, actual games of tennis – its wide content. We would want to know, in evolutionary psychology, how a mental capacity to acquire schemas of this type actually evolved, and in developmental psychology, how individuals could have acquired it as a result of experience in actual games of tennis. The two notions of content are needed for separate purposes. We need the narrow one for studying the computational nature and qualities of the internal structures and procedures, and the wide one for relating these to the external world. (For an extensive discussion of narrow and wide content, see Fodor (1987); and on evolution and intentionality, Dennett (1987).)

Intentionality and rationality are closely related. In this book, we have tried to indicate how much we already know about human inference and how much there still is to learn. The detailed structure of mental representations and processes must be discovered to assess the precise rationality of our inference, its strengths and weaknesses, and to solve the problem of its general efficiency and pragmatic appropriateness. But although we do not have god-like powers of rational thought and action, we are not so irrational that we shall find ourselves to be senseless.

References

Abelson, R.P. (1981) 'Psychological status of the script concept', *American Psychologist*, vol. 36, pp 715–29.

Achinstein, P. (ed.) (1983) *The Concept of Evidence*, Oxford, Oxford University Press.

Adams, E. (1970) 'Subjunctive mood and indicative conditionals', *Foundations of Language*, vol. 6, pp 89–94.

Akiyama, M. (1984) 'Are language-acquisition strategies universal?', *Developmental Psychology*, vol. 20, pp 219–28.

Anderson, J.R. (1983) *The Architecture of Cognition*, Cambridge, Massachusetts, Harvard University Press.

Austin, J.L. (1962) *How to Do Things with Words*, Oxford, Oxford University Press.

Baddeley, A.D. (1987) *Working Memory*, Oxford, Clarendon Press.

Bar-Hillel, M. (1979) 'The role of sample size in sample evaluation', *Organisational Behavior and Human Decision Making*, vol. 24, pp 245–57.

Baron, J. (1985) *Rationality and Intelligence*, Cambridge, Cambridge University Press.

Bartlett, F.C. (1932) *Remembering*, Cambridge, Cambridge University Press.

Barwise, J. and Perry, P. (1983) *Situations and Attitudes*, Cambridge, Massachusetts, MIT Press.

Bereiter, C. (1983) 'Story grammar as knowledge', *The Behavioral and Brain Sciences*, vol. 6, pp 593–4.

Beth, E.W. and Piaget, J. (1966) *Mathematical Epistemology and Psychology*, Dordrecht, Reidel.

Bickhard, M.H. and Richie, D.M. (1983) *On the Nature of Representation*, New York, Praeger.

Bloom, L.M. (1970) *Language Development: Form and Function in Emerging Grammars*, Cambridge, Massachusetts, MIT Press.

Bloom, L.M., Lightbrown, P. and Hood, L. (1975) 'Structure and variation in child language development', *Monographs of the Society for Research in Child Development*, vol. 40, no. 2.

Bobrow, D.G. and Collins, A.M. (eds) (1975) *Representation and Understanding*, London, Academic Press.

Boden, M. (1988) *Models of the Mind*, Cambridge, Cambridge University Press.

Bower, G.H., Black, J.B. and Turner, T.J. (1979) 'Scripts in text comprehension and memory', *Cognitive Psychology*, vol. 11, pp 177–220.

Bowerman, M. (1986) 'First steps in acquiring conditionals', in E.C. Traugott, A. ter Meulen, J.S. Reilly and C.A. Ferguson (eds) *On Conditionals*, Cambridge, Cambridge University Press.

Braine, M.D.S. and Rumain, B. (1983) 'Logical reasoning', in J.H. Flavell and E.M. Markman (eds) *Handbook of Child Psychology*, 4th edn, Chichester, John Wiley & Sons.

Brainerd, C.J. (1978) 'Learning research and Piagetian theory', in L.S. Siegel and C.J. Brainerd (eds) *Alternatives to Piaget: Critical Essays on the Theory*, New York, Academic Press.

Bransford, J.D., Barclay, J.R. and Franks, J.J. (1972) 'Sentence memory: a constructive versus interpretive approach', *Cognitive Psychology*, vol. 3, pp 193–209.

Bransford, J.D. and Johnson, M.K. (1973) 'Consideration of some problems of comprehension', in W.G. Chase (ed.) *Visual Information Processing*, London, Academic Press.

Brewer, W.F. (1983) 'Form, content, and affect in the theory of stories', *The Behavioral and Brain Sciences*, vol. 6, pp 595–6.

Brewer, W.F. and Lichtenstein, E.H. (1981) 'Event schemas, story schemas, and story grammars', in J. Long and A.D. Baddeley (eds) *Attention and Performance IX*, Hillsdale, New Jersey, Lawrence Erlbaum Associates.

Bynum, T.W., Thomas, J.A. and Weitz, L.J. (1972) 'Truth-functional logic in formal operational thinking: Inhelder and Piaget's evidence', *Developmental Psychology*, vol. 7, pp 129–32.

Campbell, D. (1974) 'Evolutionary epistemology', in P. Schillp (ed.) *The Philosophy of Karl Popper*, La Salle, Illinois, Open Court.

Campbell, R.L. and Bickhard, M.H. (1986) *Knowing Levels and Developmental Stages*, Basel, Karger.

Carey, S. (1978) '*Less* may never mean "more"', in R.N. Campbell and P.T. Smith (eds) *Recent Advances in the Psychology of Language*, London, Plenum Press.

Carey, S. (1985) *Conceptual Change in Childhood*, Cambridge, Massachusetts, MIT Press.

Carnap, R. and Jeffrey, R. (eds) (1971) *Studies in Inductive Logic and Probability*, Berkeley, University of California Press.

Carpenter, P.A. and Just, M.A. (1975) 'Sentence comprehension: a psycholinguistic processing model of verification', *Psychological Review*, vol. 82, pp 45–73.

Carston, R. (1987) 'Being explicit', *The Behavioral and Brain Sciences*, vol. 10, pp 713–14.

Chang, C.C. and Keisler, H.J. (1977) *Model Theory*, 2nd edn, Amsterdam, North–Holland.

Chellas, B.F. (1980) *Modal Logic: an Introduction*, Cambridge, Cambridge University Press.

Cheng, P.W. and Holyoak, K.J. (1985) 'Pragmatic reasoning schemas', *Cognitive Psychology*, vol. 17, pp 391–416.

Cheng, P.W. and Holyoak, K.J. (in press) 'On the natural selection of reasoning theories', *Cognition*.

Cheng, P.W., Holyoak, K.J., Nisbett, R.E. and Oliver, L.M. (1986) 'Pragmatic versus syntactic approaches to training deductive reasoning', *Cognitive Psychology*, vol. 18, pp 293–328.

Chi, M.T.H., Glaser, R. and Rees, E. (1982) 'Expertise in problem solving', in R.J. Sternberg (ed.) *Advances in the Psychology of Human Intelligence*, vol. 1, Hillsdale, New Jersey, Lawrence Erlbaum Associates.

Chomsky, C. (1969) *The Acquisition of Syntax in Children from 5 to 10*, Cambridge, Massachusetts, MIT Press.

Chomsky, N. (1965) *Aspects of the Theory of Syntax*, Cambridge, Massachusetts, MIT Press.

Chomsky, N. (1981) *Lectures on Government and Binding*, Dordrecht, Foris Publications.

Churchland, P.M. (1986) 'Some reductive strategies in cognitive neurobiology', *Mind*, vol. 95, pp 279–309.

Churchland, P.M. (1988a) *Matter and Consciousness*, rev. edn, Cambridge, Massachusetts, MIT Press.

Churchland, P.M. (1988b) 'Folk psychology and the explanation of behavior', *Proceedings of the Aristotelian Society Supplement*, vol. LXII, pp 209–21.

Churchland, P.S. (1986) *Neurophilosophy*, Cambridge, Massachusetts, MIT Press.

Clancy, P.M. (1980) 'Referential choice in English and Japanese narrative discourse', in W.L. Chafe (ed.) *The Pear Stories: Cognitive, Cultural, and Linguistic Aspects of Narrative Production*, Norwood, New Jersey, Ablex.

Clark, A. (1987) 'Connectionism and cognitive science', in J. Hallam and C. Mellish (eds) *Advances in Artificial Intelligence*, Chichester, John Wiley & Sons.

Clark, E.V. (1973) 'Non-linguistic strategies and the acquisition of word meanings', *Cognition*, vol. 2, pp 161–82.

Clark, H.H. (1974) 'Semantics and comprehension', in T.A. Sebeok (ed.) *Current Trends in Linguistics Vol. 12: Linguistics and Adjacent Arts and Sciences*, The Hague, Mouton.

Clark, H.H. (1977a) 'Bridging', in P.N. Johnson-Laird and P.C. Wason (eds) *Thinking: Readings in Cognitive Science*, Cambridge, Cambridge University Press.

Clark, H.H. (1977b) 'Inferences in comprehension', in D. Laberge and S.J. Samuels (eds) *Basic Processes in Reading*, Hillsdale, New Jersey, Lawrence Erlbaum Associates.

Clark, H.H. and Carlson, T.B. (1981) 'Contexts for comprehension', in J. Long and A.D. Baddeley (eds) *Attention and Performance IX*, Hillsdale, New Jersey, Lawrence Erlbaum Associates.

Clark, H.H. and Chase, W.G. (1972) 'On the process of comparing sentences against pictures', *Cognitive Psychology*, vol. 3, pp 472–517.

Clark, H.H. and Clark, E.V. (1977) *Psychology and Language*, New York, Harcourt Brace Jovanovich.

Clark, H.H. and Schaefer, E.F. (1987) 'Concealing meaning from overhearers', *Journal of Memory and Language*, vol. 26, pp 209–25.

Clark, H.H. and Wilkes-Gibbs, D. (1986) 'Referring as a collaborative process', *Cognition*, vol. 22, pp 1–39.

Cohen, L.J. (1981) 'Can human irrationality be experimentally demonstrated?', *The Behavioral and Brain Sciences*, vol. 4, pp 317–70.

Cohen, L.J. (1986) *The Dialogue of Reason*, Oxford, Clarendon Press.

Cosmides, L. (1985) 'Deduction or Darwinian algorithms? An explanation of the "elusive" content effect on the Wason selection task', unpublished PhD thesis, Harvard University.

Cosmides, L. (1989) 'The logic of social exchange: has natural selection shaped how humans reason?', *Cognition*, vol. 31, pp 187–276.

Cosmides, L. and Tooby, J. (1986) 'From evolution to behavior: evolutionary psychology as the missing link', in J. Duptre (ed.) *The Latest on the Best: Essays on Evolution and Optimality*, Cambridge, Massachusetts, MIT Press.

Craik, K. (1943) *The Nature of Explanation*, Cambridge, Cambridge University Press.

Dennett, D.C. (1969) *Content and Consciousness*, London, Routledge & Kegan Paul.

Dennett, D.C. (1978) *Brainstorms*, Cambridge, Massachusetts, MIT Press.

Dennett, D.C. (1984) *Elbow Room: the Varieties of Free Will Worth Having*, Cambridge, Massachusetts, MIT Press.

Dennett, D.C. (1987) *The Intentional Stance*, Cambridge, Massachusetts, MIT Press.

van Dijk, T.A. (1977) 'Semantic macro-structures and knowledge frames in discourse comprehension', in M.A. Just and P.A. Carpenter (eds) *Cognitive Processes in Comprehension*, Hillsdale, New Jersey, Lawrence Erlbaum Associates.

van Dijk, T.A. and Kintsch, W. (1983) *Strategies of Discourse Comprehension*, New York, Academic Press.

Donaldson, M. (1978) *Children's Minds*, London, Fontana.

Donaldson, M. and Balfour, G (1968) 'Less is more: a study of language comprehension in children', *British Journal of Psychology*, vol. 59, pp 461–72.

Donellan, K.S. (1966) 'Referential and definite descriptions', *Philosophical Review*, vol. LXXV, pp 281–304.

Dore, J. (1975) 'Holophrases, speech acts, and language universals', *Journal of Child Language*, vol. 2, pp 21–40.

Dudman, V.R. (1984) 'Conditional interpretations of if-sentences', *Australian Journal of Linguistics*, vol. 4, pp 143–204.

Dummett, M. (1973) *Frege: Philosophy of Language*, London, Duckworth.

Eifermann, E.R. (1961) 'Negation: a linguistic variable', *Acta Psychologica*, vol. 18, pp 258–73.

Evans, J.StB.T. (1972) 'Interpretation and matching bias in a reasoning task', *Quarterly Journal of Experimental Psychology*, vol. 24, pp 193–9.

Evans, J.StB.T. (1982) *The Psychology of Deductive Reasoning*, London, Routledge & Kegan Paul.

Evans, J.StB.T. (1983) 'Linguistic determinants of bias in conditional reasoning', *Quarterly Journal of Experimental Psychology*, vol. 36A, pp 635–44.

Evans, J.StB.T. (1984) 'Heuristic and analytic processes in reasoning', *British Journal of Psychology*, vol. 75, pp 457–68.

Evans, J.StB.T. (1986) 'Reasoning', in H. Beloff and A.M. Colman (eds) *Psychology Survey 6*, Leicester, British Psychological Society.

Evans, J.StB.T. (1989) *Bias in Reasoning: Causes and Consequences*, Hove, Sussex, Lawrence Erlbaum Associates.

Evans, J.StB.T. and Dusoir, A.E. (1977) 'Proportionality and sample size as factors in statistical judgements', *Acta Psychologica*, vol. 41, pp 129–37.

Evans, J.StB.T. and Lynch, J.S. (1973) 'Matching bias in the selection task', *British Journal of Psychology*, vol. 64, pp 391–7.

Evans, J.StB.T. and Pollard, P. (1981) 'On defining rationality unreasonably', *The Behavioral and Brain Sciences*, vol. 4, pp 335–6.

Evans, J.StB.T. and Wason, P.C. (1976) 'Rationalisation in a reasoning task', *British Journal of Psychology*, vol. 67, pp 479–86.

Fillenbaum, S. (1971) 'On coping with ordered and disordered conjunctive sentences', *Journal of Experimental Psychology*, vol. 87, pp 93–8.

Fillenbaum, S. (1974) 'Pragmatic normalization: further results for some conjunctive and disjunctive sentences', *Journal of Experimental Psychology*, vol. 102, pp 574–8.

Fillenbaum, S. (1978) 'How to do some things with IF', in J.W. Cotton and R.L. Klatzky (eds) *Semantic Factors in Cognition*, Hillsdale, New Jersey, Lawrence Erlbaum Associates.

Fillenbaum, S. (1986) 'The use of conditionals in inducements and deterrents', in E.C. Traugott, A. ter Meulen, J.S. Reilly and C.A. Ferguson (eds) *On Conditionals*, Cambridge, Cambridge University Press.

Fine, K. (1985) *Reasoning with Arbitrary Objects*, Oxford, Blackwell.

Flavell, J.H. (1963) *The Developmental Psychology of Jean Piaget*, Princeton, New Jersey, Van Nostrand.

Flavell, J.H. (1985) *Cognitive Development*, 2nd edn, Englewood Cliffs, New Jersey, Prentice-Hall.

Fodor, J. (1987) *Psychosemantics*, Cambridge, Massachusetts, MIT Press.

Fong, G.T., Krantz, D.H. and Nisbett, R.E. (1986) 'The effects of statistical training on thinking about everyday problems', *Cognitive Psychology*, vol. 18, pp 253–92.

Foss, B. (ed.) (1966) *New Horizons in Psychology*, Harmondsworth, Middlesex, Penguin Books.

Foss, D.J. and Hakes, D.T. (1978) *Psycholinguistics*, Englewood Cliffs, New Jersey, Prentice-Hall.

Frege, G. (1892/1952) 'Über Sinn und Bedeutung', translated in P.T. Geach and M. Black (eds) *Philosophical Writings of Gottlob Frege*, Oxford, Blackwell.

Gärdenfors, P. and Sahlin, N. (eds) (1988) *Decision, Probability, and Utility*, Cambridge, Cambridge University Press.

Garnham, A. (1981) 'Mental models as representations of text', *Memory and Cognition*, vol. 9, pp 560–5.

Garnham, A. (1983) 'What's wrong with story grammars?', *Cognition*, vol. 15, pp 145–54.

Garnham, A. (1984) *Psycholinguistics: Central Topics*, London, Methuen.

Garnham, A. (1988) *Artificial Intelligence: an Introduction*, London, Routledge.

Garnham, A., Oakhill, J.V. and Johnson-Laird, P.N. (1982) 'Referential continuity and the coherence of discourse', *Cognition*, vol. 11, pp 29–46.

Gazdar, G. (1979) *Pragmatics: Implicature, Presupposition, and Logical Form*, New York, Academic Press.

Gazdar, G. and Good, D. (1982) 'On the notion of relevance', in G. Gazdar and D. Good (eds) *Mutual Knowledge*, London, Academic Press.

Geber, B.A. (ed.) (1977) *Piaget and Knowing*, London, Routledge & Kegan Paul.

Gelman, R. and Baillargeon, R. (1983) 'A review of Piagetian concepts', in J.H. Flavell and E.M. Markman (eds) *Cognitive Development: Manual of Child Psychology, Vol. 3*, New York, John Wiley & Sons.

Girotto, V. (1988) 'Conditional and biconditional biases in children's reasoning', paper presented at the Conference on Cognitive Biases, Université de Provence.

Girotto, V., Light, P. and Colbourn, C. (1988) 'Pragmatic schemas and conditional reasoning in children', *Quarterly Journal of Experimental Psychology*, vol. 40A, pp 469–82.

Glenberg, A.M., Meyer, M. and Lindem, K. (1987) 'Mental models contribute to foregrounding during text comprehension', *Journal of Memory and Language*, vol. 26, pp 69–83.

Goldman, A. (1986) *Epistemology and Cognition*, Cambridge, Massachusetts, Harvard University Press.

Goodwin, R.Q. and Wason, P.C. (1972) 'Degrees of insight', *British Journal of Psychology*, vol. 63, pp 205–12.

Greene, J.M. (1970) 'Syntactic form and semantic function', *Quarterly Journal of Experimental Psychology*, vol. 22, pp 14–27.

Grice, H.P. (1967) 'Logic and conversation', unpublished MS of the William James Lectures, Harvard University.

Grice, H.P. (1975) 'Logic and conversation', in P. Cole and J.P. Morgan (eds) *Syntax and Semantics vol. 3: Speech Acts*, New York, Seminar Press.

Grice, H.P. (1978) 'Further notes on logic and conversation', in P. Cole (ed.) *Syntax and Semantics vol. 9: Pragmatics*, New York, Academic Press.

Grice, H.P. (1981) 'Presupposition and conversational implicature', in P. Cole (ed.) *Radical Pragmatics*, New York, Academic Press.

Griggs, R.A. (1981) 'Human reasoning: can we judge before we understand?', *The Behavioral and Brain Sciences*, vol. 4, pp 338–9.

Griggs, R.A. (1983) 'The role of problem content in the Wason selection task and THOG problem', in J.StB.T. Evans (ed.) *Thinking and Reasoning: Psychological Approaches*, London, Routledge & Kegan Paul.

Griggs, R.A. and Cox, J.R. (1983) 'The effects of problem content and negation on Wason's selection task', *Quarterly Journal of Experimental Psychology*, vol. 35A, pp 519–33.

Gross, T.F. (1985) *Cognitive Development*, Monterey, California, Brooks/ Cole.

Halliday, M.A.K. and Hasan, R. (1976) *Cohesion in English*, London, Longmans.

Halliday, M.S. and Hitch, G.J. (1988) 'Developmental applications of working memory', in G. Claxton (ed.) *Growth Points in Cognition*, London, Routledge.

Haviland, S.E. and Clark, H.H. (1974) 'What's new? Acquiring new information as a process in comprehension', *Journal of Verbal Learning and Verbal Behavior*, vol. 13, pp 512–21.

Hodges, W. (1977) *Logic*, Harmondsworth, Middlesex, Penguin Books.

Holland, J.H., Holyoak, K.J., Nisbett, R.E. and Thagard, P.R. (1986) *Induction*, Cambridge, Massachusetts, MIT Press.

Hood, L., Lahey, M., Lifter, K. and Bloom, L.M. (1988) 'Observation and descriptive methodology in studying child language: preliminary results in the development of complex sentences', in G. Sackett (ed.) *Observing Behavior*, Baltimore, University Park Press.

Inhelder, B. and Piaget, J. (1958) *The Growth of Logical Thinking*, New York, Basic Books.

Isaacs, E.A. and Clark, H.H. (1987) 'References in conversation between novices and experts', *Journal of Experimental Psychology: General*, vol. 116, pp 26–37.

Jackson, F. (1985) 'On the semantics and logic of obligation', *Mind*, vol. 94, pp 177–96.

Jackson, F. (1987) *Conditionals*, Oxford, Blackwell.

Johnson-Laird, P.N. (1980) 'Mental models in cognitive science', *Cognitive Science*, vol. 4, pp 71–115.

Johnson-Laird, P.N. (1982) 'Thinking as a skill', *Quarterly Journal of Experimental Psychology*, vol. 34A, pp 1–29.

Johnson-Laird, P.N. (1983) *Mental Models*, Cambridge, Cambridge University Press.

Johnson-Laird, P.N. (1985) 'Human and computer reason', *Trends in Neuroscience*, vol. 8, pp 54–7.

Johnson-Laird, P.N. (1988) *The Computer and the Mind*, London, Fontana.

Johnson-Laird, P.N., Legrenzi, P. and Legrenzi, M.S. (1972) 'Reasoning and a sense of reality', *British Journal of Psychology*, vol. 63, pp 395–400.

Johnson-Laird, P.N. and Wason, P.C. (eds) (1977) *Thinking: Readings in Cognitive Science*, Cambridge, Cambridge University Press.

Just, M.A. and Clark, H.H. (1973) 'Drawing inferences from the presuppositions and implications of negative sentences', *Journal of Verbal Learning and Verbal Behavior*, vol. 12, pp 21–31.

Kahneman, D. (1981) 'Who shall be the arbiter of our intuitions?', *The Behavioral and Brain Sciences*, vol. 4, pp 339–40.

Kahneman, D., Slovic, P. and Tversky, A. (eds) (1982) *Judgment Under Uncertainty: Heuristics and Biases*, Cambridge, Cambridge University Press.

Kahneman, D. and Tversky, A. (1972) 'Subjective probability: a judgment of representativeness', *Cognitive Psychology*, vol. 3, pp 430–54; also reprinted in D.

Kahneman *et al.* (eds) (1982) *Judgment Under Uncertainty: Heuristics and Biases*, Cambridge, Cambridge University Press.

Kahneman, D. and Tversky, A. (1982) 'Judgments of and by representativeness', in D. Kahneman *et al.* (eds) *Judgment Under Uncertainty: Heuristics and Biases*, Cambridge, Cambridge University Press.

Kamp. H. (1981) A theory of truth and semantic representation', in J. Groenendijk, T. Janssen and M. Stokhof (eds) *Formal Methods in the Study of Language*, Amsterdam, Mathematical Centre Tracts.

Keil, F.C. (1981) 'Constraints on knowledge and cognitive development', *Psychological Review*, vol. 88, pp 197–227.

Keil, F.C. (1984) 'Mechanisms of cognitive development and the structure of knowledge', in R.J. Sternberg (ed.) *Mechanisms of Cognitive Development*, New York, W.H. Freeman.

Kim, K.J. (1985) 'Development of the concept of truth-functional negation', *Developmental Psychology*, vol. 21, pp 462–72.

Kintsch, W. (1977) 'On comprehending stories', in M.A. Just and P.A. Carpenter (eds) *Cognitive Processes in Comprehension*, Hillsdale, New Jersey, Lawrence Erlbaum Associates.

Kintsch, W. (1979) 'On modeling comprehension', *Educational Psychologist*, vol. 14, pp 3–14.

Kintsch, W. and van Dijk, T.A. (1978) 'Toward a model of text comprehension and production', *Psychological Review*, vol. 85, pp 363–94.

Klayman, J. and Ha, Y-W. (1987) 'Confirmation, disconfirmation, and information in hypothesis testing', *Psychological Review*, vol. 94, pp 211–28.

Klima, E.S. (1964) 'Negation in English', in J.A. Fodor and J.J. Katz (eds) *The Structure of Language: Readings in the Philosophy of Language*, Englewood Cliffs, New Jersey, Prentice-Hall.

Klima, E.S. and Bellugi, U. (1966) 'Syntactic regularities in the speech of children', in J. Lyons and R.J. Wales (eds) *Psycholinguistics Papers*, Edinburgh, Edinburgh University Press.

Kripke, S. (1972) 'Naming and necessity', in D. Davidson and G. Harman (eds) *Semantics and Natural Language*, Dordrecht, Reidel.

Kyburg, H.E. (1983) 'Rational belief', *The Behavioral and Brain Sciences*, vol. 6, pp 231–73.

Lakoff, G. (1972) 'Structural complexity in fairy tales', *The Study of Man*, vol. 1, pp 128–90.

Leech, G.N. (1983) *Principles of Pragmatics*, London, Longmans.

Lehnert, W.G. (1981) 'Plot units and narrative structure', *Cognitive Science*, vol. 5, pp 293–331.

Lehnert, W.G. (1982) 'Plot units: a narrative summarisation strategy', in W.G. Lehnert and M.H. Ringle (eds) *Strategies for Natural Language Processing*, Hillsdale, New Jersey, Lawrence Erlbaum Associates.

Lehnert, W.G. (1983) 'Moving toward a point of some return', *The Behavioral and Brain Sciences*, vol. 6, pp 602–3.

Lesgold, A.M., Roth, S.F. and Curtis, M.E. (1979) 'Foregrounding effects in discourse comprehension', *Journal of Verbal Learning and Verbal Behavior*, vol. 18, pp 291–308.

Levinson, S.C. (1983) *Pragmatics*, Cambridge, Cambridge University Press.

Lewis, D. (1973) *Counterfactuals*, Oxford, Blackwell.

Liben, L.S. (ed.) (1983) *Piaget and the Foundations of Knowledge*, Hillsdale, New Jersey, Lawrence Erlbaum Associates.

Lichtenstein, E.H. and Brewer, W.F. (1980) 'Memory for goal-directed words', *Cognitive Psychology*, vol. 12, pp 412–45.

Lord, C., Ross, L.E. and Lepper, M.R. (1979) 'Biased assimilation and attitude polarization: effects of prior theories on subsequently considered evidence', *Journal of Personality and Social Psychology*, vol. 37, pp 2098–109.

MacDonald, R.R. (1986) 'Credible conceptions and implausible probabilities', *British Journal of Mathematical and Statistical Psychology*, vol. 39, pp 15–27.

McGee, V. (1985) 'A counterexample to modus ponens', *Journal of Philosophy*, vol. LXXXII, pp 462–71.

McKinley, R. (1986) *Black Beauty by Anna Sewell*, London, Hamish Hamilton.

MacNamara, J. (1986) *A Border Dispute: the Place of Logic in Psychology*, Cambridge, Massachusetts, MIT Press.

Maibaum, T.S.E. (1987) 'A logic for the formal requirements specification of real-time embedded systems', unpublished Manuscript, Imperial College, London.

Mandler, J.M. (1983) 'Structural invariants in development', in L.S. Liben (ed.) *Piaget and the Foundations of Knowledge*, Hillsdale, New Jersey, Lawrence Erlbaum Associates.

Mandler, J.M. (1984) *Stories, Scripts, and Scenes: Aspects of Schema Theory*, Hillsdale, New Jersey, Lawrence Erlbaum Associates.

Mandler, J.M. and Johnson, N.S. (1977) 'Remembrance of things parsed: story structure and recall', *Cognitive Psychology*, vol. 9, pp 111–51.

Manktelow, K.I. (1981) 'Recent developments in research on Wason's selection task', *Current Psychological Reviews*, vol. 1, pp 257–68.

Manktelow, K.I. and Evans, J. StB.T. (1979) 'Facilitation of reasoning by realism: effect or non-effect?', *British Journal of Psychology*, vol. 70, pp 477–88.

Manktelow, K.I. and Jones, J. (1987) 'Principles from the psychology of thinking and mental models', in M.M. Gardiner and B. Christie (eds) *Applying Cognitive Psychology to User-Interface Design*, Chichester, John Wiley & Sons.

Manktelow, K.I. and Over, D.E. (1987) 'Reasoning and rationality', *Mind and Language*, vol. 2, pp 199–219.

Manktelow, K.I. and Over, D.E. (in press, a) 'Mental logic and deontic reasoning', in R. Spencer-Smith and S. Torrance (eds) *Machinations: Computational Studies of Logic, Language, and Cognition*, Norwood, New Jersey, Ablex.

Manktelow, K.I. and Over, D.E. (in press, b) 'Deontic thought and the selection task', in K.J. Gilhooly, M. Keane, R.H. Logie and G. Erdos (eds) *Lines of Thought: Reflections on the Psychology of Thinking*, Chichester, John Wiley & Sons.

Mell, G. (1982) *This Curious Game of Cricket*, London, George Allen & Unwin.

Meyer, J-J. (1988) 'A different approach to deontic logic: deontic logic viewed as a variant of dynamic logic', *Notre Dame Journal of Formal Logic*, vol. 29, pp 109–36.

Minsky, M. (1975a) 'A framework for representing knowledge', in P. Winston (ed.) *The Psychology of Computer Vision*, New York, McGraw-Hill.

Minsky, M. (1975b) 'Frame-system theory', reprinted in P.N. Johnson-Laird and P.C.Wason (eds) (1977) *Thinking: Readings in Cognitive Science*, Cambridge, Cambridge University Press.

Modgil, S. and Modgil, C. (eds) (1982) *Jean Piaget: Consensus and Controversy*, London, Holt, Rinehart & Winston.

Montague, R. (1974) *Formal Philosophy*, New Haven and London, Yale University Press.

Natsopoulos, D. (1985) 'A verbal illusion in two languages', *Journal of Psycholinguistic Research*, vol. 14, pp 385–97.

Nisbett, R.E., Krantz, D.H., Jepson, C. and Kunda, Z. (1983) 'The use of statistical heuristics in everyday intuitive reasoning', *Psychological Review*, vol. 90, pp 339–63.

Nisbett, R.E. and Ross, L.E. (1980) *Human Inference: Strategies and Shortcomings of Social Judgment*, Englewood Cliffs, New Jersey, Prentice-Hall.

Oakhill, J.V. (1982) 'Constructive processes in skilled and less skilled compre-
henders' memory for sentences', *British Journal of Psychology*, vol. 73, pp 13–20.

Over, D.E. (1985) 'Constructivity and the referential/attributive distinction',
Linguistics and Philosophy, vol. 8, pp 415–29.

Over, D.E. (1987a) 'Russell's hierarchy of acquaintance', *Philosophical Papers*, vol.
XVI, pp 107–24.

Over, D.E. (1987b) 'Assumptions and the supposed counterexample to modus
ponens', *Analysis*, vol. 47, pp 142–6.

Pascual-Leone, J. (1970) 'A mathematical model for the transition rule in Piaget's
developmental stages', *Acta Psychologica*, vol. 32, pp 301–45.

Pea, R.D. (1979) 'The development of negation in child language', in D.R. Olson
(ed.) *The Social Foundations of Language and Thought: Essays in Honor of Jerome
Bruner*, New York, Norton.

Perrig, W. and Kintsch, W. (1985) 'Propositional and situational representations of
text', *Journal of Memory and Language*, vol. 24, pp 503–18.

Piaget, J. (1977) 'Intellectual evolution from adolescence to adulthood', in P.N.
Johnson-Laird and P.C. Wason (eds) *Thinking: Readings in Cognitive Science*,
Cambridge, Cambridge University Press.

Pinker, S. and Mehler, J. (eds) (1989) *Connections and Symbols*, Cambridge,
Massachusetts, MIT Press.

Pollard, P. and Evans, J.StB.T. (1983) 'The role of "representativeness" in statistical
inference: a critical appraisal', in J.StB.T. Evans (ed.) *Thinking and Reasoning:
Psychological Approaches*, London, Routledge & Kegan Paul.

Pollard-Gott, L., McCloskey, M. and Todres, A.K. (1979) 'Subjective story
structure', *Discourse Processes*, vol. 2, pp 251–82.

Popper, K. (1959) *The Logic of Scientific Discovery*, London, Hutchinson.

Prawitz, D. (1965) *Natural Deduction*, Stockholm-Goteborg-Uppsala, Almqvist &
Wiksell.

Propp, V. (1968) *Morphology of the Folktale*, Austin, University of Texas Press.

Pylyshyn, Z.W. (1984) *Computation and Cognition*, Cambridge, Massachusetts,
MIT Press.

Quine, W.V.O. (1969) *Ontological Relativity and Other Essays*, New York, Columbia
University Press.

Quine, W.V.O. (1972) *Methods of Logic*, 3rd edn, New York, Holt.

Quine, W.V.O. (1974) *The Roots of Reference*, La Salle, Illinois, Open Court.

Radnitzky, G. and Bartley, W.W. (eds) (1987) *Evolutionary Epistemology, Rationality,
and the Sociology of Knowledge*, La Salle, Illinois, Open Court.

Ramsey, F.P. (1931) *Foundations of Mathematics*, London, Routledge & Kegan Paul.

Reinhart, T. (1983) *Anaphora and Semantic Interpretation*, London, Croom Helm.

Rips, L.J. and Marcus, S.L. (1977) 'Suppositions and the analysis of conditional
sentences', in M.A. Just and P.A. Carpenter (eds) *Cognitive Processes in
Comprehension*, Hillsdale, New Jersey, Lawrence Erlbaum Associates.

Rosch, E. (1978) 'Principles of categorisation', in E. Rosch and B.B. Lloyd (eds)
Cognition and Categorisation, Hillsdale, New Jersey, Lawrence Erlbaum
Associates.

Ross, H.E. (1969) 'When is a weight not illusory?', *Quarterly Journal of Experimental
Psychology*, vol. 21, pp 346–55.

Rumelhart, D.E. (1975) 'Notes on a schema for stories', in D.G. Bobrow and A.M.
Collins (eds) *Representation and Understanding: Studies in Cognitive Science*, New
York, Academic Press.

Rumelhart, D.E. (1977) 'Understanding and summarizing brief stories', in D.
Laberge and S.J. Samuels (eds) *Basic Processes in Reading: Perception and
Comprehension*, Hillsdale, New Jersey, Lawrence Erlbaum Associates.

Rumelhart, D.E. (1980a) 'On evaluating story grammars', *Cognitive Science*, vol. 4, pp 313–16.

Rumelhart, D.E. (1980b) 'Schemata, the building blocks of cognition', in R.J. Spiro, B.C. Bruce and W.F. Brewer (eds) *Theoretical Issues in Reading Comprehension*, Hillsdale, New Jersey, Lawrence Erlbaum Associates.

Rumelhart, D.E. and McClelland, J. (1986) *Parallel Distributed Processing Vol 1: Foundations*, Cambridge, Massachusetts, MIT Press.

Russell, B. (1912) *The Problems of Philosophy*, Oxford, Oxford University Press.

Sag, I.A. (1979) 'On the nonunity of anaphora', *Linguistic Inquiry*, vol. 10, pp 152–64.

Salmon, N. and Soames, S.(1989) *Propositions and Attitudes*, Oxford, Oxford University Press.

van der Sandt, R.A. (1988) *Context and Presupposition*, London, Croom Helm.

Sanford, A.J. and Garrod, S.C. (1981) *Understanding Written Language*, Chichester, John Wiley & Sons.

Schank, R.C. (1982) *Dynamic Memory*, Cambridge, Cambridge University Press.

Schank, R.C. and Abelson, R.P. (1977) *Scripts, Plans, Goals, and Understanding*, Hillsdale, New Jersey, Lawrence Erlbaum Associates.

Schank, R.C., Collins, G.C., Davis, E., Johnson, P.N., Lytinen, S. and Reiser, B.J. (1982) 'What's the point?', *Cognitive Science*, vol. 6, pp 255–75.

Schiffer, S. (1987) *Remnants of Meaning*, Cambridge, Massachusetts, MIT Press.

von Schilcher, F. and Tennant, N. (1984) *Philosophy, Evolution, and Human Nature*, London, Routledge & Kegan Paul.

Schillp, P. (ed.) (1974) *The Philosophy of Karl Popper*, La Salle, Open Court.

Searle, J.R. (1969) *Speech Acts: an Essay in the Philosophy of Language*, Cambridge, Cambridge University Press.

Searle, J.R. (1975) 'A taxonomy of illocutionary acts', in K. Gunderson (ed.) *Minnesota Studies in the Philosophy of Language*, Minneapolis, University of Minnesota Press.

Searle, J.R. (1980) 'Minds, brains, and programs', *The Behavioral and Brain Sciences*, vol. 3, pp 417–58.

Sherman, M.A. (1976) 'Adjectival negation and the comprehension of multiply negated sentences', *Journal of Verbal Learning and Verbal Behavior*, vol. 15, pp 143–57.

Siegel, L.S. and Brainerd, C.J. (eds) (1978) *Alternatives to Piaget: Critical Essays on the Theory*, New York, Academic Press.

Skyrms, B. (1986) *Choice and Chance*, 3rd edn, Belmont, California, Wadsworth.

Slobin, D.I. (1974) *Psycholinguistics*, London, Scott Foresman.

Snow, C.E. and Ferguson, C.A. (eds) (1977) *Talking to Children: Language Input and Acquisition*, Cambridge, Cambridge University Press.

Spencer-Smith, R. (1987) 'Semantics and discourse representation', *Mind and Language*, vol. 2, pp 1–26.

Sperber, D. and Wilson, D. (1986) *Relevance: Communication and Cognition*, Oxford, Blackwell.

Sperber, D. and Wilson, D. (1987) 'Précis of "Relevance"', *The Behavioral and Brain Sciences*, vol. 10, pp 697–754.

Stalnaker, R.C. (1968) 'A theory of conditionals', in N. Rescher (ed.) *Studies in Logical Theory*, Oxford, Blackwell.

Stalnaker, R.C. (1972) 'Pragmatics', in D. Davidson and G. Harman (eds) *Semantics of Natural Language*, Dordrecht, Reidel.

Stalnaker, R.C. (1978) 'Assertion', in P. Cole (ed.) *Syntax and Semantics 9: Pragmatics*, New York, Academic Press.

Stalnaker, R.C. (1984) *Inquiry*, Cambridge, Massachusetts, MIT Press.

Stevenson, R.J. (1988) *Models of Language Development*, Milton Keynes, Open University Press.

Stevenson, R.J. and Pickering, M.J. (1987) 'The effects of linguistic and non-linguistic knowledge on the acquisition of pronouns', in P. Griffiths, J. Local and A.E. Mills (eds) *Proceedings of the Child Language Seminar*, University of York.

Stich, S.P. (1983) *From Folk Psychology to Cognitive Science*, Cambridge, Massachusetts, MIT Press.

Stich, S.P. (1985) 'Could man be an irrational animal?', *Synthèse*, vol. 64, pp 115–35.

Tamburrini, J. (1982) 'Some educational implications of Piaget's theory', in S. Modgil and C. Modgil (eds) *Jean Piaget: Consensus and Controversy*, London, Holt, Rinehart & Winston.

Thomason, R.H. (1970) 'A Fitch-style formulation of conditional logic', *Logique et Analyse*, vol. 52, pp 397–412.

Thorndyke, P.W. (1977) 'Cognitive structures in comprehension and memory of narrative discourse', *Cognitive Psychology*, vol. 9, pp 77–110.

Touretsky, D.S. and Hinton, G.E. (1985) 'Symbols among the neurons: details of a connectionist inference architecture', *Proceedings of the Ninth International Conference on Artificial Intelligence*, Los Altos, Morgan Kaufman.

Traugott, E.C., ter Meulen, A., Reilly, J.S. and Ferguson, C.A. (eds) (1986) *On Conditionals*, Cambridge, Cambridge University Press.

Turing, A. (1936) 'On computable numbers with an application to the *Entscheidungsproblem*', *Proceedings of the London Mathematical Society*, vol. 42, pp 230–65.

Turing, A. (1950) 'Computing machinery and intelligence', *Mind*, vol. 59, pp 430–60.

Tversky, A. and Kahneman, D. (1973) 'Availability: a heuristic for judging frequency and probability', *Cognitive Psychology*, vol. 4, pp 207–232; reprinted in D. Kahneman *et al.* (eds) *Judgment Under Uncertainty: Heuristics and Biases*, Cambridge, Cambridge University Press.

Tweney, R.D., Doherty, M.E. and Mynatt, C.R. (1981) *On Scientific Thinking*, New York, Columbia University Press.

Tweney, R.D., Doherty, M.E., Warner, W.J. and Pliske, D.B. (1980) 'Strategies of rule discovery in an inference task', *Quarterly Journal of Experimental Psychology*, vol. 32, pp 109–24.

Wason, P.C. (1959) 'The processing of positive and negative information', *Quarterly Journal of Experimental Psychology*, vol. 11, pp 92–107.

Wason, P.C. (1960) 'On the failure to eliminate hypotheses in a conceptual task', *Quarterly Journal of Experimental Psychology*, vol. 11, pp 129–40.

Wason, P.C. (1961) 'Response to affirmative and negative binary statements', *British Journal of Psychology*, vol. 52, pp 133–42.

Wason, P.C. (1965) 'The contexts of plausible denial', *Journal of Verbal Learning and Verbal Behavior*, vol. 4, pp 7–11.

Wason, P.C. (1968a) 'Reasoning about a rule', *Quarterly Journal of Experimental Psychology*, vol. 20, pp 273–81.

Wason, P.C. (1968b) '"On the failure to eliminate hypotheses ..." – a second look', in P.C. Wason and P.N. Johnson-Laird (eds) *Thinking and Reasoning*, Harmondsworth, Middlesex, Penguin Books.

Wason, P.C. (1969) 'Structural simplicity and psychological complexity: some thoughts on a novel problem', *Bulletin of the British Psychological Society*, vol. 22, pp 281–4.

Wason, P.C. (1972) 'In real life negatives are false', *Logique et Analyse*, vol. 57–8, pp 17–38.

Wason, P.C. (1977) 'The theory of formal operations: a critique', in B. Geber (ed.) *Piaget and Knowing*, London, Routledge & Kegan Paul.

Wason, P.C. (1983) 'Realism and rationality in the selection task', in J.StB.T. Evans (ed.) *Thinking and Reasoning: Psychological Approaches*, London, Routledge & Kegan Paul.

Wason, P.C. and Evans, J.StB.T. (1975) 'Dual processes in reasoning?', *Cognition*, vol. 3, pp 141–54.

Wason, P.C. and Johnson-Laird, P.N. (1972) *Psychology of Reasoning: Structure and Content*, London, Batsford.

Wason, P.C. and Jones, S. (1963) 'Negatives: denotation and connotation', *British Journal of Psychology*, vol. 54, pp 299–307.

Wason, P.C. and Reich, S.S. (1979) 'A verbal illusion', *Quarterly Journal of Experimental Psychology*, vol. 31, pp 591–7.

Wason, P.C. and Shapiro, D.A. (1971) 'Natural and contrived experience in a reasoning problem', *Quarterly Journal of Experimental Psychology*, vol. 23, pp 63–71.

Weisberg, R.W. (1980) *Memory, Thought, and Behavior*, Oxford, Oxford University Press.

Wilensky, R. (1983) 'Story grammars versus story points', *The Behavioral and Brain Sciences*, vol. 6, pp 579–623.

Wilks, Y. (1976) 'Frames, scripts, and fantasies', unpublished paper cited by A.J. Sanford and S.C. Garrod (1981) *Understanding Written Language*, Chichester, John Wiley & Sons.

Winograd, T. (1972) *Understanding Natural Language*, New York, Academic Press.

Yekovich, F.R. and Thorndyke, P.W. (1981) 'An evaluation of alternative functional models of narrative discourse', *Journal of Verbal Learning and Verbal Behavior*, vol. 20, pp 454–69.

Name index

Subject index

Where multiple references are given, important definitions or explanations are indicated in **bold type**.